Suggestibility in Legal Contexts

Wiley Series in

The Psychology of Crime, Policing and Law

Series Editors
Graham M. Davies and Ray Bull
University of Leicester, UK

The Wiley Series in the Psychology of Crime, Policing and Law publishes concise and integrative reviews on important emerging areas of contemporary research. The purpose of the series is not merely to present research findings in a clear and readable form, but also to bring out their implications for both practice and policy. In this way, it is hoped the series will not only be useful to psychologists but also to all those concerned with crime detection and prevention, policing, and the judicial process.

For other titles in this series please see www.wiley.com/go/pcpl

Suggestibility in Legal Contexts

Contexts

Psychological Research and Forensic Implications

Edited by

**Anne M. Ridley, Fiona Gabbert
and David J. La Rooy**

A John Wiley & Sons, Ltd., Publication

Library of Congress Cataloging-in-Publication Data
Suggestibility in legal contexts : psychological research and forensic implications / edited by Anne M. Ridley, Fiona Gabbert and David J. La Rooy.
    p. cm.
    Includes index.
    ISBN 978-0-470-66369-1 (cloth) – ISBN 978-0-470-66368-4 (pbk.) 1. Law–Psychological aspects. 2. Forensic psychology. 3. Evidence, Expert. 4. Recollection (Psychology) 5. Criminal investigation–Psychological aspects. 6. Judicial process–Psychological aspects. I. Ridley, Anne M. II. Gabbert, Fiona. III. La Rooy, David J.
    K487.P75S84 2012
    614′.15–dc23
                            2012029602

A catalogue record for this book is available from the British Library.

Cover image: © David Fairfield / Getty Images
Cover design by Nicki Averill Design

Set in 10/12pt Century Schoolbook by SPi Publisher Services, Pondicherry, India

Printed in Singapore by Ho Printing Singapore Pte Ltd

1   2013

Dedications

AMR: For my family – Michael, Nick, Jo and Lew
FG: For Bry, whom I married while working on this book
DJLR: For my friend, Roger Smith

Contents

Contributors

Deirdre Brown
Victoria University of Wellington

Quin M. Chrobak
University of Wisconsin-Oshkosh

Travis Conradt
University of Toledo

Ryan Corser
University of Toledo

Deborah Davis
University of Nevada, Reno

Fiona Gabbert (Editor)
Goldsmiths University of London

Gisli H. Gudjonsson
Kings College London

Lucy A. Henry
London South Bank University

Lorraine Hope
University of Portsmouth

Michael E. Lamb
University of Cambridge

David J. La Rooy (Editor)
University of Abertay Dundee

Richard A. Leo
University of San Francisco Law School

Kamala London
University of Toledo

Katie L. Maras
City University, London

James Ost
University of Portsmouth

Anne M. Ridley (Editor)
London South Bank University

Rachel Wilcock
London South Bank University

Maria S. Zaragoza
Kent State University

Series Preface

The Wiley Series in the Psychology of Crime, Policing and the Law publishes both single and multi-authored monographs and edited reviews of important and emerging areas of contemporary research. The purpose of this series is not merely to present research findings in a clear and readable form, but also to bring out their implications for both practice and policy. Books in this series are useful not only to psychologists, but also to all those involved in crime detection and prevention, child protection, policing and judicial processes.

The terms 'Suggestible' and 'Suggestibility' must be among the most widely used but least understood descriptors in law and psychology. These labels have been applied across a diverse range of persons and situations: from the character of a young offender, through the memories of a child witness, to characterizing the continuing beliefs among world leaders regarding the presence of weapons of mass destruction in Iraq. Given this ubiquity, it is perhaps surprising that so few books have been devoted to pinning down this elusive concept and exploring its impact on crime and the law.

As Anne Ridley's opening chapter makes clear, this was not always so in the history of psychology. If we go back to the dawn of empirical psychology, we find such pioneers as Alfred Binet and Hugo Münsterberg promoting suggestibility as a central concept in understanding witness testimony, while Sigmund Freud and Pierre Janet invoked it as an explanation for otherwise irrational behaviour and beliefs among their patients. While clinical psychology continued to explore the term, notably through the work of Hans Eysenck, Desmond Ferneaux and latterly, Gisli Gudjonsson, experimental psychology largely turned its back on research into this most mentalistic of concepts, under the baleful influence of Behaviourism. It was the advent of Cognitive Psychology and in particular the research of Elizabeth Loftus which saw the return of suggestibility to the mainstream. Loftus's work on post-event misinformation treated suggestibility as a consequence of situational factors impacting on the individual witness, particularly the phrasing of verbal statements and questions. This approach contrasted with the emphasis in Gudjonsson's work on individual differences in vulnerability to suggestion of defendants and its consequences for false confessions. The role of individual and situational factors in producing suggestibility had been argued over by the early pioneers and the controversy has been revived today, most notably in the ongoing debate between the followers of Stephen Ceci and Gail Goodman over the extent to which young witnesses can be said to be inherently suggestible and the consequences for the reliability of their testimony at court.

All of these key issues are given a contemporary edge by the contributors to the new volume, together with new forensic issues which have emerged in recent years. Both post-event misinformation effects and interrogative suggestibility receive widespread attention, both from a legal and psychological standpoint. The possible link between mental or emotional vulnerability and heightened suggestibility for witnesses and suspects is also thoroughly explored, while recovered memories are considered as a contemporary manifestation of suggestive responding. If Binet and Münsterberg were alive today, they would be surprised at just how much we had learned – and how many of the basic issues had stayed the same.

The Editors have done an excellent job of gathering a host of internationally known contributors for the current volume and fashioning their contributions into a coherent whole. Dr Anne Ridley is currently Principal Lecturer in Psychology at London South Bank University, with teaching and research interests in forensic psychology, who contributes to their Master's programme in Investigative Forensic Psychology, as well as acting as Faculty Director of Teaching and Learning. Anne originated and developed the idea for a book on suggestibility and has overseen its development through to press. She has been ably assisted by Dr Fiona Gabbert and Dr David J. La Rooy of the University of Abertay, Scotland, both experienced researchers on witness evidence, who have helped in reviewing and developing manuscripts. *Suggestibility in Legal Contexts: Psychological Research and Forensic Implications* can be read with profit by all practitioners and researchers who must deal with offenders and witnesses within the criminal justice system.

Graham M. Davies
University of Leicester

Preface

The seeds of this book were sown while working on my doctorate *Anxiety in Eyewitness Testimony*, completed in 2003. It was several years later during a conversation with Professor Ray Bull on a coach to a conference dinner in Maastricht that the idea of a book on suggestibility in legal contexts really started to germinate. Ray suggested that the topic might be of interest to Wiley for their Psychology of Crime, Policing and Law series. My original ambition was to write the entire book myself in order to clearly delineate the mechanisms underpinning the different 'types' of suggestibility. I soon realized, however, that undertaking such a big project was going to be much more difficult than I had originally thought! During the early stages, I worked closely with Professor Graham Davies (the Series Editor along with Ray Bull) who gave me invaluable advice including the suggestion that it might be worthwhile to consider an edited volume. Graham proved to be an excellent sounding board regarding authors who could provide as broad an overview of suggestibility as possible. I am very grateful that so many experts were willing and able to contribute.

While writing my own chapters, and receiving submissions, I soon realized that reviewing and editing would be a lonely furrow on my own. Fiona Gabbert, whom I first met when we were both PhD students, was one of the first people involved in the book, so I invited her to become a co-editor. We felt that a third editor would be ideal and that David La Rooy's knowledge of research on child interviewing and recent experience of editing Wiley's *Children's Testimony* would make him an excellent fit. We have all learned a huge amount about suggestibility from working with all our contributors and each other. What's more, it has been a very enjoyable experience.

We hope that this volume, outlining current findings and ideas for future research, makes an important, up-to-date contribution to the literature on suggestibility and that academics, students and practitioners alike will find it useful and illuminating.

Anne Ridley

Acknowledgements

Without our contributors this volume would not have been possible so we are very grateful to them all. Our thanks also go to the series editors, Professors Graham Davies and Ray Bull for their advice and encouragement. Finally, to everyone at Wiley, for the opportunity to publish this book, particularly Andrew Peart, Karen Shield and Victoria Halliday for their patience and support, and to their colleagues who helped bring it to press.

1

Suggestibility: A History and Introduction

Anne M. Ridley

KEY POINTS

This chapter will provide an overview of the conceptual and historical factors that have contributed to modern research and theories of suggestibility in legal contexts:

- Definitions of suggestibility.
- Early work to establish whether suggestibility was one or more phenomena.
- Eyewitness testimony in the early twentieth century.
- Suggestibility in the early twentieth century.
- Cognitive and social theories relevant to suggestibility.

The 1970s and early 1980s heralded a new era in the study of suggestibility in legal contexts, an area that had been largely neglected since the early twentieth century. Using experimental studies, Elizabeth Loftus in the USA demonstrated how easy it was, under certain circumstances, to mislead people into remembering incorrect details about a witnessed event (Loftus, Miller, & Burns, 1978). Loftus's was an *experimental* approach. In Europe, through his clinical and forensic work, Gisli Gudjonsson

Suggestibility in Legal Contexts: Psychological Research and Forensic Implications,
First Edition. Edited by Anne M. Ridley, Fiona Gabbert and David J. La Rooy.
© 2013 John Wiley & Sons, Ltd. Published 2013 by John Wiley & Sons, Ltd.

noted that some individuals seemed to be more suggestible than others. This approach assumed that suggestibility is a *trait* and led to the development of a model of interrogative suggestibility (Gudjonsson & Clark, 1986). Much research and debate have followed to establish whether suggestibility is a trait (i.e. some people are inherently more suggestible than others), or whether suggestibility is merely the result of situational factors that can be manipulated experimentally. Nevertheless, what both approaches have in common is the fact that they consider suggestibility from the point of view of its impact on the accuracy of information obtained during the investigation of crimes, and that is the focus of this book.

The notion of *interrogative suggestibility* was originally proposed by Binet (1900) and has been used since by others, particularly Gudjonsson (e.g. Gudjonsson 2003; Gudjonsson & Clark, 1986). Recent use of the term interrogative suggestibility is usually restricted to suggestibility that occurs in the presence of inappropriate questioning plus pressure, either in the form of negative feedback and/or coercive interview techniques. If suggestibility is indeed a trait (and the evidence is equivocal: see Baxter, 1990, for a review), then it is one that is most likely to emerge when such situational pressures are present. Nevertheless, it is also possible for individuals to be suggestible simply through exposure to incorrect information about a previously witnessed event, or in response to leading questions, in an otherwise supportive evidence-gathering interview. We would argue that the term *investigative suggestibility* should be used to distinguish suggestibility that occurs incidentally in this way from suggestibility that occurs due to interrogative pressure, and will therefore use these two terms, when appropriate in this book.

WHAT IS SUGGESTIBILITY?

Suggestibility is 'a peculiar state of mind which is favourable to suggestion.' (Sidis, 1898, p. 15)

Definitions of *suggestibility* and *suggestion* are many and varied, reflecting the difficulty in pinning down this pervasive yet perplexing aspect of human behaviour. Marcuse (1976, cited in Wagstaff, 1991) describes *suggestibility* in situational terms including 'the influence of one person on another without his or her consent, the implanting of an idea, possessing a submissive tendency, and appealing to the unconscious' (p. 132). In a similar vein, Stern (1910, p. 273), while talking of the psychology of testimony, defines *suggestion* from the influenced individual's viewpoint as 'the imitative assumption of a mental attitude under the illusion of assuming it spontaneously'. This latter definition is rather more suggestibility than suggestion, a distinction that was perhaps lost in translation from the German original.

Suggestion and suggestibility are linked but distinct concepts, with the latter generally resulting from the former. "Suggestion" refers to a type of influential communication, while "suggestibility" refers to the individual differences between those responding to suggestion under comparable circumstances' (Hilgard, 1991, p. 37), a distinction elegantly captured by Sidis's (1898) much earlier definition highlighted above. Thus, suggestion, whether in the context of hypnosis, social influence or incorrect information, can lead to a state or moment of suggestibility. In forensic psychology, suggestibility has been described in psychosocial terms as 'the extent to which, within a closed social interaction, people come to accept messages communicated during formal questioning, as the result of which their subsequent behavioural response is affected' (Gudjonsson & Clark, 1986, p. 84). In distinct contrast to the preceding definitions, Powers, Andriks, and Loftus (1979) define suggestibility in terms of memory processes, stating that it is 'the extent to which they [people] come to accept a piece of post-event information and incorporate it into their recollection' (p. 339). Whether suggestion has an impact on memory rather than behaviour, mirrors the situational versus trait approaches to suggestibility that have been the subject of sometimes strong debate since the 1980s.

IS SUGGESTIBILITY ONE CONSTRUCT OR MORE?

As illustrated in the above sections, suggestibility is hard to pin down. Many researchers have pointed out over the past century or so that there is no unitary concept of suggestibility and that the one word is used to describe a variety of phenomena (e.g. Binet, 1900; Eysenck, 1989; Wagstaff, 1991). In an attempt to resolve the issue, Eysenck (1947) proposed three types of suggestibility: primary, secondary and tertiary.

Primary suggestibility describes an ideo-motor phenomenon whereby thinking about or imagining one's body moving can cause it to occur. This has been demonstrated experimentally in the body sway test (see Box 1.1), arm lowering, and pendulum tests. Primary suggestibility correlates highly with hypnotizability and neuroticism. In contrast, secondary suggestibility is linked to indirect suggestions where the purpose of the suggestion is not clear. It is not related to hypnotizability and is negatively related to intelligence. In other words, people who are 'gullible' (Eysenck & Furneaux, 1945) tend to be more suggestible.

Studies carried out since those by Eysenck and his colleagues have supported the notion of primary suggestibility (e.g. Duke, 1964; Evans, 1966, cited in Evans, 1967; Stukat, 1958), but this is not the case for

Box 1.1 Eysenck & Furneaux (1945), Primary and Secondary Suggestibility

Eysenck and Furneaux raised the question of whether suggestibility is a single mental trait or a number of separate 'suggestibilities' (p. 485). They carried out a study among 60 neurotic patients in an army hospital. A battery of 12 different tests was administered in order to understand the relationships between them and whether they would support the notions of primary and secondary suggestibility.

Examples of tests given and the type of suggestibility it was hypothesized that they related to:

Picture Report (secondary): A picture was studied for 30 seconds, followed by 14 questions about it, of which five contained incorrect details. Suggestibility was measured by the number of suggested details accepted.

Ink Blot Suggestion Test (secondary): Typical responses to Rorschach ink blots were suggested as well as implausible responses. Suggestibility was measured by the number of implausible suggestions accepted.

Body Sway Test (primary): Participants closed their eyes and it was suggested they were falling forward. The amount of sway was measured via a thread attached to the participants' clothing. 'Complete falls are arbitrarily scored as 12 inches' (p. 487).

Odour Suggestion Test (secondary): Participants were asked to identify the scents presented in different bottles. The three final bottles presented contained water. Suggestibility was measured by the number of these placebo bottles that had an odour attributed to them.

Hypnosis (primary): Attempted induction was via 'fixation of a bright object, a constant low sound, and verbal suggestion' (p. 488). Various suggestions were made to participants such as tiredness and hallucinations. A total hypnosis score was derived from responses to the suggestions.

Analysis supported the two types of suggestibility, although more so for primary than for secondary suggestibility. The best tests of primary suggestibility were the body sway test and hypnosis, while the ink blot and odour tests were the best tests of secondary suggestibility.

Of particular relevance to suggestibility in legal contexts is the picture report test, which used a method very similar to that since adopted in studies of investigative suggestibility. The suggestibility effect was relatively small with a mean of 1.0 (SD 1.1) out of a possible 5.0, and the picture report test did not map strongly onto the concept of secondary suggestibility.

secondary suggestibility. Evans (1967) questioned the methodology of Eysenck and Furneaux (1945). He re-evaluated the data and found that the notion of secondary suggestibility could not be justified. Evans concluded that three types of suggestibility could be identified: 'primary' (passive motor), 'challenge',[1] and 'imagery' (sensory) suggestibility (p. 127). As they involve physical movement, primary and challenge suggestibility are of little relevance to investigative suggestibility. Imagery is more promising, and its relationship with investigative suggestibility has since been researched (see Eisen, Winograd, & Qin, 2002, for a review).

Eysenck (1947) also proposed a third or 'tertiary' type of suggestibility. He linked this to attitude change and persuasion, emphasizing the importance of interpersonal factors such as the perceived authority of the person providing the suggestion. Although Evans (1967) concluded that there was little evidence of this effect, more recent research in the area of suggestibility in legal contexts indicates otherwise, to the extent that there is now an acknowledged link between interrogative suggestibility and tertiary suggestibility (Eysenck, 1989; Sheehan, 1989). Furthermore, Sheehan (1989) proposed that Gudjonsson's suggestibility scales are a form of indirect suggestion. The term 'indirect' links back to secondary suggestibility. Thus it can be argued that interrogative suggestibility may bridge two of Eysenck's categories of suggestibility: secondary and tertiary.

THE HISTORY OF SUGGESTIBILITY RESEARCH

Hypnosis and Suggestibility

As the previous section illustrates, the history of suggestibility is closely intertwined with that of hypnosis. The two have been linked by Orne (1977, cited in Gheorghiu, 1989, p. 4) who defined hypnosis as 'the state in which suggestion can be used to give rise to distortions in perception and memory'.

Hypnosis is characterized by a relaxed and drowsy state, during which the influenced individual is responsive to suggestions made such as hallucinations or age-regression. A further characteristic of the state is that the person involved is subsequently able to report that he was hypnotized (Barber, Spanos, & Chaves, 1974), although amnesia for experiences during hypnosis sometimes occurs. This amnesia may either be suggested or may happen independently of a specific suggestion (Eysenck & Furneaux, 1945). Hypnosis is used widely in therapies of various kinds, from psychological distress through to treatment of

---

[1] A challenge suggestion has two stages: the suggested inhibition of a movement, followed by a challenge to overcome the initial suggestion.

addiction and relief of pain. Such therapy has sometimes resulted in recovered memories of childhood sexual abuse, and hypnotism has also been used on occasions to obtain testimony in police investigations (see Orbach, Lamb, La Rooy, & Pipe, 2012, for an example).

The use of hypnosis has a long history, dating back at least as far as de Montagne in the seventeenth century and Franz Mesmer in the eighteenth century. Mesmer believed the effects observed when he *mesmerized* or hypnotized his patients were due to animal magnetism; an external life force that was a result of his connection to the patient. He disagreed with de Montagne, who proposed that the imagination of the patient was the primary cause. With hindsight it would seem that de Montagne was closer to the mark. The study of hypnotism continued through the work of Freud, Janet and Binet among others, although it was probably Bernheim (1888/1964) who first linked hypnosis to suggestibility. He proposed that the former was a heightened state of the latter. Modern researchers do not agree with this position due, in part, to the circular nature of the theory (suggestibility leads to hypnosis leads to suggestibility), although it is generally accepted that the two phenomena are closely linked. According to Edmonston (1989):

> ... although suggestion may be a route for establishing the condition of hypnosis, we should agree that hypnosis is not suggestion and suggestion is not hypnosis, and that to study one is not necessarily to study the other. (p. 73)

Edmonston also points out that an important aspect of the relationship between hypnotism and suggestibility is that the effects of suggestion are *greater* when under hypnosis than when in a waking state.

The issue of hypnosis and suggestibility has direct relevance to suggestibility in legal contexts. Under certain circumstances, hypnosis increases the likelihood of the recall of misleading information, creation of pseudomemories and acceptance of the persuasive messages contained in leading questions (Sheehan, 1989). However, Orbach *et al.* (2012) report the case of a child interviewed under hypnosis who provided details that were crucial to the apprehension of the person who had abducted her sister. Analysis of the interview indicated that no suggestive questions were used.

Early Work on Eyewitness Testimony

Münsterberg (1863–1916) has been described as the father of eyewitness testimony research (e.g. Wrightsman, 2001). Furthermore, as articles in a Special Issue of *Applied Cognitive Psychology* (2008) demonstrate (e.g. Bornstein & Penrod, 2008; Sporer, 2008), the early twentieth century was a boom period for psychology and law. What follows will be a brief summary of the work of Münsterburg, Stern, Binet and other early investigative psychologists.

Münsterberg's book *On the Witness Stand* (1908/1925) contains a series of essays about psychology and law. Titles include 'The Memory of the Witness', 'Untrue Confessions' and 'Suggestions in Court'. (See Box 1.2 for a section from the first of these essays.) Hugo Münsterberg, a student of Wilhelm Wundt, advocated an experimental approach to the study of eyewitness memory. He referred to the recent proliferation of psychological research in the USA and Europe, and lamented the fact that the courts took little notice of it, yet allowed findings from

---

Box 1.2 A Section from Münsterberg's (1908/1925) Essay from *On the Witness Stand* about 'The Memory of the Witness'

This is based on his own memory for events surrounding a burglary at his house.

In this way, in spite of my best intentions, in spite of good memory and calm mood, a whole series of confusions, of illusions, of forgetting, of wrong conclusions, and of yielding to suggestions were mingled with what I had to report under oath, and my only consolation is the fact that in a thousand courts at a thousand places all over the world, witnesses every day affirm by oath in exactly the same way much worse mixtures of truth and untruth, combinations of memory and of illusion, of knowledge and of suggestion, of experience and wrong conclusions. Not one of my mistakes was of the slightest consequence. But is it probable that this is always so? Is it not more natural to suppose that every day errors creep into the work of justice through wrong evidence which has the outer marks of truth and trust-worthiness? Of course, judge and jury and, later, the newspaper reader try their best to weigh the evidence. Not every sworn statement is accepted as absolute reality. Contradictions between witnesses are too familiar. But the instinctive doubt refers primarily to veracity. The public in the main suspects that the witness lies, while taking for granted that if he is normal and conscious of responsibility he may forget a thing, but it would not believe that he could remember the wrong thing. The confidence in the reliability of memory is so general that the suspicion of memory illusions evidently plays a small rôle in the mind of the juryman, and even the cross-examining lawyer is mostly dominated by the idea that a false statement is the product of intentional falsehood.

other sciences like medicine and even what he called pseudosciences such as graphology to be presented as expert evidence in court. Münsterberg's work has stood the test of time because it is accessible to read, and possibly, as Bornstein and Penrod (2008) suggest, because (on the basis that there is no such thing as bad publicity) it was pilloried by Wigmore (1909) in the *Illinois Law Review*.

Siegfried Sporer (2008) argues that modern researchers of eyewitness testimony owe at least as much to William Stern (1871–1938) as they do to Münsterberg. Although both Münsterberg and Stern were German, Münsterberg moved to Harvard, a move that facilitated the influence of his work in English-speaking countries. Much of Stern's work, in contrast (as with Binet, 1900) has never been translated into English. Stern was well aware of the problems posed by post-event information, suggestive questions and false memory induction. He placed error and deception on a continuum of intention to illustrate the fact that individual witnesses may apply different standards of truthfulness when questioned. Thus truthfulness may vary as a function of the task and perceived consequences. In an experimental study, Stern found that taking an oath improved accuracy, although by no means eliminated error altogether (Stern, 1902, cited in Sporer, 2008). These issues reflect a theme that has been picked up more recently in many studies of confidence and accuracy as well as a series of papers by Asher Koriat and Morris Goldsmith in Haifa (e.g. Koriat & Goldsmith, 1996; Koriat, Goldsmith & Pansky, 2000) looking at factors that affect what people report, the level of specificity and the goal-dependent criteria they adopt when deciding how to respond.

Suggestibility in Legal Contexts

Much of the early research on suggestibility in legal contexts was carried out on children. Based on his book *La Suggestibilité*, Alfred Binet (1900) could certainly claim to have been one of the first to highlight its importance, pointing out 'the advantage that would accrue from the creation of a practical science of testimony' (Whipple, 1909, p. 154). Binet (1900) emphasized that he wished to investigate suggestibility that was *not* a result of hypnotism. He did this using an individual differences approach, acknowledging that an individual who is susceptible to suggestion on one task may not demonstrate similar levels of suggestibility on another. He proposed that suggestibility is in fact a number of phenomena (with contemporary equivalence in brackets): obedience to an authority figure, which he felt is the true meaning of the word suggestibility; imitation (conformity); a preconceived notion that prevents critical thought (bias and stereotyping); unconscious errors of a vivid imagination (confabulation); and unconscious processes due to distraction or an altered state of consciousness.

Table 1.1 Mean scores in response to suggestion (Binet, 1900)

Questionnaire 1 (cued questions)		Questionnaire 2 (moderate suggestion)		Questionnaire 3 (strong suggestion)	
Mean errors	Mean correct	Mean suggestible	Mean correct	Mean suggestible	Mean correct
2.9	8.1	4.9	8.09	7.9	5.09

Binet conducted a number of studies on 'l'interrogatoire' (p. 244), probably the first reference to interrogative suggestibility. He showed schoolchildren an array of six everyday objects attached to a card. In the first study he tested to see how many objects they remembered seeing, which ranged from all six down to a minimum of three. The children were then asked 41 questions about the objects. One object was a picture of an industrial strike scene. Several different types of error were noted, including incorrect recall of particular details, through to descriptions that did not resemble the scene at all – something that might be identified as confabulation today. Binet described these as errors of memory. The number of errors varied from 5 to 14, with the mode being 11. He then carried out a similar exercise, but this time with children writing down their own free account. The number of errors reduced dramatically. In a third study, Binet used questionnaires that contained either questions that were not misleading; questions that were 'moderate suggestion' using tags such as 'isn't it?' and finally 'strong suggestions' which were forced choice questions that contained misleading information. The results showed that responses to the third questionnaire were more likely to be suggestible than correct (see Table 1.1). Binet described the evident discomfort of the children when being required to give answers to strong suggestions, indicating there may not have been private acceptance of the suggested information.

'Our results show incontrovertibly that even the phrasing of the question can influence the response and produce errors of fact' (Binet, 1900, p. 316, my translation). Binet argued that direct questions can make a child feel they have to respond even though their memory may be uncertain, resulting in suggestibility. He therefore proposed that the best evidence

> ... is given spontaneously, without precise questions, without pro-gression of any sort; we have seen that with spontaneous testimony errors still occur but they are fewer than for interrogative questions. (pp. 316–317, my translation)

In addition to testing suggestibility, Binet also found evidence of compliance and conformity (defined more fully later in this chapter).

In his study of compliance, he noted that most children agreed with suggestions, but when asked afterwards were well aware that the information they gave (about colours and length of lines) was incorrect. In the study of conformity, Binet compared children who worked together in groups of three to answer suggestive questions with children who worked alone. To his surprise, those who worked in groups were suggestible in 12 out of 13 questions while those who worked alone were less suggestible, averaging 8 out of 13. He proposed that those working in the group may have given less attention to the task. As a result of this finding he expressed concern about the political and social dangers of the suggestibility of crowds.

Binet's series of studies was comprehensive in its scope and methodologically sound. It addressed three key areas still of major concern today: suggestibility, conformity and compliance. All have been widely researched since and have serious implications for eyewitness testimony and how to achieve best evidence.

Moving from research carried out in France to that carried out in Germany, William Stern gave a series of invited lectures about his work to Clark University in the USA. He reported a picture memory study in which:

> ... the 'narrative' resulted in 5–10% of errors and the 'interrogatory' in 25–30%. The power of the 'suggestive' question showed itself to be dependent in large measure on age with 50% of errors in the case of 7-year-olds, 20% in that of 18-year-olds. (Stern, 1910, p. 272)

Stern went on to discuss why there should be reduced accuracy associated with interrogatory questions rather than narrative or free-recall accounts. He proposed that specific questions act as an imperative, and that as detailed memories may be limited, an individual answering interrogatory questions may have to rely on more fragmentary information. An answer provided in a question, particularly if it invites a positive response, is therefore particularly easy to accept. According to Stern:

> The naïve human being is much inclined to affirm any idea presented to him, that is, to credit it with an objective existence. Suggestive questions of this sort operate with especial force in the case of young and uneducated persons; more with women than with men. (p. 273)

While the first part of this quotation correctly concludes that both social factors and memory are implicated in suggestibility, the second part is a somewhat rash overgeneralization.

In addition to investigating the effects of narrative and specific questions on suggestibility, Stern (cited in Whipple, 1909) went further, describing various types of interrogatory questions with increasing levels of suggestion. For example, *completely disjunctive* or leading questions such as 'Is there a dog in the picture?' (p. 158), and *expectative* questions that strongly indicate an answer: 'Was there not a dog in the picture?' Not only do these echo Binet's classifications earlier in this section but they have also been reflected in contemporary classifications used by researchers such as Michael Lamb and his colleagues (see Lamb, Hershkowitz, Orbach, & Esplin, 2008, for a review).

Varendonck (1911, cited in Whipple, 1913, and Goodman, 1984) was a Belgian psychologist whose experimental work and case studies demonstrated the effects of suggestive questioning and suggestions on children. Varendonck acted as expert witness in a case where a man had been incriminated for the murder and rape of a 9-year-old girl by the evidence of two playmates. He carried out a number of experiments to establish whether children were suggestible, as a basis for deciding if the evidence of the two girls was likely to be reliable. He concluded that children were highly suggestible if questions were phrased inappropriately. He therefore assumed children made poor witnesses and went on to say 'When are we going to give up, in all civilized nations, listening to children in courts of law?' (cited in Goodman, 1984, p. 27). However, Gross (1910, cited in Whipple, 1911, p. 308) argued the opposite, saying that a 'healthy half grown boy' made the best witness!

The benefits of free recall, and the dangers associated with overuse of specific questions (as demonstrated by Binet, Stern, Varendonck, and many since) are reflected in methods advocated in modern questioning techniques for vulnerable witnesses, such as *Achieving Best Evidence* (Ministry of Justice, 2011) and the NICHD protocol (Lamb *et al.*, 2008).

There has been less obvious change in the courts, however. It is worth noting that Stern's *expectative* phraseology is commonly used by contemporary barristers in an attempt to lead witnesses. Apparently this is not new for, as Whipple (1909) elegantly put it:

> ... the browbeating of the average court lawyer does not suggest extraordinary caution in the avoidance of suggestibility. (p. 165)

COGNITIVE FACTORS ASSOCIATED WITH SUGGESTIBILITY: MEMORY AND ATTENTION

Some of the early work discussed above acknowledges that aspects of memory may contribute to suggestibility, so it is important to mention perhaps the most influential work from the twentieth century on the fallibility of memory – which lends itself to suggestibility – that of Sir Frederick Bartlett.

Remembering appears to be far more decisively an affair of construction rather than one of mere reproduction. (Bartlett, 1932, p. 205)

The relationship between suggestibility and memory is far from clear-cut and much of the debate over the past 25 years has focused on whether suggestibility has anything to do with memory at all. Nevertheless what we know about memory tends to suggest that under certain conditions, incorrect information can become embedded in memory for an event.

On the basis of a number of studies, Bartlett proposed that memory is primarily a *reconstructive* process, although some rote memories such as songs and poems do persist. He noted that when asked to recall an Indian folklore story *The War of the Ghosts* with repeated recall either from one individual to another, or serial recall by one person over time, participants tended to make errors of four kinds: (1) omission (particularly of details that were peripheral or outside the readers' own cultural experience); (2) rationalization (a quest after meaning); (3) transformation of detail (particularly from the unusual to the commonplace); and (4) changing the order of events (e.g. giving priority to details to which the reader related). As a result of these observations, Bartlett proposed that memory is schematic: 'Schema refers to an active *organisation* [my emphasis] of past reactions, or of past experiences' (p. 201). This organization is thought to be necessary because of the vast amount of information that we are continually encoding and subsequently storing in memory. Memories for events are therefore prone to being reconstructed in the light of relevant available schemata. Furthermore, if leading questions or incorrect post-event information allow rationalization or translation from the unusual to the commonplace, it is easy to see how a witness might incorporate these suggestions in recall of an event, thereby making it schema-consistent.

Bartlett is also credited with being the forerunner of the accuracy-oriented approach to memory research (Koriat *et al.*, 2000). In distinct contrast to the quantity-oriented research attributed originally to Ebbinghaus (1885/1964), accuracy-oriented research explicitly takes into account errors made and the nature of those errors, seeking to establish how closely recollections *correspond* to the original stimulus. Research into eyewitness memory, including suggestibility, fits very much into the accuracy-oriented approach.

On the basis of the work by Bartlett and others since, it has been amply demonstrated that humans are quite capable of altering the detail of memory themselves. It therefore seems entirely plausible that under certain circumstances information provided by an external source can also lead to reconstruction. Nevertheless, Ost and Costall

(2002) pointed out that even some of Bartlett's own findings showed that memory can be very accurate and there is much evidence, even within the suggestibility research, that true memories can be resilient in the face of suggestive stimuli.

Memory for a to-be-remembered event is dependent on an individual focusing their attention on it. Further, as Binet (1900) indicated, attention is also likely to be a factor in suggestibility. He noted this in the context of the distraction that he believes may have taken place to account for the greater suggestibility when children were working as a group to answer questions compared to a child working alone. Lipmann (1911) also talked about the importance of attention when encoding information and pointed out that details that catch the attention of a child are likely to be different to those that capture an adult's attention. If an adult then questions a child about an aspect of a witnessed event that they too have seen, they will assume that the other has a faulty memory if they cannot recall that particular detail, whereas in fact the child may simply have a different but true memory for the same event. The focus of attention is likely to contribute to the reconstructive nature of memory and this refers to both attention to the original event and attention to suggestions made afterwards. The devil is in teasing out the differences.

SUGGESTIBILITY AND SOCIAL FACTORS

Above, it was outlined how Binet conducted studies not only into suggestibility but also compliance and conformity among children. It has been made clear throughout this chapter that suggestibility is about either a social interaction, memory or both. Social influence is a powerful phenomenon and two key concepts are compliance and conformity. Although these notions will be explored in more detail elsewhere in this book, it is worth briefly outlining two classic studies that illustrate the similarities and differences between compliance and conformity, both of which are examples of social influence.

The first study, demonstrating conformity, was by Asch (1951, 1955). In his study, 50 participants individually joined a group that ostensibly was made up of seven other participants. The group were shown lines of various lengths and were asked whether they were the same or different in length to a comparison or reference line. In fact, the seven co-participants were confederates of the experimenter and gave pre-determined answers that were clearly incorrect. Nevertheless, about one-third of participants gave incorrect responses that conformed to the majority. They did not privately believe the answers they gave, but assumed other members of the group knew something they did not. Numerous studies have since confirmed the strength of the conformity effect.

The second (now famous) study by Stanley Milgram (1963) demonstrated compliance. Participants (designated as teachers for the experiment) were required to administer electric shocks to an unseen 'student' (a confederate of the experimenter) if they made errors in a memory task. The intensity of the shocks increased with each mistake. The participant administering the shocks could hear the pained reactions of the confederate. Milgram found that about two-thirds of participants continued to administer shocks when instructed to do so by the 'teacher' even when they knew they were administering potentially lethal levels. Gudjonsson (2003) points out that compliance is the result of eagerness to please and/or avoidance of conflict with somebody in authority.

Suggestibility differs in an important way from both conformity and compliance. Suggestible responses are believed to be true by the person concerned. In contrast, with conformity and compliance there is not always private acceptance that the suggested information is correct. Like suggestibility, compliance and conformity help to explain why some people report incorrect information they have been exposed to. A number of social theories can also help to explain why some people may be *less* suggestible than others. These are cognitive dissonance, reactance and belief perseverance.

The theory of cognitive dissonance (Festinger, 1957) was developed to explain the discomfort people can feel when their attitudes and behaviour do not match each other. For example, if somebody is on a diet, their attitude is likely to be that they should not eat chocolate. If they do, their behaviour is at odds with their attitude, which causes cognitive dissonance. In order to reduce this cognitive dissonance, an individual might adjust their attitude to eating chocolate: 'Well, it is only 180 calories.' In the case of a police interview, if a person is asked a leading question, the knowledge that they are being led, perhaps about a detail they are uncertain of, may cause cognitive dissonance. To alleviate the associated discomfort, the witness might rationalize that the police officer must know the truth and therefore conclude that it is reasonable to accept the suggestion. Alternatively, the person may reject the suggested information to keep their behaviour (response) in line with their memory of the information in question.

Reactance (Brehm, 1966) can occur if somebody tries to persuade another to adopt a particular attitude (e.g. a hard-sell by a political campaigner). In such circumstances, individuals frequently respond by taking the *opposite* position in order to protect their personal free-dom to choose. This can even happen if the individual would, under other circumstances, agree with the proposition. The situation of a police interview, particularly for a suspect, provides an interesting example of how this might work. When a leading question is asked, some individuals may comply with the suggestion, whether or not it is true, others may *react* against it by disagreeing with the suggestion even if they know it to be true. A guilty suspect is likely to do this in any case in their own self-interest. It can become difficult to maintain this position in the face of, say, overwhelming evidence, yet some individuals may continue to exert reactance, even when it is no longer in their best interests to do so.

Belief perseverance explains the tendency to stick to an original opinion or hypothesis about people and/or social situations, despite subsequent evidence or attempted influence to the contrary (Anderson, 2007). This is of course the *opposite* of what happens in suggestibility where misinformation provided is accepted, recalled or judged to be true. Nevertheless, Bierhoff and Klein (1989) argued that the mechanisms behind belief perseverance closely resemble those used to explain secondary suggestibility, namely expectations that bias cognitive processes. The issue of belief perseverance is important in forensic contexts, for example, when it occurs among police officers interviewing suspects. Modern interview techniques emphasize the importance of keeping an open mind, yet once an investigator has decided a suspect is guilty and an interrogation starts, an innocent suspect may find that their adversary's mind is anything but open, even in the face of evidence that contradicts guilt. According to Meissner and Kassin (2004, p. 94), the interviewer may 'unwittingly create behavioral information that verifies that belief [of guilt]'.

In summary, both cognitive and social psychology contribute considerably to our understanding of factors that underpin suggestibility and, conversely, factors that might protect us from these influences.

ABOUT THIS BOOK

The purpose of this book is to review the evidence for suggestibility in legal contexts, considering research, associated theories and implications for practitioners. In each chapter, the content and conclusions are clearly stated using bullet points and forensic implications are highlighted at the end.

Chapter 2 by Quin M. Chrobak and Maria S. Zaragoza provides an overview of the various experimental methodologies used to study the misinformation effect and outlines the theoretical debates that have followed. The chapter concludes with recent work on the forced fabrication of entire fictitious events.

Chapter 3 explores the closely related area of interrogative suggestibility as conceptualized by the author, Gisli H. Gudjonsson. The chapter describes the development and applied use of the Gudjonsson Suggestibility Scales (1983, 1984) and outlines a model of interrogative suggestibility.

Chapter 4 considers memory conformity between co-witnesses who discuss their memories. Fiona Gabbert and Lorraine Hope review the methodologies that researchers have used to examine this phenomenon. Findings from this field of research, theoretical explanations and forensic implications are discussed.

Chapter 5 by Anne M. Ridley and Gisli H. Gudjonsson considers how the study of individual differences can further our understanding of suggestibility. In this review, they focus on psychosocial measures (anxiety, self-esteem and life adversity) and memory-related factors.

Chapter 6 by James Ost considers the controversial issue of recovered memories of childhood sexual abuse. He considers the likelihood that such memories can be completely forgotten for many years and reviews the evidence that false memories for traumatic and personally experienced events can be experimentally induced.

In Chapter 7, Kamala London, Lucy A. Henry, Travis Conradt and Ryan Corser outline recent work on individual differences in children's suggestibility, focusing on narrative ability, theory of mind, emotional states and intellectual disabilities.

Chapter 8 reviews research on suggestibility in three vulnerable groups. Katie L. Maras considers adults with intellectual disabilities and autism spectrum disorder, while Rachel Wilcock provides an overview of research on older witnesses.

In Chapter 9, Deborah Davis and Richard A. Leo review factors that can induce acute interrogative suggestibility when suspects are interviewed using coercive interrogation methods.

Chapter 10 by David J. La Rooy, Deirdre Brown and Michael E. Lamb considers how interview techniques (the Cognitive Interview and NICHD protocol) developed in recent years have helped to reduce the likelihood that witnesses will give suggestible responses that might mislead an investigation.

In Chapter 11 the editors summarize key findings from the book and consider the forensic implications.

CONCLUSIONS

- Suggestibility can be defined and conceptualized in a number of ways reflecting its complexity as a phenomenon of human behaviour.
- Early work on eyewitness testimony in the early twentieth century is still highly relevant.
- Binet, Stern and others who carried out early research on suggestibility, primarily among children, developed methods and protocols that are still relevant to researchers today.
- Bartlett's work on the constructive nature of memory helps to explain how suggestible responding can occur, as do social theories of conformity and compliance.

REFERENCES

Anderson, C.A. (2007). Belief perseverance. In R.F. Baumeister, & K.D. Vohs (Eds), *Encyclopedia of Social Psychology*. Thousand Oaks, CA: Sage.

Asch, S.E. (1951). Effects of group pressure upon the modification and distortion of judgment. In H. Guetzkow (Ed.), *Groups, Leadership, and Men*. Pittsburgh: Carnegie.

Asch, S.E. (1955). Opinions and social pressure. *Scientific American, 193*, 31–35.

Barber, T.X., Spanos, N.P., & Chaves, J.F. (1974). *Hypnosis, Imagination and Human Potentialities*. New York: Pergamon Press.

Bartlett, F.C. (1932). *Remembering: A Study in Experimental and Social Psychology*. Cambridge: Cambridge University Press.

Baxter, J.S. (1990). The suggestibility of child witnesses: A review. *Applied Cognitive Psychology, 4*, 393–407.

Bernheim, H. (1888). *Hypnosis and Suggestion in Psychotherapy*. (Reprinted New York: University Books, 1964).

Bierhoff, H.W., & Klein, R. (1989). Expectations, confirmation bias, and suggestibility. In V.A. Gheorghiu, P. Netter, H.J. Eysenck, & R. Rosenthal (Eds), *Suggestion and Suggestibility: Theory and Research*. Berlin: Springer-Verlag.

Binet, A. (1900). *La Suggestibilité*. Paris: Schleicher Frères.

Bornstein, B.H., & Penrod, S.D. (2008) Hugo Who? G. F. Arnold's alternative early approach to psychology and law. *Applied Cognitive Psychology, 22*, 759–768.

Brehm, J.W. (1966). *A Theory of Psychological Reactance*. New York: Academic Press.

Duke, J.D. (1964). Intercorrelational status of suggestibility tests and hypnotisability. *Psychological Record, 14*, 71–80.

Ebbinghaus, H.E. (1885). *Memory: A Contribution to Experimental Psychology*. New York: Dover (Translated 1964).

Edmonston, W.E. (1989). Conceptual clarification of hypnosis and its relationship to suggestibility. In V.A. Gheorghiu, P. Netter, H.J. Eysenck, & R. Rosenthal (Eds), *Suggestion and Suggestibility: Theory and Research*. Berlin: Springer-Verlag.

Eisen, M.L., Winograd, E., & Qin, J. (2002). Individual differences in adults' suggestibility and memory performance. In M.L. Eisen, J.A. Quas, & G.S. Goodman (Eds), *Memory and Suggestibility in the Forensic Interview*. Mahwah, NJ: Lawrence Erlbaum.

Evans, F.J. (1967). Suggestibility in the normal waking state. *Psychological Bulletin, 67*, 114–129.

Eysenck, H.J. (1947). *Dimensions of Personality*. London: Routledge & Kegan Paul.

Eysenck, H.J. (1989). Personality, primary and secondary suggestibility, and hypnosis. In V.A. Gheorghiu, P. Netter, H.J. Eysenck, & R. Rosenthal (Eds), *Suggestion and Suggestibility: Theory and Research*. Berlin: Springer-Verlag.

Eysenck, H.J., & Furneaux, W.D. (1945). Primary and secondary suggestibility: An experimental and statistical study. *Journal of Experimental Psychology, 35*, 485–503.

Festinger, L. (1957). *A Theory of Cognitive Dissonance*. Evanston, IL: Row, Peterson.

Gheorgiu, V.A. (1989). The development of research on suggestibility: Critical considerations. In V.A. Gheorghiu, P. Netter, H.J. Eysenck, & R. Rosenthal

(Eds), *Suggestion and Suggestibility: Theory and Research*. Berlin: Springer-Verlag.

Goodman, G.S. (1984). Children's testimony in historical perspective. *Journal of Social Issues, 40,* 9–31.

Gudjonsson, G.H. (2003). *The Psychology of Interrogations, Confessions, and Testimony: A Handbook*. Chichester: John Wiley & Sons, Ltd.

Gudjonsson, G.H., & Clark, N.K. (1986). Suggestibility in police interrogation: A social psychological model. *Social Behaviour, 1,* 83–104.

Hilgard, E.R. (1991). Suggestibility and suggestions as related to hypnosis. In J. F. Schumaker (Ed.), *Human Suggestibility*. New York & London: Routledge.

Koriat, A., & Goldsmith, M. (1996). Monitoring and control processes in the strategic regulation of memory accuracy. *Psychological Review, 3,* 490–517.

Koriat, A., Goldsmith, M., & Pansky, A. (2000). Towards a psychology of memory accuracy. *Annual Review of Psychology, 51,* 481–537.

Lamb, M.E., Hershkowitz, I., Orbach, Y., & Esplin, P.W. (2008). *Tell Me What Happened: Structured Investigative Interviews of Child Victims and Witnesses*. Chichester: John Wiley & Sons, Ltd.

Lipmann, O. (1911). Pedagogical psychology of report. *Journal of Educational Psychology, 2,* 253–260.

Loftus, E.F., Miller, D.G., & Burns, H.J. (1978). Semantic integration of verbal information into a visual memory. *Journal of Experimental Psychology: Human Learning & Memory, 4,* 19–31.

Meissner, C., & Kassin, S. (2004). 'You're guilty, so just confess!': Cognitive and behavioral confirmation biases in the interrogation room. In G.D. Lassiter (Ed.), *Interrogations, Confessions, and Entrapment*. New York: Springer.

Milgram, S. (1963). Behavioral study of obedience. *Journal of Abnormal and Social Psychology, 67,* 371–378.

Ministry of Justice (2011). *Achieving Best Evidence in Criminal Proceedings: Guidance on Interviewing Victims and Witnesses, and Guidance on using special Measures* (3rd edition). London: Ministry of Justice.

Münsterberg, H. (1908/1925). *On the Witness Stand: Essays on Psychology and Crime*. http://psychclassics.yorku.ca/Munster/Witness/ (accessed 20 March 2012).

Orbach, Y., Lamb, M.E., La Rooy, D., & Pipe, M.-E. (2012). A case study of witness consistency and memory recovery across multiple investigative interviews. *Applied Cognitive Psychology, 26,* 118–129.

Ost, J., & Costall, A. (2002). Misremembering Bartlett: A study in serial reproduction. *British Journal of Psychology, 93,* 243–255.

Powers, P.A., Andriks, J.L., & Loftus, E.F. (1979). Eyewitness accounts of females and males. *Journal of Applied Psychology, 64,* 339–347.

Sheehan, P.W. (1989). Commentary on 'Theoretical and Historical Perspectives'. In V.A. Gheorghiu, P. Netter, H.J. Eysenck, & R. Rosenthal (Eds), *Suggestion and Suggestibility: Theory and Research*. Berlin: Springer-Verlag.

Sidis, B. (1898). *The Psychology of Suggestion*. New York: Appleton.

Sporer, S.L. (2008). Lessons from the origins of eyewitness testimony research in Europe. *Applied Cognitive Psychology, 22 (6),* 737–758.

Stern, W. (1910). Abstracts of lectures on the psychology of testimony and on the study of individuality. *The American Journal of Psychology, 21,* 270–282.

Stukat, K.G. (1958). *Suggestibility: A Factor and Experimental Analysis*. Stockholm: Almquist & Wiksell.

Wagstaff, G. (1991). Suggestibility: A social psychological approach. In J.F. Schumaker (Ed.), *Human Suggestibility*. New York & London: Routledge.

Whipple, G.M. (1909). The observer as reporter: A survey of the 'psychology of testimony'. *Psychological Bulletin, 6,* 153–170.

Whipple, G.M. (1911). The psychology of testimony. *Psychological Bulletin, 8,* 307–309.

Whipple, G.M. (1913). Psychology of testimony and report. *Psychological Bulletin, 10,* 264–268.

Wigmore, J.H. (1909). Professor Munsterberg and the psychology of testimony. *Illinois Law Review,* 399–445.

Wrightsman, L.S. (2001). *Forensic Psychology.* Belmont, CA: Wadsworth.

2

The Misinformation Effect: Past Research and Recent Advances

QUIN M. CHROBAK AND MARIA S. ZARAGOZA

KEY POINTS

This chapter will provide a comprehensive review of the *misinformation effect*. Specifically it will:

- Provide a historical overview of research on misinformation effects and trace the evolution of research and theory on these and related phenomena.
- Discuss methodological issues relevant to studies of misinformation phenomena, with an emphasis on their implications for interpreting experimental findings.
- Describe the various theoretical proposals that have been put forward to explain misinformation phenomena.
- Describe recent, more ecologically valid extensions of the misinformation effect, new theoretical developments, and implications for real life forensic situations.

Although psychologists had long suspected that investigative interviews have the potential to distort eyewitness testimony (Binet, 1900; Münsterburg, 1908), modern research on the topic did not begin

Suggestibility in Legal Contexts: Psychological Research and Forensic Implications,
First Edition. Edited by Anne M. Ridley, Fiona Gabbert and David J. La Rooy.
© 2013 John Wiley & Sons, Ltd. Published 2013 by John Wiley & Sons, Ltd.

until the 1970s, when a series of studies by Elizabeth Loftus and colleagues on the 'misinformation effect' confirmed their suspicions and ushered in a new era of psychological research on memory. The *misinformation effect* is the finding that misleading post-event suggestions introduced after an eyewitness event are highly likely to contaminate eyewitness memory, in some cases resulting in confident recollections of suggested events that never actually transpired (see Zaragoza, Belli, & Payment, 2007, for a review).

The misinformation effect is one of the most influential findings in experimental psychology. A google.scholar search for the term yields almost 2000 hits, a rather staggering number given the sheer simplicity of the experimental paradigm that produces it. In a typical experiment, participants view a slide sequence depicting a complex and forensically relevant event, such as a traffic accident or theft. Immediately thereafter, participants are questioned about the event they witnessed. The critical manipulation is that the post-event questioning includes false or misleading suggestions, typically introduced in the form of presuppositions or leading questions. Finally, participants are tested on their memory for the witnessed event. The 'misinformation effect' is the finding that, when compared to control participants who were not misinformed, participants in the misled group are likely to report the misleading suggestions, rather than the events they actually witnessed. Because the misinformation was introduced in an incidental way that does not draw attention to it, the misinformation effect is a type of suggestibility referred to in this volume as *investigative suggestibility*.

To what can we attribute the surprising longevity of research on the misinformation effect? First, it is one of the most robust and reliable findings in experimental psychology, having been replicated across countless laboratories, using a variety of both witnessed and suggested items/events, and utilizing a wide range of test conditions. A second reason for the longstanding interest is that it raises fundamental questions about human memory and its validity: How faithfully are the events we experience stored in memory? Are memories permanent, or might they be susceptible to irreversible loss and even alteration? What is the nature of the memory representations that underlie our recollections of the past? Is it possible to develop genuine false memories for fictitious events that never actually transpired? These are just some of the basic questions that have been investigated in the context of misinformation phenomena. Finally, the misinformation effect has important implications for legal systems that rely on eyewitness evidence in the administration of justice. The fallibility of eyewitness memory has been a central issue in many well-publicized cases (e.g. Thompson-Cannino, Cotton, & Toreneo, 2009), and reinforces concerns about the reliability and validity of eyewitness testimony. Clearly, advancing our scientific understanding of eyewitness memory and its susceptibility to post-event suggestion is critical from both a theoretical and practical point of view. In what follows, we will review the range of phenomena that can be classified as 'misinformation effects' and describe some prominent theoretical accounts that have been put forward to explain them.

CONTRADICTORY MISINFORMATION AND INTERFERENCE ACCOUNTS OF MISINFORMATION PHENOMENA

The basic 'misinformation effect' was first demonstrated in a seminal paper by Loftus, Miller, and Burns (1978). In this study, all participants first viewed a slide sequence depicting an auto-pedestrian accident that took place near a *stop sign*. When subsequently interviewed about the events they had seen, participants in the misled condition were asked the following suggestive question, 'Did another car pass the red Datsun when it was stopped at the *yield sign*?' Participants in the corresponding control condition were not exposed to misinformation about a yield sign during the post-event interview. At the time of a final memory test for the witnessed event, all participants were given a two-alternative forced-choice recognition test that presented them with a stop sign (originally witnessed) and a yield sign (post-event misinformation for participants in the misled group). In this case, the relationship between the post-event misinformation and the corresponding original detail is contradictory in that the two items are mutually exclusive – there could only be one traffic sign on the street corner, and hence only one of the two test alternatives could be correct. The critical finding was that whereas 75% of the control participants correctly selected the stop sign on the test, only 41% of misled participants correctly identified the sign as a stop sign. Similar demonstrations of profound decrements in memory performance that result from exposure to misinformation have been replicated in countless studies (see Ayers & Reder, 1998; Zaragoza *et al.*, 2007, for reviews).

Initially, theoretical accounts of the misinformation effect focused on the 'fate' of the original memory. Were misled participants actually able to recover the originally witnessed details, but simply failed to report them on the test for some reason (e.g. because the misinformation occurred more recently)? In order to address this issue, subsequent studies by Loftus and colleagues required participants who selected the misinformation to give a second guess (e.g. was it a 'stop sign' or a 'no parking' sign?). Presumably, if participants had access to the original information – they would demonstrate an increased likelihood of selecting the original information when given a second chance. However, results indicated that performance was not greater than chance. This led Loftus (1979a, b; Loftus & Loftus, 1980) to propose that exposure to contradictory misinformation resulted in 'destructive updating' of the original memory trace, whereby the misleading suggestion permanently replaces the originally seen item from memory.

In a significant departure from the mainstream view, McCloskey and Zaragoza (1985a) argued that the misinformation effect did not provide conclusive evidence that the original memory had been impaired by the misleading suggestion. They noted that participants in misinformation experiments (like eyewitnesses to forensically relevant events) do not have perfect recall of the original eyewitness event, *even in the absence of misleading post-event information*. This is clearly illustrated in data from Loftus *et al.* (1978), as control performance (for participants who did not receive the misinformation) for the critical items was well below ceiling. Thus, for those misled participants who do not remember what type of traffic sign they saw (e.g. because they failed to encode it), the misinformation about a yield sign fills a gap in memory. Further, because these participants have no memory of the stop sign to contradict it, they are likely to be systematically biased to report the misinformation at test. In contrast, control participants who failed to encode the stop sign should not be uniformly inclined to select the incorrect response (yield sign) because they were never exposed to it during the intervening phase of the experiment.

In order to assess whether exposure to misinformation erased originally witnessed details, McCloskey and Zaragoza (1985a) conducted a series of experiments using the same basic paradigm as Loftus *et al.* (1978), but using a different eyewitness event – in this case, an office theft. Briefly, participants viewed a slide show depicting a maintenance man stealing some money from an office, and stashing it in his toolbox. Some participants who had witnessed the man lift a hammer from his tool box, later read an account of the office theft containing the misinformation that he had lifted a wrench from the toolbox. Hence, in this example, the type of tool was the critical item, with 'hammer' as the originally witnessed item and 'wrench' serving as the misleading post-event information. McCloskey and Zaragoza (1985a) showed that when they used the standard test that gave participants a forced-choice between the originally seen and the suggested item (e.g. hammer vs. wrench), they obtained robust misinformation effects (collapsing across six experiments, mean accuracy was 37% versus 72% for misled and control conditions, respectively), thus replicating the misinformation effects documented by Loftus *et al.* (1978). In order to assess whether the original memory (e.g. hammer) had been erased by exposure to the misinformation (e.g. wrench), McCloskey and Zaragoza (1985a) devised a modified version of the final recognition test that did not include the misleading post-event suggestion as an option on the test. In the Modified Recognition Test, participants were forced to choose between the originally presented detail (e.g. hammer) and a *new* item from the same category (e.g. a screwdriver) – the misleading item (e.g. wrench) was not a test option. McCloskey and Zaragoza reasoned that if misled participants' original memory of the 'hammer' had been destructively updated by exposure to 'wrench', misled participants should perform more poorly than control participants (who had not been misled) on the Modified Recognition Test. The results were clear – across a series of six experiments using the Modified Recognition Test, misled participants correctly identified the original item (e.g. hammer) on the test as often as control participants did (collapsing across six experiments, mean accuracy was 72% vs. 75%, for the misled and control conditions, respectively) thus providing strong evidence that exposure to misinformation had not erased the original item from memory.

In summary, McCloskey and Zaragoza (1985a) demonstrated that the performance of misled participants was due entirely to whether or not the suggested misinformation was an option on the test. When given a choice between the original and suggested item, misled participants overwhelmingly selected the incorrect suggested item over the item they had actually seen. However, when given the choice between the original (correct) item and a similar, but new, item, misled performance was as accurate as control performance. Based on the evidence that there was no decrement in misled performance on this Modified Test, McCloskey and Zaragoza (1985a) argued that exposure to misinformation neither erases nor impairs access to original event details. Rather, they concluded that the misinformation effect is probably due to gap filling – the tendency for misled participants who failed to encode/remember the originally seen item to accept the suggested item, and systematically report it on the test.

Consistent with McCloskey and Zaragoza's (1985a) arguments, empirical evidence supports the contention that contradictory misinformation effects are most likely to be observed in situations where memory for the originally witnessed details are weak or non-existent. For example, misinformation effects are typically limited to peripheral details (e.g. stop signs), that are not central to the story line and are typically not well remembered (e.g. Tousignant, Hall, & Loftus, 1986). Moreover, there is abundant evidence that misinformation effects increase as a function of the delay between the witnessed event and exposure to misinformation, presumably because memory for the originally witnessed item becomes weaker over time (e.g. Loftus *et al.*, 1978; see also Paz-Alonso & Goodman, 2008; Pezdek & Roe,1995; see also, e.g. Brainerd & Reyna, 1998, for related arguments that rapid forgetting of verbatim, as opposed to gist, memories underlies misinformation effects). Conversely, manipulations that serve to enhance participants' memory for the originally witnessed detail *before* contradictory misinformation is introduced have been shown to inoculate participants against misinformation effects. For example, Pansky and Tenenboim (2011) recently showed that participants who were asked to recall the specific item they had witnessed immediately after viewing an event – and did so correctly – were resistant to the contradictory misinformation presented later. Collectively, these findings support the view that participants will be influenced by contradictory misinformation when it fills a gap in their memory, and will be resistant to it otherwise.

McCloskey and Zaragoza's (1985a) claims that misleading post-event information did not impair original memories sparked a great deal of research and debate (Belli, 1989, 1993; Belli, Windschitl, McCarthy, & Winfrey, 1992; Bowman & Zaragoza, 1989; Chandler, 1989; Eakin, Schreiber, & Sergent-Marshall, 2003; Lindsay, 1990; Loftus, Donders, Hoffman, & Schooler, 1989; Loftus & Hoffman, 1989; Loftus, Schooler, & Wagenaar, 1985; McCloskey & Zaragoza, 1985b; Metcalfe, 1990; Paz-Alonso & Goodman, 2008; Schooler, Foster, & Loftus, 1988; Schreiber & Sergent, 1998; Tversky & Tuchin, 1989; see Ayers & Reder, 1998 and Zaragoza *et al.*, 2007, for reviews). Although McCloskey and Zaragoza's (1985a) findings with the Modified Test has been replicated many times and under many conditions, there is now clear evidence that reliable, albeit small, memory impairment effects *can be* obtained even when the Modified Test is used (though the exact conditions that result in impairment effects have been difficult to identify, see Zaragoza *et al.*, 2007, for discussion). In a meta-analysis of 44 published experiments that used the Modified Recognition Test (Payne, Toglia, & Anastasi, 1994), only 14 of the 44 experiments obtained significantly poorer performance in the misled condition relative to the control condition, although collectively the overall memory impairment effect was statistically significant.

In conclusion, there is now empirical evidence that misleading post-event information does sometimes impair originally witnessed memories, although these impairment effects are small and inconsistent. Whether such impairment effects are due to destructive updating of the original memory trace or impaired access to an intact trace cannot be determined conclusively. Indeed, the fundamental question of whether human memory representations can be permanently altered by subsequent experiences continues to be the subject of intense interest and debate among neuroscientists (see, for example, Schiller & Phelps, 2011).

Collectively, the empirical research on the potential memory impairing effects of post-event misinformation shows that interference caused by misinformation (be it by destructive updating or impaired accessibility) plays, at best, a small role in participants' tendency to incorporate misleading suggestions into their recollections of witnessed events. However, the memory impairment account of misinformation effects leaves unanswered some important questions regarding these phenomena. Why are participants so prone to incorporating the suggested post-event information into their memory reports of the witnessed event, and by what mechanisms do they do so? Do misled participants come to develop genuine false recollections of having witnessed the misleading details? Clearly, answers to such questions are critical for predicting when misinformation effects are likely to occur, and developing interventions that might prevent them. The next section reviews evidence bearing on these questions.

In order to address these issues, many subsequent eyewitness sug-gestibility studies have used misleading post-event information that serves to supplement, rather than contradict, originally witnessed details (the post-event source might suggest that a thief carried a gun, when in fact he carried no weapon) (cf., Gabbert, Memon, & Wright, 2006). The use of supplementary misinformation allows one to sepa-rate questions about why participant/witnesses come to embrace misleading suggestions from questions about the potential memory impairing effects of misinformation. In situations involving supple-mentary or additive misinformation, there is no original object or detail that is contradicted by the misinformation, and the misinformation is not in direct conflict with an original memory. Thus, 'impairment' of an original memory is not relevant to explaining suggestibility in situ-ations involving supplementary misinformation.

FALSE RECOLLECTIONS OF SUGGESTED DETAILS
AND CONSTRUCTIVIST ACCOUNTS
OF MISINFORMATION EFFECTS

A review of the scientific literature reveals that misinformation phenomena are often described as providing evidence that 'false memo-ries' can be caused by exposure to post-event suggestions. However, it is often unclear what exactly is meant by the term 'false memory'. In some cases, investigators use the term 'false memory' as a shorthand description of participants' performance. That is, the term is used to indicate that participants are reporting and/or selecting false informa-tion on a test of memory for the witnessed event. The use of the term 'false memory' in this way makes no assumptions about the partici-pants' beliefs, mental experience, or the basis for their incorrect response. In other cases, however, the term is used to indicate that participants have developed genuine false *recollections* of having witnessed the misinformation. As we discuss below, the finding that participants select the misleading alternative (or report it) on a test of memory for the event does not necessarily imply that participants have a false recollection of having witnessed the misleading details. Indeed, there are several reasons why participants can be expected to report the misinformation on forced choice recognition tests of the witnessed event, even if they do not falsely recollect it. Hence, if *false recollection* is the sense in which the term 'false memory' is being used, the misinformation effects that have been obtained with the standard paradigm cannot be taken as conclusive evidence of 'false memory'. In the next section, we describe techniques researchers have used to probe the basis of misled participants' responses. These techniques have allowed researchers to more directly assess whether misled participants develop genuine false recollections as a consequence of having been exposed to misinformation.

The situation faced by participants in the typical misinformation experiment is imbued with considerable demand. The misinformation is presented as 'truth' by an experimenter whom participants probably view as knowledgeable and in a position of authority. Hence, it is possible that participants select the misleading alternative because they feel some pressure or demand to conform to the suggestion provided by the experimenter, or alternatively, they select the misleading alternative because they assume the experimenter is correct. For these reasons, misled participants might choose to *report* the misinformation even if they know they do not remember witnessing it.

One technique investigators have used to minimize the contribution of demand on final memory test performance is to warn participants, typically before the final memory test, that the information contained in the post-event narrative or questionnaire is not trustworthy. This is typically done by informing participants that the post-event source contained (or may have contained) misinformation that was not in the witnessed event, or by providing a 'social' warning informing participants that the post-event source had intentions to mislead (see Echterhoff, Hirst, & Hussy, 2005, for a review). A consistent finding is that warnings tend to reduce, but do not eliminate, the reporting of misinformation (see, e.g. Chambers & Zaragoza, 2001; Echterhoff *et al.*, 2005). This demonstrates that in some cases participants report the misinformation even when they are aware that they have been misled and are presumably motivated to avoid being influenced by the misinformation.

Of course, the finding that participants report the misinformation even when warned, does not necessarily imply that they have developed a false recollection. As McCloskey and Zaragoza (1985a) noted, many participants fail to remember/encode aspects of the originally witnessed event, and hence have no memory of their own that directly refutes the suggested misinformation. Hence, warnings may be ineffective because such participants have no basis for rejecting the misinformation as 'false' – because they do not have access to disconfirming information. Note that the task demands of the standard misinformation experiment are such that participants are expected to select a response on the final recognition test – 'don't know' or 'neither' are typically not provided as response options. Hence, if the misleading item is highly famil-iar and participants have no reason to believe it is false, they may select it on the test even if they know they do not remember witnessing it.

To more directly assess whether misled participants misremember the post-event information as part of the witnessed event, researchers have used source recognition tests as the final test of memory for the witnessed event. The typical source test presents participants with the possible sources of information in memory (i.e. the originally witnessed event, the post-event questions/or narrative, both the originally witnessed event and post-event source, or neither), and requires that participants identify the true source of each item at test. In this way, source recognition tests eliminate the demand inherent in the standard procedure, as they inform participants that the post-event source contained information that was not in the original event and allow them to choose that as the source of the misleading information. The question of interest is whether or not participants incorrectly identify the original event as the source of the misinformation.

The consistent finding across a large number of studies is that misled participants claim to remember witnessing the misinformation more often than controls, even when a source recognition test is used, and even when the source test is accompanied by direct and explicit warnings (Ackil & Zaragoza, 2011; Belli, Lindsay, Gales, & McCarthy, 1994; Chambers & Zaragoza, 2001; Drivdahl & Zaragoza, 2001; Frost, Ingraham, & Wilson, 2002; Hekkanen & McEvoy, 2002; Lane, Mather, Villa, & Morita, 2001; Lindsay, 1990; Mitchell & Zaragoza, 1996, 2001; Zaragoza & Lane, 1994; Zaragoza & Mitchell, 1996). Nevertheless, it is also true that relative to the standard recognition tests, source monitor-ing tests tend to reduce claims of having witnessed the misleading items in the originally witnessed event. Presumably, the discriminations required by the source recognition tests induce participants to retrieve more source-specifying information than they would spontaneously retrieve in other testing situations.

Although the finding that participants misattribute post-event suggestions to the witnessed event on a source recognition test would seem to provide strong evidence of 'false recollection', it is possible that these findings reflect a highly confident false *belief* that the misinfor-mation came from the witnessed event, rather than a false recollection, per se. In other words, participants may believe the information occurred, even though they cannot specifically recollect it. More convincing evidence that participants sometimes develop genuine false recollec-tions comes from studies that have used measures of phenomenological experience (Tulving, 1985). For example, participants who claim they remember the misinformation from the witnessed event are subse-quently asked whether they *recollect* witnessing the suggested item in the original event or simply *believe* it was in the original event (e.g. Lane & Zaragoza, 2007; Zaragoza & Mitchell, 1996; Zaragoza, Mitchell, Payment & Drivdahl, *et al* 2011). Evidence shows that some, though not all, participants who claim to remember witnessing the misinformation on a source test also claim to 'recollect' witnessing it – thus showing that some participants falsely recollect witnessing the misinformation that was only suggested to them.

In summary, not all reports of misleading suggestions can be taken as evidence of false recollections, as there are many factors that can lead participant-witnesses to report the misinformation on a test. Participants may report the misinformation because of a perceived demand to conform or play along with the information provided by the experimenter, or because they believe the misinformation to be true. Hence, assessing whether participants develop false recollections requires the use of memory measures (e.g. source recognition tests and measures of phenomenological experience) that provide more precise information about participants' memory for the misinformation and the nature of their recollective experience. The results of studies using these measures provide strong evidence that exposure to misinformation can sometimes lead to genuine false recollections.

What are the cognitive mechanisms that underlie these false recollection effects? Misinformation phenomena are often viewed by researchers as instances of a more general class of constructive memory errors known as *source monitoring errors* (Lindsay & Johnson, 1989; Zaragoza & Lane, 1994). A source monitoring error (or *source misattribution error*) occurs when information from one source is misattributed to a different source (e.g. confusing something one only thought about doing with something one actually did, such as believing one locked the front door before leaving the house, when in fact one only thought about doing so). In the case of suggestibility phenomena, participant-witnesses are incorrectly attributing information gleaned from a post-event source to the originally witnessed event. Marcia Johnson and colleagues (Johnson, Hashtroudi, & Lindsay, 1993; Lindsay, 2008) developed a general theoretical framework, the Source Monitoring Framework (SMF) that has proven quite useful in predicting and explaining the memory errors that result from exposure to misleading post-event information.

According to the SMF, information about an item's source is typically not stored explicitly in memory. Rather, source identification is an *attribution* that involves assessing the qualitative and quantitative characteristics of an activated memory. Importantly, the SMF emphasizes that the attribution of source will be heavily influenced by the rememberer's goals, motivations and agenda. From this view, errors in source monitoring arise either because people fail to encode or activate the memory characteristics necessary to support accurate source monitoring, or because they fail to engage in the systematic and effortful decision-making processes that accurate source monitoring sometimes requires.

As predicted by the SMF, a consistent finding in the eyewitness suggestibility literature is that misattributions of post-event suggestions to the originally witnessed events are most likely to occur when the following two conditions occur simultaneously: (1) the activated memory of the suggested information has qualities or characteristics that resemble those of witnessed events; and (2) no information is retrieved that indicates the true source of the suggested event.

In general, source confusions are most often observed when people attempt to discriminate between sources that are very similar, or overlap, on a variety of characteristics. For example, the tendency to confuse imagined events for real events can be attributed to representations of imagined events having high levels of sensory-perceptual details – a characteristic that overlaps with representations of real events. In the eyewitness suggestibility paradigm, there are multiple sources of overlap between the witnessed event and the post-event narrative/questionnaire about the event (see Mitchell & Zaragoza, 2001, for discussion). Specifically, the post-event narrative/questionnaire is about the very same people and events the participants witnessed, resulting in a great deal of overlap in semantic content. Moreover, processing of the post-event narrative/questions is likely to be accompanied by active rehearsal and mental reconstruction of the witnessed event. Reflecting on the originally witnessed events while processing the post-event information may serve to increase the overlap between the two sources even further. Given that much of the information encountered in the post-event session is true of the witnessed event, simply knowing that the suggested item came from the post-event source does not necessarily imply that it was not witnessed (i.e. Gallo, 2004). Hence, even accurate memory for the suggestion's true source (e.g. a post-event narrative) does not prevent the participant from misattributing it to the witnessed event.

Consistent with the SMF, studies have shown that encouraging participants to reflectively elaborate on suggested events in ways that imbue them with characteristics that are similar to real events promotes false memory development. For example, there is considerable evidence that visual imagery can serve as a potent catalyst to false memory creation (Goff & Roediger, 1998; Hyman & Pentland, 1996). Specifically, imagining suggested events imbues the mental experience of the suggested event with sensory and perceptual details similar to those of perceived events (see Drivdahl & Zaragoza, 2001; Thomas, Bulevich, & Loftus, 2003). Similarly, asking participants/witnesses questions which encourage them to reflectively elaborate on the emotional implications (Drivdahl, Zaragoza, & Learned, 2009) or meaning and implications of suggested events (Zaragoza et al., 2011) similarly increases false recollections of suggested items.

RECENT EXTENSIONS OF THE MISINFORMATION PARADIGM: FORCED FABRICATION AND FALSE RECOLLECTION OF KNOWINGLY FABRICATED DETAILS

As mentioned at the outset of this chapter, misinformation phenomena provide an example of *investigative suggestibility*, insofar as participants/ witnesses fall prey to misleading details that are presented in an indirect fashion (e.g. embedded in post-event questions as presuppositions rather than as the focus of the question). However, in real-world forensic investigations, suggestive interviews are not restricted to situations where an interviewer *provides* or implants some piece of false information in a way that does not call attention to it. Rather, in an attempt to gather evidence, forensic interviewers sometimes attempt to *elicit* from witnesses information about events they do not remember well, did not see, or that may not have actually taken place. In other words, interviewers may press witnesses to go beyond their actual memory, pressuring them to speculate or even fabricate information (Gudjonsson, 1992; Kassin, 1997; Leo, 1996). Hence, the traditional misinformation paradigm does not address whether more overt and coercive efforts to elicit desired testimony from witnesses might later lead to false eyewitness accounts or false recollections. This latter type of suggestibility is referred to in this volume as *interrogative suggestibility*.

The memorial impact of encouraging participant/witnesses to speculate has been explored in variants of the misinformation paradigm. As in the standard paradigm, participants view an eyewitness event and are then tested on their memory. The critical difference between the standard and elicited misinformation paradigms occurs during the second phase of the experiment. In elicited misinformation paradigms, participants are encouraged to speculate or guess about a piece of information that they had not originally witnessed. This is in contrast to the standard paradigms, where the false information is provided by the experimenter. Hence, we use the term *elicited misinformation* to refer to those situations where the misinformation has been actively generated by the participant, who would not have done so without the explicit instruction (and in some cases coercion) of the experimenter.

In some experimental designs, the pressure exerted on participants to produce an answer is minimal. For example, a number of studies have examined the impact on later memory of asking participants to provide guesses to false-event questions on a pencil and paper questionnaire (Pezdek, Lam, & Sperry, 2009; Pezdek, Sperry, & Owens, 2007). For example, participants in Pezdek *et al.* (2007) viewed a 5-minute video of a carjacking and were later asked to provide a written description of the victim's wristwatch – even though no watch had been worn. At the start of the post-event questioning, participants were instructed to answer every question. When asked to complete the same questionnaire again at some later point, participants report their previously false answers at a high rate and with increased confidence. These findings suggest that participants forgot that their initial responses were mere guesses. Similar results have been found on studies investigating the memorial consequence of invited speculation in children (e.g. Compo & Parker, 2010; Schreiber & Parker, 2004; Schreiber, Wentura, & Bilsky, 2001). In these studies, children view an eyewitness event (e.g. a clown performance) in which the principal actor performs a number of uncommon actions with a number of known objects (e.g. slipping on a banana). At the time of the post-event interview, children are asked to speculate about what else the clown may have done with the common object. A natural consequence of this paradigm is that children are induced to all produce the same false information (e.g. 'He ate it.'). Results suggest that children display false memory effects for their speculations up to 5–6 months after the event, and often are quite poor at recanting their previous speculations when given the opportunity. Although both of these experimental paradigms elicit speculative information from participants, they lack a component typical of coerced forensic testimony. Specifically, in such situations the interviewer actively pressures the witness to describe events they do not remember, even if they actively resist doing so. In the aforementioned studies, participants freely complied with the request to guess or speculate or, in some cases, chose to ignore the instructions.

By contrast, the *forced fabrication paradigm* introduced by Zaragoza and colleagues is more analogous to coercive forensic interviews (see also, e.g. Kassin, 1997, for experimental studies on the related phenomenon of forced confessions). In the *forced fabrication paradigm*, participants view an event and then engage in individual, face-to-face interviews with an experimenter who presses them to answer false-event questions about items or events that, although plausible, were never actually witnessed (e.g. Zaragoza, Payment, Ackil, Drivdahl, & Beck, 2001). For example, in Zaragoza *et al.* (2001) participants watched a short video about two brothers at a summer camp. Afterwards, they were required to answer questions about information not included in the eyewitness event. For example, participants were asked where the protagonist was bleeding after he fell in the cafeteria. Such false-event questions required a fabricated response, because although participants saw the protagonist fall, they did not see him bleed. Hence, in order to answer these questions, participants had to make up, or fabricate, a response. Although participants were instructed at the outset of the experiment that they were required to answer every question – even if they had to guess – participants almost always resisted answering these false event questions. Participants resisted in a variety of ways: by remaining silent until prompted to respond, by evading the question, or by overtly resisting with statements such as 'I don't remember' or 'I didn't see that'. In response to this resistance, the experimenter repeatedly pressed the participant to provide an answer (e.g. 'just give me your best guess') until the participant eventually acquiesced. Thus participants were 'forced' into fabricating information they would not have provided had they not been pressed to do so (see Zaragoza *et al.*, 2001, for empirical evidence that participants refrain from answering these questions when given the option of doing so). One week later, participants returned to the lab individually, and were greeted by a different experimenter than the person who had interviewed them initially. This experimenter informed the participant that the person who had interviewed them earlier had asked them some questions about things that never actually happened (this warning was provided to minimize any demand). Participants were then given a source test of their memory for both witnessed and fabricated events. For example, a participant who had earlier fabricated the response that the protagonist's *knee* was bleeding, was asked 'When you watched the video, did you see Delaney's *knee* bleeding after he fell?'.

Intuitively, it seems that participants would remember which test items they had been pressed into fabricating, especially given the discomfort and uncertainty they evidenced when fabricating these responses. To the contrary, however, there is now considerable evidence that, in retention intervals as short as one week, participants are prone to developing false recollections of having witnessed the items they had knowingly fabricated earlier (Ackil & Zaragoza, 1998; Frost, LaCroix, & Sanborn, 2003; Hanba & Zaragoza, 2007; Zaragoza *et al.*, 2001).

In attempting to understand the reasons why participants develop these false recollections, many of the same factors that contribute to source confusion in the standard paradigm are present (e.g. the high degree of overlap between the eyewitness event and the post-event interview, e.g. Mitchell & Zaragoza, 2001; the likelihood that participants actively imagine the fabricated events, Goff & Roediger, 1998; Hyman & Pentland, 1996). However, there are a number of unique factors associated with forced fabrication that probably contribute to false recollection in this paradigm. First, participants' forced fabrications are self-generated, and as a result of the effort and elaboration that goes into generating these responses, the content of their fabricated accounts are likely to be highly memorable (Hirshman & Bjork, 1988; Slamecka & Graf, 1978). Moreover, because the self-generated fabrication is constructed within the constraints of a person's idiosyncratic knowledge and beliefs, this information may later be perceived by the participant as especially plausible. What is surprising about these findings is that participants so quickly forget that these items are mere guesses that they had earlier provided only after being pressed to do so. In the next section, we provide evidence for an additional mechanism that contributes to the development of false recollections following forced fabrication interviews.

FORCED FABRICATION OF ENTIRE FICTITIOUS EVENTS
AND THE EXPLANATORY ROLE HYPOTHESIS

As mentioned previously, one motivation for understanding the contaminating effects of suggestive interviews on eyewitness memory is the relevance of these phenomena for real-world forensic situations. In this regard, one limitation of the forced fabrication studies described above (as well as all of the studies reviewed thus far) is that the forced fabrications were restricted to specific items or details, most of which were not central to the storyline (e.g. the kind of hat the protagonist was wearing). In contrast, the goal of many forensic interviews is to elicit testimony that is much broader in scope and more consequential. Hence, the aforementioned empirical evidence regarding forced fabrication effects does not address whether suggestive interviews can induce false recollections of fictitious recent events that are broad in scope and extended in time, and that involve people and events that never actually transpired.[1]

To address this gap in the literature, Chrobak and Zaragoza (2008) set out to determine whether participants who were forced to fabricate entire fictitious events might eventually come to misremember witnessing these fictitious events. Of course, one consequence of pressing participants to fabricate an entire fictitious event is increased resistance on the part of participants. To illustrate the coercive nature of these interviews and participants' resistance to fabricating an entire fictitious event, we provide below a portion of an interview with a participant from one of our studies (Chrobak & Zaragoza, 2008). In the example, the participant had earlier witnessed a video clip from a movie involving two brothers at a summer camp. In one of the scenes that the participant actually witnessed, two camp counsellors, Delaney and Moe, are seen sneaking out at night on canoes as the sun sets. The next scene in the movie then depicts Delaney getting in big trouble with the camp director the following day. These two scenes were used as the basis for a false event question that required participants to fabricate where the two counsellors went and what they did when they went out on canoes – even though this information was not depicted in the original eyewitness event:

> E: Towards the end of the movie, Delaney and Moe use a canoe and sneak off at night. After sneaking out where do they go and what did they do that caused them to get into big trouble?

[1] Several studies have shown that it is possible to implant in adult participants a false memory of an entire fictitious event that allegedly occurred in their childhood (e.g. that they got lost in a mall; Loftus & Pickrell, 1995). Although these studies show that it is possible to implant false memories for broader events that are extended in time, they do not address whether participants will similarly develop false recollections of entire fictitious events that are forcibly fabricated and are from the recent past (as opposed to childhood).

P: Uhh … See I don't remember that scene at all.
E: I just need your best guess as to what they did.
P: Um … Uhh maybe they went to go see some girls. I don't know.
E: Ok, where specifically did they go?
P: I … I don't know maybe there's a girls' camp around. I don't know.
E: Um what specifically did they do at the girls' camp?
P: I don't, I don't know [nervous laughter].
E: I just need an answer.
P: Maybe try to mess with the girls. I don't know.
E: OK, how specifically did they try to mess with the girls?
P: Uhhh maybe try to make out with them. I don't know.
E: OK
P: Again that's probably wrong.
E: Who was there?
P: Uh …
E: At the girls' camp.
P: Uh. I guess just those two, I really don't know.

When participants were tested after 1 week with a recognition test procedure similar to that employed in earlier studies, participants correctly rejected their fabrications (e.g. they tried to make out with the girls at the girls' camp) as 'not witnessed'. Presumably, participants remembered that these events were 'guesses' that they had earlier been pressured to provide. The critical finding occurred 2 months after the witnessed event, when participants returned to the lab and were asked to freely recall what they remembered from the originally witnessed event. On this delayed free recall test, Chrobak and Zaragoza (2008) found that participants reported their forced fabrications nearly 50% of the time, even in cases where they had correctly rejected them as false on the 1-week recognition test. To be certain, the long retention interval led participants to forget that these events were forced fabrications, thus predisposing them to falsely remember their fabrications as part of the witnessed event. However, Chrobak and Zaragoza (2008) proposed that another factor also likely contributed to the development of these false recollections. Specifically, they hypothesized that participants were prone to developing false recollections for their forced fabrications (e.g. that the counsellors went to the girls' camp) because the fabricated events helped to explain an outcome that they had actually witnessed (one of the counsellors getting in serious trouble with the camp director the following day). This hypothesis, which we refer to as the *explanatory role hypothesis*, is consistent with a large body of research demonstrating that people are highly motivated to seek out the causes of the events they experience (e.g. Schank & Abelson, 1977).

In a recent study, Q.M. Chrobak and M.S. Zaragoza (under review) tested the 'explanatory role hypothesis' by manipulating the relationship between participants' forced fabrications and the events they had witnessed. Participants viewed one of two versions of the video clip used in Chrobak and Zaragoza (2008). In some situations (Outcome condition) participants witnessed an outcome (e.g. the counsellors getting in trouble) that could be explained by an event they would later be required to fabricate in the post-event interview (e.g. 'Where did they go and what did they do when they snuck out at night on canoes?'). However, in other cases (No Outcome condition), participants were required to fabricate an answer to the same false event question (e.g. 'Where did they go and what did they do when they snuck out at night on canoes?') but in this case they had *not* witnessed the scene where the counsellors get in trouble – as it had been replaced by an unrelated scene (a counsellor horseback riding). Thus, in the No Outcome condition, participants' fabrications (e.g. going to the girls' camp) did not explain an outcome they had witnessed. In two separate experiments, participants tested 6 weeks after being interviewed were roughly three times as likely to freely report (Experiment 1) and falsely assent to (Experiment 2) having witnessed their forced fabrications when the fabricated event helped to explain a witnessed outcome (Outcome condition) than when it did not (No Outcome condition). These results support the conclusion that participants are more likely to develop false memories for forcibly fabricated entire events when they serve an explanatory function.

In a follow-up experiment, Chrobak and Zaragoza (under review) provide additional evidence that participants are more likely to develop false memories for their forced fabrication when they serve an explanatory role. In this experiment (Experiment 3), all participants fabricated an event that explained an outcome they had witnessed. For example, participants who viewed a counsellor named Delaney fall flat on his face when he stood up to make an announcement in the dining hall, were forced to fabricate a prank that someone had pulled on Delaney that caused him to fall – when in fact they had not viewed a prank. In this case the fabricated prank (e.g. 'Ratface tied his shoe laces together') provides a causal explanation for the observed outcome (Delaney falling in the dining hall). The innovation introduced in this experiment was manipulating whether or not participants later learned some information that could serve as a potential alternative explanation for the outcome they had observed (i.e. Delaney falling in the dining hall). For example, some participants (Alternative Explanation Condition) later learned that Delaney had Meniere's disease, an inner ear disorder which can cause balance problems. In this case, his medical condition provides a potential alternative explanation (to the fabricated 'prank') for why he fell in the dining hall, although participants were not explicitly made aware of the potential connection between the additional information and the events witnessed in video. In a comparison condition (No Alternative

Explanation), other participants later learned that Delaney had a skin condition called phlemphigus, a medical condition that could not readily account for his fall in the dining hall. Research on causal reasoning has shown that the strength of a perceived causal relationship is highly influenced by the presence of alternative explanations, such that multiple possible explanations for a particular consequence reduce the extent to which people view any one event as causally related to that outcome (Einhorn & Hogarth, 1986; Kelley, 1973). By the same token, having only one causal explanation for an event increases the perceived strength of a causal relationship. Hence, the presence of a potential alternative explanation for the witnessed outcome should reduce the explanatory strength of the fabricated event. Consistent with the explanatory role hypothesis, participants in the Alternative Explanation condition evidenced lower levels of false recall of the fabricated prank than participants in the No Alternative Explanation condition.

Collectively, the above studies provide strong evidence that participants are more likely to develop false recollections of forced fabrications when the fabricated event serves an explanatory function. These findings are of particular relevance to real-world forensic situations, because in most cases, the purpose of eyewitness testimony is to provide an explanation for an outcome (e.g. an accident, robbery, or murder) that does not have a well-determined cause. In such situations, the stakes associated with 'solving' a crime can be very high. As a result, forensic interviewers may push witnesses beyond their actual memories, encouraging them or even coercing them to describe events they do not remember or never witnessed. The results reported here suggest that, because of the explanatory function eyewitness testimony serves, witnesses may be especially predisposed to developing false recollections of events that were at one time mere speculation or even forced fabrications. Indeed, these results may underestimate the extent to which eyewitnesses are prone to false memory development, as research has shown that people are especially likely to seek causal explanations for negative, unexpected and consequential outcomes (e.g. Weiner, 1985) – characteristics typical of forensically relevant outcomes.

In summary, from a source monitoring perspective, eyewitness memory is easily contaminated by post-event misinformation for two reasons. First, there exists a high degree of overlap between the original and misleading episodes – thus making the two sources highly confusable. Second, memory for the source of misinformation in memory is much more susceptible to forgetting than memory for its content. This dissociation between memory for *source* vs. *content* is especially evident in studies of forced fabrication, where participant-witnesses freely incorporate forcibly fabricated events into their eyewitness accounts after long retention intervals of 8 weeks. This demonstrates that after long delays, participants remember the content of the fabricated event, but fail to remember that they invented it. An exciting recent development is the finding that participants are more likely to develop these false recollections when the fabricated event serves to explain a witnessed outcome than when it does not serve this explanatory role. These findings suggest that a promising new direction for future research is understanding how people's search for causal explanations might influence their susceptibility to suggestive influences.

CONCLUSIONS

- Misinformation effects are among the most reliable and robust experimental findings in all of psychology. Countless studies have documented how easily eyewitness reports can become tainted by misleading post-event suggestions.
- Theoretical accounts of misinformation phenomena have centred on several questions:
  - Does misinformation impair memory for the originally-witnessed detail? The extant evidence shows some evidence of memory impairment effects, though the effects are small and inconsistent. Whether such impairment effects are permanent, or irreversible remains to be determined.
  - Do misled participants develop genuine false recollections of suggested events? Although misled participants may report misinformation for a number of reasons, there is convincing evidence that some of these reports reflect genuine false recollections.
  - What are the cognitive mechanisms that underlie these false recollection effects? We demonstrate how the Source Monitoring Framework predicts the incidence and magnitude of false recollections.
- Recent extensions of the misinformation paradigm: studies using the forced fabrication paradigm have extended the study of suggestive interviews to situations where interviewers elicit fabricated information from witnesses in a coercive manner. These findings show that, over time, participants come to develop false recollections of their forced fabrications, even in those cases where participants have been forced to fabricate entire fictitious events that are broad in scope.
- A novel finding that has emerged from studies involving entire fabricated events is that false recollection is a function of the explanatory role the fabrication serves. This is an important finding, given that in many real-world situations the purpose of eyewitness testimony is to provide an explanation for a poorly understood outcome.

FORENSIC IMPLICATIONS

• Memory for experienced events is often vague and incomplete, especially with regard to incidental details. As a consequence, there are often gaps in memory, which become more pervasive with the passage of time.
• Eyewitness memory is highly prone to contamination from post-event sources (e.g. information encountered in news stories, forensic interviews, conversations with others), especially when the new information fills a gap in memory. Hence, all things being equal, the most accurate testimony is likely to be obtained immediately following the witness event, before there is any opportunity for contamination to occur.
• When participants encounter post-event information that is false, or misleading (e.g. in suggestive forensic interviews), they sometimes come to develop genuine *false recollections* of having witnessed events that they in fact never saw. When memory has been tainted in this way, even an honest witness can be mistaken, and provide high confidence testimony that is false.
• Over the long term, coercive forensic interviews can result in false recollections. That is, even testimony that is *knowingly* fabricated with great resistance and under duress can develop into false recollections over a period of just a few weeks. Hence, false testimony that is initially provided with great uncertainty can become more confident over time.
• Recent research shows that witnesses are especially prone to developing false recollections for post-event suggestions (or coerced fabrications) that serve to explain a consequential outcome they have witnessed. Given that the goal of most forensic investigations is to gather evidence that can explain a consequential outcome (e.g. an accident, theft, murder, etc.), investigators should be careful not to press witnesses to go beyond their actual memory in explaining the causes of a witnessed event, as these 'explanatory' speculations are especially likely to develop into false recollections.
• Leading or suggestive forensic interviews can seriously undermine the accuracy of eyewitness recollections, and should be avoided. However, because it may be impossible to prevent all instances of leading or suggestive interviews, audio or video recording of all forensic interviews would provide a means of identifying those cases where contaminating influences were present.

REFERENCES

Ackil, J.K., & Zaragoza, M.S. (1998). Memorial consequences of forced confabulation: Age differences in susceptibility to false memories. *Developmental Psychology, 34*(6), 1358–1372.

Ackil, J.K., & Zaragoza, M.S. (2011). Forced fabrication versus interviewer suggestions: Differences in false memory depend on how memory is assessed. *Applied Cognitive Psychology, 25*(6), 933–942.

Ayers, M.S., & Reder, L.M. (1998). A theoretical review of the misinformation effect: Predictions from an activation-based memory model. *Psychonomic Bulletin & Review, 5*(1), 1–21.

Belli, R.F. (1989). Influences of misleading postevent information: Misinformation interference and acceptance. *Journal of Experimental Psychology: General, 118*, 72–85.

Belli, R.F. (1993). Failure of interpolated tests in inducing memory impairment with final modified tests: Evidence unfavorable to the blocking hypothesis. *American Journal of Psychology, 106*, 407–427.

Belli, R.F., Lindsay, D.S., Gales, M.S., & McCarthy, T.T. (1994). Memory impairment and source misattribution in postevent misinformation experiments with short retention intervals. *Memory & Cognition, 22*, 40–54.

Belli, R.F., Windschitl, P.D., McCarthy, T.T., & Winfrey, S.E. (1992). Detecting memory impairment with a modified test procedure: Manipulating retention interval with centrally presented event items. *Journal of Experimental Psychology: Learning, Memory, and Cognition, 18*, 356–367.

Binet, A. (1900). *La suggestibilité*. Paris: Schleicher.

Bowman, L.L., & Zaragoza, M.S. (1989). Similarity of encoding context does not influence resistance to memory impairment following misinformation. *American Journal of Psychology, 102*, 249–264.

Brainerd, C.J., & Reyna, V.F. (1998). Fuzzy-trace theory and children's false memories. *Journal of Experimental Child Psychology, 71*, 81–129.

Chambers, K.L., & Zaragoza, M.S. (2001). Intended and unintended effects of explicit warnings on eyewitness suggestibility: Evidence from source identification tests. *Memory & Cognition, 29*, 1120–1129.

Chandler, C.C. (1989). Specific retroactive interference in modified recognition tests: Evidence for an unknown cause of interference. *Journal of Experimental Psychology: Learning, Memory, and Cognition, 15*, 256–265.

Chrobak, Q.M. & Zaragoza, M.S. (2008). Inventing stories: Forcing witnesses to fabricate entire fictitious events leads to freely reported false memories. *Psychonomic Bulletin & Review, 15*(6), 1190–1195.

Chrobak, Q.M., & Zaragoza, M.S. (under review). When forced fabrications become truth: Causal explanations and false memory development. *Journal of Experimental Psychology: General*.

Compo, N.S., & Parker, J.F. (2010). Gaining insight into long-term effects of inviting speculation: Does recantation help? *Applied Cognitive Psychology, 24*, 969–990.

Drivdahl, S.B., & Zaragoza, M.S. (2001). The role of perceptual elaboration and individual differences in the creation of false memories for suggested events. *Applied Cognitive Psychology, 15*, 265–281.

Drivdahl, S.B., Zaragoza, M.S., & Learned, D.M. (2009). The role of emotional elaboration in the creation of false memories. *Applied Cognitive Psychology, 23*, 13–35.

Eakin, D.K., Schreiber, T.A., & Sergent-Marshall, S. (2003). Misinformation effects in eyewitness memory: The presence and absence of memory impairment as a function of warning and misinformation accessibility. *Journal of Experimental Psychology: Learning, Memory, and Cognition, 29*, 813–825.

Echterhoff, G., Hirst, W., & Hussy, W. (2005). How eyewitnesses resist misinformation. Social postwarnings and the monitoring of memory characteristics. *Memory & Cognition, 33*, 770–782.

Einhorn, H. J., & Hogarth, M. (1986). Judging probable cause. *Psychological Bulletin, 99*(1), 3–19.

Frost, P., Ingraham, M., & Wilson, B. (2002). Why misinformation is more likely to be recognised over time. A source monitoring account. *Memory, 10*(3), 179–185.

Frost, P., Lacroix, D., & Sanborn, N. (2003). Increasing false recognition rates with confirmatory feedback: A phenomenological analysis. *American Journal of Psychology, 116,* 515–525.

Gabbert, F., Memon, A., & Wright, D.B. (2006). Memory conformity: Disentangling the steps toward influence during a discussion. *Psychonomic Bulletin & Review, 139*(3), 480–485.

Gallo, D.A. (2004). Using recall to reduce false recognition: Diagnostic and disqualifying monitoring. *Journal of Experimental Psychology: Learning, Memory, and Cognition, 30*(1), 120–128.

Goff, L.M., & Roediger, H.L. (1998). Imagination inflation for action events: Repeated imaginings lead to illusory recollections. *Memory & Cognition, 26,* 20–33.

Gudjonsson, G.H. (1992). *The Psychology of Interrogations, Confessions and Testimony*. Oxford, England: John Wiley & Sons, Ltd.

Hanba, J.M., & Zaragoza, M.S. (2007). Interviewer feedback in repeated interviews involving forced confabulation. *Applied Cognitive Psychology, 21,* 433–455.

Hekkanen, S.T., & McEvoy, C. (2002). False memories and source-monitoring problems: Criterion differences. *Applied Cognitive Psychology, 16,* 73–85.

Hirshman, E., & Bjork, A. (1988). The generation effect: Support for a two-factor theory. *Journal of Experimental Psychology: Learning, Memory, and Cognition, 14*(3), 484–494.

Hyman, I.E., & Pentland, J. (1996). The role of mental imagery in the creation of false childhood memories. *Journal of Memory and Language, 35,* 101–117.

Johnson, M.K., Hashtroudi, S., & Lindsay, D.S. (1993). Source monitoring. *Psychological Bulletin, 114,* 3–28.

Kassin, S.M. (1997). The psychology of confession evidence. *American Psychologist, 52*(3), 221–233.

Kelley, H.H. (1973). The process of causal attribution. *American Psychologist, 78,* 107–128.

Lane, S.M., Mather, M., Villa, D., & Morita, S.K. (2001). How events are reviewed matters: Effects of varied focus on eyewitness suggestibility. *Memory & Cognition, 29,* 940–947.

Lane, S.M., & Zaragoza, S. (2007). A little elaboration goes a long way: The role of generation in eyewitness suggestibility. *Memory & Cognition, 35*(6), 1255–1266.

Leo, R.A. (1996). Inside the interrogation room. *The Journal of Criminal Law and Criminology, 86,* 266–303.

Lindsay, D.S. (1990). Misleading suggestions can impair eyewitnesses' ability to remember event details. *Journal of Experimental Psychology: Learning, Memory, and Cognition, 16,* 1077–1083.

Lindsay, D.S. (2008). Source monitoring. In J. Byrne (Series Ed.) & H.L. Roediger, III (Vol. Ed.), *Learning and Memory: A Comprehensive Reference: Vol. 2. Cognitive Psychology of Memory* (pp. 325–348). Oxford: Elsevier.

Lindsay, D.S., & Johnson, M.K. (1989). The eyewitness suggestibility effect and memory for source. *Memory & Cognition, 17,* 349–358.

Loftus, E.F. (1979a). *Eyewitness Testimony*. Cambridge, MA: Harvard University Press.

Loftus, E.F. (1979b). The malleability of memory. *American Scientist, 67,* 312–320.

Loftus, E.F., Donders, K., Hoffman, H.G., & Schooler, J.W. (1989). Creating new memories that are quickly accessed and confidently held. *Memory & Cognition, 17,* 607–616.

Loftus, E.F., & Hoffman, H. G. (1989). Misinformation and memory: The creation of new memories. *Journal of Experimental Psychology: General, 118,* 100–104.

Loftus, E.F., & Loftus, G.R. (1980). On the permanence of stored information in the human brain. *American Psychologist, 35,* 409–420.

Loftus, E.F., Miller, D.G., & Burns, H.J. (1978). Semantic integration of verbal information into a visual memory. *Journal of Experimental Psychology: Human Learning & Memory, 4,* 19–31.

Loftus, E.F., Schooler, J.W., & Wagenaar, W. (1985). The fate of memory: Comment on McCloskey and Zaragoza. *Journal of Experimental Psychology: General, 114,* 375–380.

McCloskey, M., & Zaragoza, M. (1985a). Misleading postevent information and memory for events: Arguments and evidence against memory impairment hypotheses. *Journal of Experimental Psychology: General, 114,* 1–16.

McCloskey, M., & Zaragoza, M. (1985b). Postevent information and memory: Reply to Loftus, Schooler, and Wagenaar. *Journal of Experimental Psychology: General, 114,* 381–387.

Metcalfe, J. (1990). Composite Holographic Associative Recall Model (CHARM) and blended memories in eyewitness testimony. *Journal of Experimental Psychology: General, 119,* 145–160.

Mitchell, K.J., & Zaragoza, S. (1996). Repeated exposure to suggestion and false memory: The role of contextual variablity. *Journal of Memory and Language, 35*(2), 246–260.

Mitchell, K.J., & Zaragoza, M.S. (2001). Contextual overlap and eyewitness suggestibility. *Memory & Cognition, 29,* 616–626.

Münsterberg, H. (1908). *On the Witness Stand.* Garden City, NY: Doubleday.

Panksy, A., & Tenenboim, E. (2011). Inoculating against eyewitness suggestibility via interpolated verbatim vs. gist testing. *Memory & Cognition, 39,* 155–170.

Payne, D.G., Toglia, M.P., & Anastasi, J.S. (1994). Recognition performance level and the magnitude of the misinformation effect in eyewitness memory. *Psychonomic Bulletin & Review, 1,* 376–382.

Paz-Alonso, P.M., & Goodman, G.S. (2008). Trauma and memory: Effects of post-event misinformation, retrieval order, and retention interval. *Memory, 16*(1), 58–75.

Pezdek, K., Lam, S.T., & Sperry, K. (2009). Forced confabulation more strongly influences event memory if suggestions are other-generated than self-generated. *Legal and Criminological Psychology, 14,* 241–252.

Pezdek, K., & Roe, C. (1995). The effect of memory trace strength on suggestibility. *Journal of Experimental Child Psychology, 60,* 116–128.

Pezdek, K., Sperry, K., & Owens, S.M. (2007). Interviewing witnesses: The effect of forced confabulation on event memory. *Law and Human Behavior, 31*(5), 463–478.

Schank, R.C., & Abelson, R.P. (1977). *Scripts, Plans, Goals, and Understanding: An Inquiry into Human Knowledge Structures.* Hillsdale, NJ: Erlbaum.

Schiller, D., & Phelps, E.A. (2011). Does reconsolidation occur in humans? *Frontiers in Behavioral Neuroscience, 5*(24), 1–12.

Schooler, J.W., Foster, R. A., & Loftus, E. F. (1988). Some deleterious consequences of the act of recollection. *Memory & Cognition, 16,* 243–251.

Schreiber, N., & Paker, J.F. (2004). Inviting witnesses to speculate: Effects of age and interaction on children's recall. *Journal of Experimental Child Psychology, 89*(1), 31–52.

Schreiber, T.A., & Sergent, S.D. (1998). The role of commitment in producing *misinformation effects in eyewitness memory*. Psychonomic Bulletin & Review, 5, 443–448.

Schreiber, N., Wentura, D., & Bilsky, W. (2001). 'What else could he have done?' Creating false answers in children witnesses by inviting speculation. *Journal of Applied Psychology, 86*(3), 525–532.

Slamecka, N.J., & Graf, P. (1978). The generation effect: Delineation of a phenomenon. *Journal of Experimental Psychology: Human Learning and Memory, 4*(6), 592–604.

Thomas, A.K., Bulevich, J.B., & Loftus, E.F. (2003). Exploring the role of repetition and sensory elaboration in the imagination inflation effect. *Memory & Cognition, 31*(4), 630–640.

Thompson-Cannino, J., Cotton, R., & Torneo, E. (2009). *Picking Cotton: Our Memoir of Injustice and Redemption*. New York: St. Martin's Press.

Tousignant, J.P., Hall, D., & Loftus, E.F. (1986). Discrepancy detection and vulnerability to misleading postevent information. *Memory & Cognition, 14,* 329–338.

Tulving, E. (1985). Memory and consciousness. *Canadian Psychology, 26,* 1–12.

Tversky, B., & Tuchin, M. (1989). A reconciliation of the evidence on eyewitness testimony: Comments on McCloskey and Zaragoza. *Journal of Experimental Psychology: General, 118,* 86–91.

Weiner, B. (1985). 'Spontaneous' causal thinking. *Psychological Bulletin, 97*(1), 74–84.

Zaragoza, M.S., Belli, R.S., & Payment, K.E. (2007). Misinformation effects and the suggestibility of eyewitness memory. In M. Garry, & H. Hayne (Eds), *Do Justice and Let the Sky Fall: Elizabeth F. Loftus and Her Contributions to Science, Law, and Academic Freedom* (pp. 35–63). Hillsdale, NJ: Lawrence Erlbaum Associates.

Zaragoza, M. S.,& Lane, S. M. (1994). Source misattributions and the suggestibility of eyewitness memory. *Journal of Experimental Psychology: Learning, Memory, & Cognition, 20,* 934–945.

Zaragoza, M.S., & Mitchell, J. (1996). Repeated exposure to suggestion and the creation of false memories. *Psychological Science, 7*(5), 294–300.

Zaragoza, M.S., Mitchell, K.J., Payment, K., & Drivdahl, S. (2011). False memories for suggestions: The impact of conceptual elaboration. *Journal of Memory and Language, 64,* 18–31.

Zaragoza, M.S., Payment, K.E., Ackil, J.K., Drivdahl, S.B., & Beck, M. (2001). Interviewing witnesses: Forced confabulation and confirmatory feedback increase false memories. *Psychological Science, 12,* 473–477.

3

Interrogative Suggestibility and Compliance

Gisli H. Gudjonsson

KEY POINTS

The purpose of this chapter is to consider theory and research related to:

- The development of the Gudjonsson Suggestibility Scales (GSS 1 and GSS 2) and the Gudjonsson Compliance Scale (GCS).
- A model of interrogative suggestibility.
- Individual differences in suggestibility and compliance.
- The relationship between suggestibility, compliance and false confessions.
- The role of memory distrust in suggestibility and compliance.
- Malingering on the GSS and GCS.

In the early 1980s there no tests were available for measuring interrogative suggestibility as an individual differences variable that could be used for clinical and research purposes (Gudjonsson, 1992; Gudjonsson & Gunn, 1982). In view of this, Gudjonsson constructed and developed the GSS 1 (Gudjonsson, 1983, 1984), which was followed by a theoretical formulation of interrogative suggestibility (Gudjonsson & Clark, 1986), and the publications of the GSS 2 (Gudjonsson, 1987) and

Suggestibility in Legal Contexts: Psychological Research and Forensic Implications,
First Edition. Edited by Anne M. Ridley, Fiona Gabbert and David J. La Rooy.
© 2013 John Wiley & Sons, Ltd. Published 2013 by John Wiley & Sons, Ltd.

the GCS (Gudjonsson, 1989). The Manual to the Scales was published in 1997 (Gudjonsson, 1997). Extensive research has been conducted into the Scales and the key studies will be reviewed in this Chapter. Gudjonsson (1992, 1997, 2003a, b) has reviewed the development of the Scales and their application to forensic practice. In addition, there have been two rigorous independent reviews of the Scales. The first review was that by Grisso (1986) of the early development of the GSS 1, which led to the development of the GSS 2, and a more recent review in Buros' *The Seventeenth Mental Measurement Yearbook* (Janoson & Frumkin, 2007). This chapter will build on the previous reviews, highlight the most relevant findings to forensic use of the Scales, and present the most recent findings.

DEFINITION AND EARLY DEVELOPMENT
OF INTERROGATIVE SUGGESTIBILITY

The concept of suggestibility was originally developed in order to explain hypnotic phenomena, which is why the early tests of suggestibility measured the influence of suggestion upon the motor and sensory systems. In contrast, interrogative suggestibility is mainly concerned with past experiences and events, recollections, and remembered states of knowledge (Gudjonsson, 2003a). This is why it is relevant to the police questioning of suspects, victims and witnesses. In their theoretical development of interrogative suggestibility, Gudjonsson and Clark (1986) define it as: 'The extent to which, within a closed social interaction, people come to accept messages communicated during formal questioning, as the result of which their subsequent behavioural response is affected' (p. 84).

The idea of 'interrogative suggestibility' was first introduced by Binet (1900), and was subsequently used by other researchers, such as Stern (1939) to show that leading questions can produce distorted responses due to being phrased in such a way as to suggest the wanted or expected answer. Later researchers have used a similar or modified procedure to that of Stern to elicit this type of suggestibility (e.g. Loftus, 1979; Stukat, 1958). Gudjonsson (1983) introduced the idea of another type of interview (interrogative) suggestibility. This relates to the extent to which interviewers are able to 'shift' unwanted but perhaps accurate answers by challenge and negative feedback (i.e. informing interviewees that they have made a number of mistakes and that they should try to do better). These are two distinct types of suggestibility, referred to in the literature as 'Yield' and 'Shift'. These terms are incorporated into the Gudjonsson Suggestibility Scales (Gudjonsson, 1997) (Box 3.1), which provide empirical measurements of interrogative suggestibility (Gudjonsson, 2003a).

Box 3.1 Procedure for the Gudjonsson Suggestibility Scales

The GSS 1 and GSS 2 consist of a short story plus 20 questions, 15 of which are leading. The two Scales are parallel forms of the same kind of test, but differ in that the GSS 1 includes a crime-related narrative, whereas the GSS 2 has a more neutral family-related content.

The story is read out by the person administering the test. Participants are then asked to recall everything they can remember about the story and this is repeated 50 minutes later. Following this, they are asked the 20 questions. Participants are then given negative feedback and the questions are repeated. (i.e. they are informed that they have made a number of errors and that it is therefore necessary to go through all the questions again, and that this time they should try to provide more accurate answers).

The Scales provide the following measures:
- immediate free recall (range of scores 0–40);
- delayed free recall (range of scores 0–40; normally 50-minute interval);
- confabulation on immediate recall (confabulated answers are incorrect responses that have not been suggested);
- confabulation on delayed recall;
- yield 1 (extent to which people give in to leading questions prior to negative feedback; range of scores 0–15);
- yield 2 (extent to which people give in to leading questions after negative feedback; range of scores 0–15);
- shift (how many times during the 20 questions people change their answers; range of scores 0–20);
- total Suggestibility (Yield 1 and Shift added together; range of scores 0–35).

The reliability of the GSS is good. Internal consistency of the GSS 1 as measured by Cronbach's alpha is 0.77 and 0.71 for Yield 1 and Shift, respectively (Gudjonsson, 1984; Singh & Gudjonsson, 1987). The correlations between the suggestibility measures of the GSS 1 and GSS 2 are high. For Total Suggestibility they range from 0.92 for forensic patients tested on both measures at the same time dropping to 0.81 for forensic patients tested on two separate occasions (Gudjonsson, 1987). This indicates reasonable stability in suggestibility over time.

The GSS Manual recommends a delay of about 50 minutes between immediate and delayed free recall tests. Smeets, Leppink, Jelicic, and Merckelbach (2009) investigated whether varying this memory administration procedure would affect the suggestibility scores on the

GSS 1. The participants were 80 undergraduates who were randomly assigned to four experimental conditions with 20 participants in each group: (1) standard procedure in accordance to the GSS manual (i.e. 50-minute interval between immediate and delayed recall) followed by specific questions which are repeated again with negative feedback (GSS questions); (2) the GSS questions were administered after immediate recall (i.e. there was no 50-minute retention interval); (3) the GSS questions were administered immediately after the narrative had been read out to them (i.e. without immediate or delayed recall); and (4) the GSS questions were administered 50 minutes after the narrative had been read out, but without any immediate and delayed recall (i.e. there was no rehearsal of the story).

No significant differences emerged in the Yield 1, Yield 2, Shift or Total Suggestibility scores between the four experimental conditions. The results suggest that the suggestibility scores are not affected by manipulation of the memory recall procedure either in terms of time interval (i.e. absence or presence of the 50-minute retention interval) or whether the GSS questions follow without rehearsal of the narrative (i.e. no immediate recall). The authors of the article suggest that if there is pressure of time during the testing procedure, the GSS could be administered without a retention interval or multiple memory recall testing without it having detrimental effect on the suggestibility scores. Nevertheless, they rightly suggest caution about generalizing from their results to forensic populations without replication of the study among that population.

THE GUDJONSSON AND CLARK MODEL OF INTERROGATIVE SUGGESTIBILITY (1986)

This model of interrogative suggestibility integrates the 'leading questions' and 'negative feedback' aspects of suggestibility first introduced by Gudjonsson (1983). The model postulates that suggestibility arises out of the way the individual interacts with others within the social and physical environment. The basic assumption of the model is that interrogative suggestibility is dependent upon the coping strategies that people can generate and implement when faced with two important aspects of the interrogative situation – uncertainty and expectations. When interviewed, people have to cognitively process the question and context in which the questioning takes place. In order to do this they employ one or more strategies of general coping. This process involves the interviewee having to cope with *uncertainty* and *interpersonal trust* on the one hand and *expectations* on the other. These three components are seen as essential prerequisites for the suggestibility process and can be manipulated during an interview in order to influence the answers given. Gudjonsson (2003a) provides detailed information about studies that have successfully tested different aspects of the model (e.g. raising expectations, the use of warnings regarding leading questions, types of coping strategies used during the questioning).

The Gudjonsson and Clark model differs in several respects from the typical Loftus paradigm (Gudjonsson, 2003a). Schooler and Loftus (1986) argue that the principal differences represent two complementary approaches, the 'individual differences' and 'experimental' approaches, respectively. The experimental approach focuses on the timing (i.e. length of time after observing the event) and the nature of the questions (e.g. whether the question contains misleading post-event information), where suggestibility is seen to be principally mediated by a central cognitive mechanism referred to as 'discrepancy detection' (i.e. the ability of the individual to detect discrepancies between what is observed and that suggested). The individual differences approach, in contrast, construes suggestibility as a potential vulnerability during questioning in terms of giving in to leading questions and interrogative pressure.

Modified Versions of the GSS

There are a small number of modified versions of the GSS that have been developed by other researchers. Rationales for their development, and accompanying research findings, will be reviewed in this section.

Scullin and Ceci (2001) used the GSS Yield and Shift format to develop a suggestibility scale for very young children (aged 3–5 years) where the to-be-remembered event was presented on video (Video SSC or VSSC). The participants were 195 American children (97 boys and 98 girls), Yield and Shift scores loaded on separate factors as predicted on the basis of previous research on the GSS and had good internal consistency (Cronbach alpha for Yield 1 and Shift were 0.85 and 0.75, respectively). The authors of the article concluded that interview suggestibility can be reliably measured in very young children. McFarlane and Powell (2002) partly validated the VSSC against other measures of suggestibility among 77 Australian children aged between 46 and 67 months (mean = 4.9 years). Yield was found to be a significant predictor of acceptance of an independently presented false event and the number of false details reported. In contrast, Shift did not relate to any of the other suggestibility measures. The authors reached two conclusions. First, susceptibility to suggestions on one measure may not generalize to a measure in another context (i.e. how children's memory is elicited and suggestibility is measured affects the results). This implies that context is important. Second, Yield may be a more reliable and valid measure of suggestibility than Shift in preschool children.

Candel, Merckelbach, & Muris (2000) have also developed a suggestibility scale for children based on the GSS Yield and Shift format. It is referred to as the 'Bonn Test of Statement Suggestibility' (BTSS) and was developed in Holland to measure interview suggestibility in 4- to 10-year-old children. There were 48 Dutch participants in the study (24 boys and 25 girls). Cronbach's alpha for Yield 1, Shift and Total Suggestibility were 0.78, 0.82, and 0.87, respectively. The test–retest score, 6-weeks apart, were 0.90 for Yield 1, 0.78 for Shift, and 0.90 for Total Suggestibility. The concurrent validity of the BTSS is provided by showing that the Yield 1 suggestibility score was being confirmed by teachers' ratings of the children's suggestibility. The authors suggest that the advantage of the BTSS over the GSS is that it can be used with younger children.

Gorassini, Harris, Diamond, and Flynn-Dastoor (2006) developed a computerized administration of the GSS 1. The main purpose of the study was to investigate whether feedback could be adequately delivered during a computerized administration of the GSS 1. The participants were 40 women and 36 men from an introductory psychology course. Approximately half the participants were given neutral feedback and half standard feedback from the GSS Manual. Significant differences emerged between the two feedback instructions as predicted (i.e. the standard feedback elicited significantly higher Shift than the neutral feedback). The findings showed that the GSS can be satisfactorily administered on a computer, including the feedback part of the scale. However, the authors recommended further modification to computer interface to replicate the standard GSS conditions (e.g. the story being read out, questions asked, verbal feedback).

Attempts to modify the GSS have recognized the importance of measuring both the extent to which people give in to leading questions (Yield) and interrogative pressure (Shift). The GSS was the first scale to incorporate these two separate measures of suggestibility, which is seen as fundamental to the theory and measurement of interrogative suggestibility (Gudjonsson, 2003a).

Compliance

Gudjonsson (2003a) defines compliance as: 'the tendency of the individual to go along with propositions, requests or instructions, for some immediate instrumental gain' (p. 370). The main difference between suggestibility and compliance is that suggestibility, unlike compliance, implies personal acceptance of the information suggested (i.e. it is more relevant to the person's belief system). Another difference is that whereas suggestibility can be measured by an experimental procedure in the form of a 'mini' interrogation, which is the basis of the GSS 1 and GSS 2, compliance is difficult to measure in an experimental way and typically relies on self-report or ratings from informants (Gudjonsson, 2003a). The Gudjonsson Compliance Scale (GCS; Gudjonsson, 1997) consists of 20 statements, which respondents are asked to rate in terms of 'true' or 'false' responses as it relates to them, providing possible scores between 0 and 20. Examples of questions include 'I tend to give in to people who insist they are right' and 'I try to do what is expected of me'. The scale has moderate internal reliability (Cronbach's alpha = 0.71) and test–retest reliability was 0.88 (Gudjonsson, 1987).

In contrast to suggestibility, the background to the development of the GCS relates to the work of Milgram into obedience (Milgram, 1974), where eagerness to please and avoidance of conflict and confrontation are the key components to compliant behaviour (Gudjonsson, 1989, 1997). According to Gudjonsson (1989), whereas the suggestibility scales were developed specifically to address vulnerabilities in police interviews, the GCS was developed for one additional purpose: to measure susceptibility to exploitation by another person (e.g. susceptibility to be manipulated, tricked or pressured to participate in criminal activity). This aspect of compliance has been studied and validated in relation to compliance motivation in offending (Gudjonsson & Sigurdsson, 2004, 2007) and taking blame for antisocial acts not committed (Gudjonsson, Sigurdsson, & Einarsson, 2007). Research with the GCS suggests that the tendency to comply in one situation increases the likelihood that the person is susceptible to complying with requests in other situations (Gudjonsson, Sigurdsson, Einarsson, & Einarsson, 2008). Compliance has been found to be associated with a background history of childhood sexual abuse (Gudjonsson, Sigurdsson, & Tryggvadottir, 2011).

INDIVIDUAL DIFFERENCES AND THE GSS AND GCS

Suggestibility and compliance are seen as being potentially moderated by factors such as low intelligence (IQ), poor memory, anxiety, low self-esteem, and history of life adversity, that impair the ability of the person to cope with the uncertainty and expectations contained within questioning.

Gudjonsson (2003a) has reviewed the relationship between IQ, memory and suggestibility and concluded that low IQ and poor memory are positively correlated with suggestibility. However, the evidence supports Gudjonsson and Clark's (1986) theory that Yield 1 type of suggestibility is more strongly associated with cognitive factors such as memory than Shift. In contrast, Shift is more strongly associated with anxiety and poor coping strategies than Yield 1 (Gudjonsson, 2003a). Shift is also more affected than Yield 1 by sleep deprivation (Blagrove, 1996; Blagrove & Akehurst, 2000) and alcohol/substance withdrawal (Gudjonsson *et al.*, 2004; Gudjonsson, Hannesdottir, Petursson, & Bjornsson, 2002).

A number of studies have investigated the relationship between intelligence (IQ) and compliance. In the original study of the GCS, Gudjonsson (1989) did not find a significant relationship between full-scale IQ, as measured by the Wechsler Adult Intelligence Scale–Revised (WAIS-R), and compliance. He argued that 'since compliance is not related to memory processes like suggestibility, it should not correlate with IQ to the same extent' (p. 538). However, in a study of 60 court referrals, compliance correlated negatively with full-scale verbal and performance IQ scores (measured by the WAIS-R). The correlations ranged between -0.25 and -0.29 ($p < 0.05$).

Two more recent studies have found a significant negative relationship between compliance and IQ (Gudjonsson & Young, 2010; Sondenaa et al., 2010). Both studies used the WASI (Wechsler, 1999). This test contains two verbal (vocabulary, similarities) and two non-verbal (matrix reasoning, block design) subtests. Gudjonsson and Young (2010) found among a sample of 102 unemployed persons that full-scale IQ correlated negatively with compliance ($r = -0.59$). The correlations with IQ were lower for suggestibility and acquiescence. It was found that the shared variance between acquiescence and compliance was almost fully mediated by IQ; in other words, the relationship between acquiescence and compliance was driven by intelligence. This sample was biased towards the lower end of the IQ range (mean = 91.7, SD = 17.8, range 53–131) and 10% of the participants had an IQ score below 70.

Sondenaa, Rasmussen, Palmstierna, and Nottestad (2010) used the Norwegian translation of both the GSS 1 and GCS with prisoners. The prisoners also completed the WASI. The WASI IQ scores correlated significantly with all the GSS 1 suggestibility scales as well as immediate recall (delayed recall was not measured). The correlation between full-scale IQ and compliance was -0.36, ($n = 119$) and similar to that of total suggestibility on the GSS 1. The authors found that the GCS could be used for prisoners with IQ scores below 70 (those with an IQ score below 70 were significantly more compliant than the more intellectually able prisoners, with a large effect size). However, Gudjonsson (1997) recommends that the GCS should be used cautiously with people of low intellectual abilities, because of their limited reading and comprehension skills. The findings from a study by Gudjonsson and Young (2010) confirm this. The high level of acquiescence of people with low IQ scores may artificially inflate their compliance score on the GCS due to the fact that most of the items indicating a compliant response are scored in the affirmative. In view of this, practitioners should, whenever possible, assess acquiescence of persons with low IQ at the same time as compliance in order to assist with the interpretation of the compliance score. See Chapters 5 and 7 for further research on individual differences in suggestibility.

Lack of Confidence in Memory and Suggestibility

A suspect's lack of confidence in his or her memory has been found to be an important precursor to 'internalized' false confessions in murder cases, including the case of Andrew Evans who was convicted of murdering a teenage girl in 1973 and released on appeal in 1992 (Gudjonsson, 2003a, pp. 482–493; Gudjonsson, Kopleman, & MacKeith, 1999) and the cousin in the Birgitte Tengs case (Gudjonsson, 2003a, Chapter 23). In this context, Gudjonsson and MacKeith (1982) introduced the concept of 'memory distrust syndrome' (MDS). Gudjonsson (2003a) defines this mental state as 'a condition where people develop profound distrust of their memory recollections, as a result of which they are particularly susceptible to relying on external cues and suggestions' (p. 196). MDS is associated with two distinct conditions. First, where due to some medical (organic problems, alcohol intoxication or blackout) or psychological (psychogenic amnesia) conditions the interviewee has no clear recollection of what he or she was doing at the time of the alleged offence. Second, interviewees have a reasonably clear recollection of events, but their confidence in their memory is undermined by the way they are interviewed and manipulated by police (e.g. by suggesting that they have memory problems in relation to the reporting of a specific, crime-related, event). An experimental study by van Bergen, Jelicic, and Merckelbach (2008) found support for a relationship between memory distrust and false confessions and the deleterious impact of confidence-undermining questioning techniques.

A lack of confidence in memory has been found to be related to suggestibility as measured by the GSS 1. In the first study of the GSS 1 (Gudjonsson, 1983), after each question participants were asked to rate their level of confidence in the answer on a scale from 0 to 100. It was found that confidence in memory was negatively associated with Yield 1 type suggestibility (explaining about 9% of the variance, indicating a medium effect size), but not with Shift. Apart from directly asking participants to rate their level of confidence in their answers, there are two other indicators on possible lack of confidence in memory. First, when the person tested is hesitant in his or her replies by giving several replies to the same question (e.g. 'yes', 'not sure', 'yes, think so'). Second, by counting the proportion of replies where participants give 'don't know' replies (Gudjonsson, Young, & Bramham, 2007).

Suggestibility, Compliance and Disputed/False Confessions

As already discussed, the GSS 1, the GSS 2 and the GCS were designed to measure individual differences in vulnerabilities that are relevant to some police interviews (i.e. susceptibility to giving misleading or false information if asked leading questions or pressured in an interview). The Scales were first accepted in the Court of Appeal in the United Kingdom in 1991 in the case of Engin Raghip, one of the so-called 'Tottenham Three' who was convicted of murdering a police officer during the Tottenham riots in 1985. They are cited in many subsequent UK appeal judgments and were accepted by the House of Lords in December 2001 in the case of Donald Pendleton (Gudjonsson, 2003a, b; Gudjonsson, 2006, 2010a, b). The Scales have also been accepted in court cases in the United States and elsewhere (Frumkin, 2008; Fulero, 2010; Gudjonsson, 2003a, 2010b; Gudjonsson & Sigurdsson, 2010a).

Not all disputed confessions are false confessions (Gudjonsson, 2003a). Kassin and Gudjonsson (2004) define false confession in a police interview as 'any detailed admission to a criminal act that the confessor did not commit' (p. 48). False confessions do sometimes occur and the reasons are multifaceted (Gudjonsson, 2003a; Kassin et al., 2010). Susceptibility to leading questions, inability to cope with interrogative pressure, and high compliance are seen as key vulnerabilities in a police interview in terms of producing false confessions (Kassin et al., 2010).

Sigurdsson and Gudjonsson (1996) found that confabulation and suggestibility on the GSS 1 discriminated between 'false confessors' and 'non-false confessors' of the internalized type (i.e. false confessors who believe that they are guilty), whereas compliance was discriminative with all types of false confessions (voluntary, compliant and internalized). Since false confessions of the internalized type are most related to changes in belief systems, rather than mere compliance to a request, this finding is consistent with the Gudjonsson and Clark model of interrogative suggestibility.

False confessors identified in anecdotal case studies typically have higher GSS and GCS scores than non-false confessors (Gudjonsson, 2003a, 2010a). However, the GSS 1, GSS 2 and GCS are not intended to measure whether a confession is true or false; the Scales only measure vulnerabilities that are potentially important in some cases where confessions are disputed. This is the most common misconception found in practice (Gudjonsson, 2010c). In fact, there are no psychological tests available for detecting whether or not a confession is false.

It is important to acknowledge that the outcome of a police interview typically involves a dynamic process that comprises the interaction between circumstances, custodial pressures (i.e. confinement and interrogation), physical and mental health factors, psychological vulnerabilities (e.g. suggestibility, compliance), and support factors (i.e. access to legal advice, and an 'appropriate adult' while in custody). Further, suspects with intellectual/learning disabilities are typically assumed to be more susceptible to making false confessions than other vulnerable groups (Gudjonsson, 2003a, 2010a).

Box 3.2 Attention Deficit Hyperactive Disorder (ADHD), False Confessions, Suggestibility and Compliance

In a recent study among prisoners with ADHD, Gudjonsson, Sigurdsson, Einarsson, Bragason, and Newton (2008) found that the reported rate of false confessions among prisoners who are symptomatic for ADHD in adulthood was 41% in comparison to 18% of the remaining prisoners, suggesting a strong association between ADHD symptoms and false confessions. As suggestibility and compliance may predispose individuals to confess falsely, a number of studies have been conducted to investigate whether prisoners with ADHD are particularly compliant and/or suggestible.

Gudjonsson *et al.* (2007) compared suggestibility scores on the GSS 2 of 36 patients diagnosed with ADHD with 36 healthy controls. In spite of significantly lower immediate and delayed memory scores, people with ADHD were not significantly more suggestible than the controls. They coped during questioning by giving a disproportionate number of 'don't know' replies rather than yielding to suggestions and interrogative pressure. The authors suggest that behavioural inhibition and lack of confidence in memory may be more important than memory deficits in understanding how people with ADHD cope with questioning. There is evidence that lack of confidence in memory makes some people susceptible to the memory distrust syndrome (see earlier section, this chapter), which has been associated with false confession (Gudjonsson, 2003a; Gudjonsson *et al.*, 1999).

Gudjonsson *et al.* (2008) investigated the relationship of suggestibility and compliance with ADHD screened symptoms. Participants consisted of 90 Icelandic prisoners, 27 (30%) were currently symptomatic for ADHD. No differences were found between the symptomatic and non-symptomatic prisoners with regard to the memory recall and suggestibility scores on the GSS 1. In contrast, the symptomatic group were significantly more compliant on the GCS. There was a correlation of 0.45 between compliance and current ADHD symptoms (i.e. a shared variance of 20%).

Finally, Gudjonsson and Sigurdsson (2010b) analysed which of the core ADHD symptoms were most highly correlated with compliance. The correlations of inattention and hyperactivity/impulsivity with compliance were 0.50 and 0.29, respectively. Regression analysis showed that inattention predicted compliance well above and beyond hyperactivity/impulsivity symptoms. The authors considered this to be a novel and important finding, which possibly linked inattention to social passivity and the disorganized aspects of ADHD as the most relevant salient functional impairments (Gudjonsson, Wells, & Young, 2012).

> Overall, the findings indicate that ADHD is associated more with compliance than suggestibility. The findings also raise interesting questions about a possible connection between memory distrust and the tendency to give 'don't know' responses in prisoners with ADHD.

Elevated scores on suggestibility and compliance are commonly, but not exclusively, found in cases where convictions have been overturned on appeal (Gudjonsson, 2006), or in cases of proven false confessions (Gudjonsson, 2003a). There are many different reasons why suspects give false confessions and each case needs to be considered on its own merit (Gudjonsson, 2010a). Test scores should not be interpreted in isolation to other information, including salient background information and the nature of the police interview and other custodial pressures. Considering the type and nature of the interview technique used by police when interpreting test scores is essential in most cases (Gudjonsson & Pearse, 2011). In view of the fact that the GSS 1, the GSS 2 and GCS do not measure susceptibility to making false confessions directly, it is not appropriate to produce figures for false positive and negative error rates (Gudjonsson, 2010c) (Box 3.2).

MALINGERING ON THE GSS AND GCS

The GCS often presents more problems in Court than the GSS 1 and GSS 2, because it is based on self-report, the direct meaning of the items is quite transparent, and a high score may be construed as self-serving by lawyers. Therefore, independent corroboration of high compliance, for example, from reliable informants, or salient background information is helpful (Gudjonsson, Sigurdsson, & Einarsson, 2004). Importantly, Gudjonsson (2003a) provides a detailed assessment model to assist 'confession experts' when instructed in cases of disputed confessions, which sometimes involve the assessment of traits of suggestibility and compliance, using the GSS 1, GSS 2, and GCS.

Nevertheless, malingering (i.e. deliberate faking on psychological tests) sometimes occurs during a forensic evaluation and a number of methods have been devised to detect this when it occurs (Gudjonsson & Young, 2009). Gudjonsson (1997, 2003a) has raised concerns about the self-report nature of the GCS and the apparent transparency of the items. For this reason he recommended corroborative information when interpreting the score obtained in court referral cases, such as a parallel questionnaire to the GCS (GCS Form E) that is completed by independent informants, evidence of compliance from independent records, and evidence of psychological traits that are related to compliance (e.g. anxiety, low self-esteem).

Hansen, Smeets, and Jelicic (2010) investigated the susceptibility of both the GSS 1 and GCS to malingering using an experimental design. There were three experimental conditions with each condition consisting of 30 participants. In Condition 1 ('misled group'), the participants were instructed to play the role of a person who is being interviewed as a suspect during a criminal investigation and convince the interviewer that they are easily influenced and give in readily to leading questions. Participants in Condition 2 ('compliant group') were instructed to play the role of a person who is being interviewed as a suspect during a criminal investigation and convince the interviewer that they are eager to please and to avoid conflicts with others (i.e. that they comply easily with requests and demands from others). Condition 3 ('standard group') followed the standard instructions (i.e. no reference is made to a criminal investigation or malingering). The results showed the GSS 1, Yield 1, and Shift scores were unaffected by the faking instructions even though the participants in Condition 1 were specifically instructed to 'accept leading questions' suggesting that 'instructed malingerers fail to fully grasp the idea behind the GSS' (p. 227). In contrast, the study showed that it was much easier to fake a high score on the GCS (i.e. the participants in Conditions 1 and 2 had significantly higher GCS score than those in the standard condition).

Other studies on malingering have focused on the GSS rather than the GCS. These studies have given participants more explicit instructions about how to fake on the tests (e.g. instructing them to give in to leading questions, try to appear affected by pressure, and go along with what the interviewer says). The instructions provided to participants in the malingering conditions by their nature reveal the nature of the test and are contrary to the instructions provided for the tests in a real-life examination. The key studies are those of Baxter and Bain (2002), Boon, Gozna, and Hall (2008), Hansen et al. (2010), Smith and Gudjonsson (1986), and Woolston, Bain, and Baxter (2006). The studies by Baxter and Bain (2002) and Woolston et al. (2006) showed that Yield 1 was easier to fake than Shift (i.e. participants primed to expect leading questions can identify them and inflate the score if instructed to do so).

Hansen et al. (2010) make the important point that research into malingering on the GCS and GSS Scales does not apply in practice unless people are aware of the purpose of the tests and are specifically instructed to malinger. With regard to the GSS, people are informed that their memory is being tested (i.e. they are not told their suggestibility is being measured). Similarly, with regard to the GCS, people are not told that their compliance is being measured, but since some of the items are quite transparent, the purpose of the test may become apparent to some people during a forensic evaluation. If motivated to malinger on the test, people can, and even if they do not malinger, the prosecution will often argue that a high score is the result of malingering (Gudjonsson *et al.*, 2004). However, malingering with regard to suggestibility is rarely an issue in forensic cases in view of the subtlety of the test (i.e. the scores are not based on self-report).

CONCLUSIONS AND FORENSIC IMPLICATIONS

- The concepts and empirical measurement of interview (interrogative) suggestibility and compliance are now well established and validated for identifying vulnerabilities relevant to assessing cases of disputed confession and witness statements more generally.
- Suggestibility as measured by the GSS and later adaptations is conceptualized in a model of interrogative suggestibility that encompasses coping strategies for dealing with uncertainty, interpersonal trust and expectations in the interview situation.
- Both suggestibility and compliance are influenced by a number of factors, such as IQ and memory, anxiety, self-esteem and memory distrust. The distinction between Yield (giving in to leading questions) and Shift (giving in to interrogative pressure) is fundamental to both the theory and measurement of suggestibility. The GSS 1, GSS 2 and GCS do not directly assess whether or not a confession or statement is true or false. The focus of the psychological evaluation should be on identifying vulnerabilities (i.e. risk factors) that are relevant to evaluating the reliability of answers and accounts given in police interviews. Translating the psychological findings to the legal issues in the case (e.g. 'Is the confession/statement given in the police interview reliable?') is typically the most difficult part of the evaluation and this is an area where results from tests are sometimes misinterpreted, or there is a failure to properly interpret the findings within the totality of material available in the case (i.e. the expert witness fails to satisfactorily translate the findings within the context of the legal issues).
- Psychometric tests such as the GSS and GCS should only be used in conjunction with other assessment tools (which also provide a check against malingering, particularly in the case of the GCS). These include an interview and a careful consideration of other relevant material in the case.

REFERENCES

Baxter, J.S., & Bain, S.A. (2002). Faking interrogative suggestibility: The truth machine. *Legal and Criminological Psychology, 7,* 219–225.
Binet, A. (1900). *La Suggestibilitè*. Paris: Doin et Fils.

Blagrove, M. (1996). Effects of length of sleep deprivation on interrogative suggestibility. *Journal of Experimental Psychology: Applied, 2*(1), 48–59.

Blagrove, M., & Akehurst, L. (2000). Effects of sleep loss on confidence–accuracy relationships for reasoning and eyewitness memory. *Journal of Experimental Psychology: Applied, 6,* 59–73.

Boon, J., Gozna, L., & Hall, S. (2008). Detecting 'faking bad' on the Gudjonsson Suggestibility Scales. *Personality and Individual Differences, 44,* 263–272.

Candel, I., Merckelbach, H., & Muris, P. (2000). Measuring interrogative suggestibility in children: Reliability and validity of the Bonn Test of statement suggestibility. *Psychology, Crime and Law, 6,* 61–70.

Frumkin, I.B. (2008). Psychological evaluation in Miranda waiver and confession cases. In R. Denny, & J. Sullivan (Eds.), *Clinical Neuropsychology in the Criminal Forensic Setting* (pp. 135–175). New York: Guilford Press.

Fulero, S.M. (2010). Admissibility of expert testimony based on the Grisso and Gudjonsson Scales in disputed confession cases. *The Journal of Psychiatry and Law, 38,* 193–214.

Gorassini, D.R., Harris, J.A., Diamond, A., & Flynn-Dastoor, E. (2006). Computer assessment of interrogative suggestibility. *Personality and Individual Differences, 40,* 569–577.

Grisso, T. (1986). *Evaluating Competencies; Forensic Assessments and Instruments.* New York: Plenum Press.

Gudjonsson, G.H. (1983). Suggestibility, intelligence, memory recall and personality: An experimental study. *British Journal of Psychiatry, 142,* 35–37.

Gudjonsson, G.H. (1984). A new scale of interrogative suggestibility. *Personality and Individual Difference, 5,* 303–314.

Gudjonsson, G.H. (1987). A parallel form of the Gudjonsson Suggestibility Scale. *British Journal of Clinical Psychology, 26,* 215–221.

Gudjonsson, G.H. (1989). Compliance in an interrogation situation: A new scale. *Personality and Individual Differences, 10,* 535–540.

Gudjonsson, G.H. (1992). *The Psychology of Interrogations, Confessions, and Testimony.* Chichester: John Wiley & Sons, Ltd.

Gudjonsson, G.H. (1997). *The Gudjonsson Suggestibility Scales Manual.* Hove, Sussex: Psychology Press.

Gudjonsson, G.H. (2003a). *The Psychology of Interrogations and Confessions. A Handbook.* Chichester: John Wiley & Sons, Ltd.

Gudjonsson, G.H. (2003b). Psychology brings justice: The science of forensic psychology. *Criminal Behaviour and Mental Health, 13,* 159–167.

Gudjonsson, G.H. (2006). Disputed confessions and miscarriages of justice in Britain: Expert psychological and psychiatric evidence in Court of Appeal. *The Manitoba Law Journal, 31,* 489–521.

Gudjonsson, G.H. (2010a). Psychological vulnerabilities during police interviews: Why are they important? *Legal and Criminological Psychology, 15,* 161–175.

Gudjonsson, G.H. (2010b). The psychology of false confessions: A review of the current evidence. In G.D. Lassiter, & C.A. Meissner (Eds), *Police Interrogations and False Confessions* (pp. 31–47). New York: American Psychological Association.

Gudjonsson, G.H. (2010c). Interrogative suggestibility and false confessions. In J.M. Brown, & E.A. Campbell (Eds), *The Cambridge Handbook of Forensic Psychology* (pp. 202–207). Cambridge: Cambridge University Press.

Gudjonsson, G.H., & Clark, N.K. (1986). Suggestibility in police interrogation: A social psychological model. *Social Behaviour, 1,* 83–104.

Gudjonsson, G.H., & Gunn, J. (1982). The competence and reliability of a witness in a criminal court. *British Journal of Psychiatry, 141,* 624–627.

Gudjonsson, G.H., Hannesdottir, K., Agustsson, T.P., Sigurdsson, J.F., Gudmundsdottir, A., Pordardottir, P., Tyrfingsson, P., & Petursson, H. (2004). The relationship of alcohol withdrawal symptoms to suggestibility and compliance. *Psychology, Crime and Law, 10,* 169–177.
Gudjonsson, G.H., Hannesdottir, K., Petursson, H., & Bjornsson, G. (2002). The effects of alcohol withdrawal on mental state, interrogative suggestibility, and compliance: An experimental study. *Journal of Forensic Psychology, 13,* 53–67.
Gudjonsson, G.H., Kopelman, M.D., & MacKeith, J.A.C. (1999). Unreliable admissions to homicide: A case of misdiagnosis of amnesia and misuse of abreaction technique. *British Journal of Psychiatry, 174,* 455–459.
Gudjonsson, G.H., & MacKeith, J.A.C. (1982). False confessions. Psychological effects of interrogation. A discussion paper. In A. Trankell (Ed.), *Reconstructing the Past: The Role of Psychologists in Criminal Trial* (pp. 253–269). Deventer, The Netherlands: Kluwer.
Gudjonsson, G.H., & Pearse, J. (2011). Suspect interviews and false confessions. *Current Directions in Psychological Science, 20,* 33–37.
Gudjonsson, G.H., & Sigurdsson, J.F. (2004). Motivation for offending and personality. *Legal and Criminological Psychology, 9,* 69–81.
Gudjonsson, G.H., & Sigurdsson, J.F. (2007). Motivation for offending and personality. A study among young offenders on probation. *Personality and Individual Differences, 43,* 1243–1253.
Gudjonsson, G.H., & Sigurdsson, J.F. (2010a). False confessions in the Nordic countires Backgound and current landscape. In P.A. Granhag (Ed.), *Forensic Psychology in Context; Nordic and International Approaches* (pp. 94–116). Devon: Willan Publishing.
Gudjonsson, G.H., & Sigurdsson, J.F. (2010b). The relationship of compliance with inattention and hyperactivity/impulsivity. *Personality and Individual Differences, 49,* 651–654.
Gudjonsson, G.H., Sigurdsson, J.F., & Einarsson, E. (2004). Compliance and personality: The vulnerability of the unstable-introvert. *European Journal of Personality, 18,* 435–443.
Gudjonsson, G.H., Sigurdsson, J.F., & Einarsson, E. (2007). Taking blame for antisocial acts and its relationship with personality. *Personality and Individual Differences, 43,* 3–13.
Gudjonsson, G.H., Sigurdsson, J.F., Einarsson, E., Bragason, O.O., & Newton, A.K. (2008). Interrogative suggestibility, compliance and false confessions among prisoners and their relationship with attention deficit hyperactivity disorder (ADHD) symptoms. *Psychological Medicine, 38,* 1037–1044.
Gudjonsson, G.H., Sigurdsson, J.F., Einarsson, E., & Einarsson, J.H. (2008). Personal versus impersonal relationship compliance and their relationship with personality. *The Journal of Forensic Psychiatry and Psychology, 19,* 502–516.
Gudjonsson, G.H., Sigurdsson, J.F., & Tryggvadottir, H.B. (2011). The relationship of compliance with a background of childhood neglect and physical and sexual abuse. *The Journal of Forensic Psychiatry and Psychology, 22,* 87–98.
Gudjonsson, G.H., Wells, J., & Young, S. (2012). Personality disorders and clinical syndromes in ADHD prisoners. *Journal of Attention Disorders, 16,* 305–314.
Gudjonsson, G., & Young, S. (2009). Suboptimal effort and malingering. In S. Young, M. Kopelman, & G. Gudjonsson (Eds), *Forensic Neuropsychology in Practice; A Guide to Assessment and Legal Processes* (pp. 267–299). Oxford: Oxford University Press.
Gudjonsson, G.H., & Young, S. (2010). Personality and deception. Are suggestibility, compliance and acquiescence related to socially desirable responding? *Personality and Individual Differences, 50,* 192–195.

Gudjonsson, G.H., Young, S., & Bramham, J. (2007). Interrogative suggestibility in adults diagnosed with attention-deficit hyperactivity disorder (ADHD): A potential vulnerability during police questioning. *Personality and Individual Differences, 43,* 737–745.

Hansen, I., Smeets, T., & Jelicic, M. (2010). Further data on interrogative suggestibility and compliance scores following instructed malingering. *Legal and Criminological Psychology, 15,* 221–228.

Janoson, M., & Frumkin, B. (2007). Gudjonsson Suggestibility Scales. In K.F. Geisinger, R.A. Spies, J.F. Carlson, & B.S. Plake (Eds), *The Seventeenth Mental Measurement Yearbook.* Lincoln, NE: Buros Institute of Mental Measurements.

Kassin, S.M., Drizin, S. A., Grisso, T., Gudjonsson, G.H., Leo, R.A., & Redlich, A.P. (2010). Police-induced confessions: Risk factors and recommendations. *Law and Human Behavior, 34,* 3–38.

Kassin, S.M., & Gudjonsson, G.H. (2004). The psychology of confessions. A review of the literature and issues. *Psychological Science in the Public Interest, 5,* 33–67.

Loftus, E.F. (1979). *Eyewitness Testimony.* London: Harvard University Press.

McFarlane, F., & Powell (2002). The Video Suggestibility Scale for children: How generalizable is children's performance to other measures of suggestibility? *Behavioral Sciences and the Law, 20,* 699–716.

Milgram, S. (1974). *Obedience to Authority.* London: Tavistock.

Schooler, J.W., & Loftus, E.F. (1986). Individual differences and experimentation: Complementary approaches to interrogative suggestibility. *Social Behaviour, 1,* 105–112.

Scullin, M.H., & Ceci, S.J. (2001). A suggestibility scale for children. *Personality and Individual Differences, 30,* 843–856.

Sigurdsson, J.F., & Gudjonsson, G.H. (1996). Psychological characteristics of 'false confessors': A study among Icelandic prison inmates and juvenile offenders. *Personality and Individual Differences, 20,* 321–329.

Singh, K., & Gudjonsson, G.H. (1987). The internal consistency of the 'shift' factor on the Gudjonsson Suggestibility Scale. *Personality and Individual Differences, 8,* 265–266.

Smeets, T., Leppink, J., Jelicic, M., & Merckelbach, H. (2009). Shortened versions of the Gudjonsson Suggestibility Scale meet the standards. *Legal and Criminological Psychology, 14,* 149–155.

Smith, K., & Gudjonsson, G.H. (1986). Investigation of the responses of 'fakers' and 'non-fakers' on the Gudjonsson Suggestibility Scale. *Medicine, Science and the Law, 26,* 66–71.

Sondenaa, E., Rasmussen, K., Palmstierna, T., & Nottestad, J.A. (2010). The usefulness of assessing suggestibility and compliance in prisoners with unidentified intellectual disabilities. *Scandinavian Journal of Psychology, 51,* 434–438.

Stern, W. (1939). The psychology of testimony. *Journal of Abnormal and Social Psychology, 34,* 3–20.

Stukat, K.G. (1958). *Suggestibility: A Factor and Experimental Analysis.* Stockholm: Almgvist & Wiksell.

Van Bergen, S., Jelicic, M., & Merckelbach, H. (2008). Interrogation techniques and memory distrust. *Psychology, Crime & Law, 14,* 425–434.

Wechsler, D. (1999). *Wechsler Abbreviated Scale of Intelligence (WASI).* New York: The Psychological Corporation.

Woolston, R., Bain, S.A., & Baxter, J.S. (2006). Patterns of malingering and compliance in measures of interrogative suggestibility. *Personality and Individual Differences, 40,* 453–461.

4

Suggestibility and Memory Conformity

FIONA GABBERT AND LORRAINE HOPE

INTRODUCTION

What happens to our personal memories for a witnessed incident if we discuss them with another person who witnessed the same event? If the other person mentions details to us that we do not remember ourselves, or describes the event in a way that does not correspond with our own recollections, how is this apparent discrepancy resolved? To address these questions, this chapter will explore recent research on *memory conformity*.

KEY POINTS

The chapter will address the following;

- The impact of memory conformity in real life.
- Methodological approaches to investigating memory conformity.
- Theoretical accounts of why memory conformity occurs.
- Future directions for research.

Suggestibility in Legal Contexts: Psychological Research and Forensic Implications,
First Edition. Edited by Anne M. Ridley, Fiona Gabbert and David J. La Rooy.
© 2013 John Wiley & Sons, Ltd. Published 2013 by John Wiley & Sons, Ltd.

The research summarised in the chapter shows that people sometimes 'conform' to another person's version of events when discussing their recollections together, such that their subsequent individual memory reports converge and become similar. The phenomenon occurs because witnesses accept, and later report, information that is suggested to them in the course of the discussion. As such, this area of suggestibility research relates to what Schooler and Loftus (1993) refer to as 'delayed suggestibility', as found in misinformation studies, and referred to as investigative suggestibility in Chapter 1 (see also Chapters 2 and 5). The difference between 'memory conformity' studies and more general 'misinformation studies' is that participants are exposed to misleading post-event information in the social context of a discussion. As both social and cognitive factors can play a role in determining whether someone will become influenced, exposure to misleading post-event information during discussions with others is a particularly powerful form of suggestion. Individuals are not always aware of this process, and so do not realize that their memory has been influenced. Sometimes, however, memory conformity occurs because people consciously choose to report the suggested items in a bid to improve the accuracy of their own memory, or because, as social beings, we are keen to agree with others.

THE IMPACT OF MEMORY CONFORMITY IN REAL LIFE

Eyewitness research has consistently shown that memory is fallible, and that recollections can be influenced by information encountered after an incident has been witnessed. Exposure to post-event information that is inconsistent with one's own original memory reduces the likelihood that the original memory will subsequently be reported (see Chapter 2; also, Ayers & Reder, 1998; Ceci & Bruck, 1993; Loftus, Miller, & Burns, 1978; Payne, Toglia, & Anastasi, 1994). In everyday life, one of the most *common* and *natural* ways to encounter post-event information is when individuals who have shared the same experience discuss this with one another. In the case of witnessing a crime, individuals might be particularly motivated to discuss what happened and who was involved because of the significance of the event. The information encountered during this discussion with a co-witness might be largely accurate, and consistent with one's own recollections of the event. However, some details may differ between witnesses. Such differences can occur for a variety of reasons including idiosyncratic differences at encoding or retrieval, or if one person was in error.

Given the vulnerability of memory to misleading post-event information, and the importance of independent and reliable individual accounts within the investigative process and legal system, recent research has investigated the consequences of witnesses discussing their memories together prior to providing a police statement. Crimes often have more than one eyewitness (Valentine, Pickering, & Darling, 2003; Wright & McDaid, 1996), and surveys completed by real eyewitnesses reveal that discussion between witnesses is common. For example, Skagerberg and Wright (2008) reported that the majority of witnesses who completed their UK survey saw the crime with other people present, and over half of these people talked with the co-witnesses. Similarly, an Australian survey of eyewitnesses by Paterson and Kemp (2006) found that where multiple witnesses had been present, 86% of respondents admitted to discussing the event with a co-witness. Although good police practice advises witnesses not to talk to each other in order to avoid evidence contamination, discussions could take place before the police arrive at the crime scene, or afterwards if witnesses ignore police advice.

A striking example of how the memory report of one witness may influence that of another witness during a discussion was revealed in an analysis of witness evidence in the Oklahoma bombing in 1995. The key prosecution evidence in this case came from interviews with witnesses who worked at Elliot's Body Shop where the perpetrator, Timothy McVeigh, rented the truck used in the bombing. McVeigh was arrested for the mass murder but questions remained as to whether he carried out the bombing with an accomplice. Three witnesses encountered McVeigh when he hired the truck. One of these witnesses claimed, with some confidence, that he was accompanied by a second man. Initially, the other witnesses gave no description of this apparent accomplice. However, later they too claimed to remember details of a second person. This led to a costly police search for an accomplice which ultimately proved futile. Months later, the first witness acknowledged that he may have simply been recalling another customer. So, why did all three witnesses provide a description of an accomplice when McVeigh had actually entered the shop alone? The most likely explanation stems from the fact that the witnesses indicated in court that they had discussed their memories before being questioned by investigators (Memon & Wright, 1999). From a psychological perspective, it is likely that the confident witness unintentionally influenced the others, leading them to report that they also recalled a second man (Memon & Wright, 1999; Schacter, 2001).

A second real-life example of memory conformity comes from another high profile case; the murder investigation of the Swedish foreign minister, Anna Lindh (September, 2003). The attack took place in a busy shopping centre. Witnesses were placed together in a small room to prevent them leaving the scene of the crime prior to being interviewed. When in the room, the witnesses admitted to talking with one another (Granhag, Ask, & Rebelius, 2005). During these discussions, one witness mentioned to others present in the room that the perpetrator wore a camouflage patterned military jacket. As a result, a number of witnesses subsequently reported this clothing detail to the investigating officers. This description was used in an immediate search for the perpetrator in the surrounding area, and also featured in the release of a national police alert. The detail, however, was later revealed to be incorrect. Footage from surveillance cameras showed that the killer, Mijailo Mijailovic, was in fact wearing a grey hooded sweatshirt. Again, contaminated witness accounts resulted in wasted time and resources, as well as false leads based on incorrect information. Given that witnesses were free to discuss the incident with each other at some length, it is reasonable to conclude that co-witness influence was the source of error in the immediate stages of this investigation (Granhag *et al.*, 2005).

A final example from the UK illustrates how witnesses' recognition decisions can also be vulnerable to suggestion. Here, a witness central to the Jill Dando murder investigation (April, 2001) became increasingly confident that the main suspect, Barry George, was responsible for the crime after discussing the identification parade with another witness who had identified George. This witness, who had not felt confident enough to make an identification originally, subsequently revealed that, following discussions with the other witness, they felt '95% sure' that George was the man she had seen at the crime scene (Cathcart, 2002). Thus, both recall and recognition are vulnerable to the suggestions of others.

As these examples show, when memory conformity occurs in the context of a forensic investigation, there can be serious and costly implications. In such cases, consistent statements obtained from witnesses might be seized upon as valuable corroborative evidence from independent witnesses when in fact the evidence might be contaminated if the witnesses had discussed their memories prior to being interviewed by the police. This can lead to misdirected lines of enquiry, and has the the the potential to lead to miscarriages of justice.

DIFFERENT METHODOLOGICAL APPROACHES TO INVESTIGATING MEMORY CONFORMITY

The phenomenon of memory conformity has typically been examined in laboratory or relatively controlled experimental settings. Broadly speaking, researchers have adopted three main paradigms in order to explore the phenomenon. These include: (1) examining the extent of memory conformity between participants who unwittingly share different information when engaging in collaborative retrieval due to (unbeknownst to them) having viewed different versions of an event;

(2) the use of a confederate acting as a co-witness who deliberately reports some incorrect details during a collaborative recall task; and (3) providing participants with information about what other co-witnesses have allegedly said, for example, via the experimenter revealing responses that have been given by another witness. Irrespective of the method used, and whether the research is conducted in a laboratory or field setting (such as a street, beach or other public space), the primary interest is whether participants go on to report items of information that they had not originally seen themselves, and critically, information that could only have been obtained from the 'co-witness' informant.

The first method, of tracking the emergence of memory conformity during interactions between participants, is the most ecologically valid of the methodological paradigms listed above because co-witnesses naively share both correct and incorrect items of post-event information while discussing their memories, much like in real life. To achieve this, researchers lead pairs of participants to believe that they have encoded the same stimuli (often a simulated crime event shown on video or slides), when in reality they are shown stimuli that bear a similarity but differ in critical ways. For example, Gabbert, Memon, and Allan (2003) showed participants the same mock-crime, however, the event was filmed from two different eyewitness perspectives such that certain details could only be seen from one viewpoint only. Usually in a study of this nature, only a small number of misleading critical differences are manipulated between perspectives to ensure that participants do not become suspicious that they have in fact seen different events. The critical differences can take the form of added items (where one person sees an item that the other person did not) or contradictory items (where both individuals see the same item, but the exact details of this item differ in terms of key properties such as the colour). This method therefore allows different features of the event in question to be observed by the witnesses. After encoding the event, participants are given time to discuss what they have seen. In the course of conversation each witness naturally reveals their unique perspectives. When later questioned individually, the effects of the co-witness discussion on memory become readily apparent: witnesses report information they could only have learnt about from the co-witness as opposed to what they had seen themselves.

Wright, Self, and Justice (2000) were among the first researchers to use this method to investigate memory conformity between co-witnesses. In their study, pairs of witnesses viewed a storybook containing 21 colour pictures depicting a crime event. They were then asked 'true'/'false' questions about what they had seen, and rated their confidence in their answers after each question. Following this task, they discussed their memories about the sequence of events with the co-witness before answering the same questions again. Crucially, each witness had in fact seen a different critical detail in the story-book. In one version an accomplice had been present while in the other version there was no accomplice at all (similar to the situation in the McVeigh case study). Of the 20 pairs of witnesses tested in this study, 19 were initially accurate in their memory for the accomplice. Consequently, there was a high level of disagreement when the witnesses discussed their memories for what they had seen. However, when the same questionnaire was given to witnesses after they had discussed the contents of the story book, 15 of the 19 pairs (79%) came to agree on whether or not an accomplice had been seen. Given the high levels of accuracy of the witnesses' original memory, this is clear evidence of memory conformity between witnesses. There was no general tendency for the conformity to be in one direction or another (i.e. agreeing that there was, or was not, an accomplice). However, confidence ratings predicted which person in the pair per-suaded the other. Specifically, pairs tended to conform to the partici-pant with the higher level of confidence, but only for participants who *had* actually seen the accomplice. The confidence rating of the person who did *not* see the accomplice had little value in determining the direction of conformity.

Following Wright *et al.*'s (2000) study, Gabbert *et al.* (2003) also used this method to investigate memory conformity, and found similar results. Participants viewed a simulated crime event. Two versions of the event were prepared, each of which contained the same sequence of events but had been filmed from different angles to simulate different witness vantage points, allowing for unique features of the event to be observed by each witness. After viewing the event, witnesses were asked to recall it either alone or in pairs. Subsequent memory reports showed that a large proportion (71%) of witnesses who had discussed the event reported at least one (of two) erroneous detail acquired during the discussion with their co-witness.

The second approach to memory conformity has been to employ a confederate to act as a co-witness to purposefully introduce items of misleading post-event information into the discussion with the naive co-witness (Gabbert, Memon, Allan, & Wright, 2004; Hollin & Clifford, 1983; Meade & Roediger, 2002; Paterson, Kemp, & Forgas, 2009; Shaw, Garven, & Wood, 1997, Experiment 2). This method has advantages over other methods of studying witness conformity because a well-trained confederate can impart the same information (including misinformation) to all the naive witnesses during the course of a discussion. For example, Shaw *et al.* (1997) showed pairs of participants (comprising one actual participant and a confederate) a short video of a simulated robbery and then interviewed them together after a short delay. Participants took turns in being the first to provide their answers to the questions. For one-third of the questions, the actual participant responded first, thus receiving no co-witness information prior to giving their response. Here, the correct response was given 58% of the time. For the remaining items, the confederate co-witness responded first, either providing an accurate or an inaccurate response before the actual participant gave their answer. When accurate information had been encountered prior to responding, participants' accuracy level elevated to 67%, however, when inaccurate information was encountered, the accuracy level dropped to 42%.

Gabbert *et al.* (2004) used a confederate to examine whether participants are more suggestible when post-event misinformation is encountered socially via a face-to-face discussion, than when it is encountered via non-social means. Suggestions encountered socially can be particularly influential due to the combination of social and cognitive factors at play. Young (17–33 years) and older (58–80 years) adults viewed a simulated crime event and were later exposed to four items of misinformation about it within the context of a discussion with a confederate whom they believed to be a fellow participant, or within a written narrative that was alleged to have been written by a previous participant. The use of a confederate in this study enabled control over the information imparted to participants during the course of the discussion. Specifically, the confederate was trained to disclose the same items of correct and misleading post-event information, as was present in the misleading narrative. In a final recall test about the crime event, both young and older adults who had encountered the misinformation in the course of a social interaction with the confederate were more likely to report the misinformation than those who had encountered the same misinformation while reading the narrative. Similar findings demonstrating the potent influence of misinformation conveyed to an eyewitness in the context of a discussion have also been reported by Paterson and Kemp (2006) (although also see Bodner, Musch, & Azad, 2009).

The final method used to examine memory conformity provides participants with information about what other co-witnesses have supposedly said. Here, co-witness information is imparted *indirectly*, either by incorporating it into a recall questionnaire, where previously given responses are visible (see Betz, Skowronski, & Ostrom, 1996; Meade & Roediger, 2002, Experiment 3), or via the experimenter revealing responses that have purportedly been given by other witnesses (see Corey & Wood, 2002; Gabbert *et al.*, 2004; Paterson & Kemp, 2006). For example, Corey and Wood (2002) staged a live simulated theft in front of a group of participants. These participants were then interviewed about the incident individually. The interviewer asked 18 questions about the event, six of which were paired with alleged co-witness information that was accurate (e.g. 'What colour was the thief's hat? . . . The other witnesses said it was black'), six were paired with alleged co-witness information that was inaccurate (e.g. 'What colour was the thief's jacket? . . .The other witnesses said it was red'), and the remaining six were not paired with any co-witness information. Participants' immediate responses to these questions were influenced by the co-witness information, where accuracy was highest when correct co-witness information had been encountered, and lowest when incorrect co-witness information had been encountered.

To summarize, regardless of the method used to investigate memory conformity, results reveal that people are often influenced by post-event information suggested by another person. However, research by Gabbert *et al*. (2004) and Paterson and Kemp (2006) have both found that people are *most* suggestible when post-event information is encountered directly from a co-witness in the context of a social interaction, than when it is encountered indirectly. Furthermore, Meade and Roediger (2002, Experiment 4) found that the *quality* of co-witness influence can be dependent on whether an actual or implied co-witness imparted the post-event information. Specifically, participants were more likely to make source-misattribution errors for items of misinformation encountered from a co-witness who was physically present (versus co-witness information encountered indirectly), reporting that they could remember seeing items that had in fact only been suggested. It is possible that information encountered during a face-to-face interaction is attended to more fully and deemed to be more credible than information from an absent and anonymous source. The dynamic nature of the interaction might encourage more active and deeper processing of the information, making it more difficult to later discriminate from the originally encoded information, hence the source errors observed in Meade and Roediger's research (2002). This interpretation fits with findings by Zaragoza and Lane (1994) who found that participants were significantly more likely to make source-misattribution errors when they were required to actively retrieve (i.e. 'reactivate') the originally encoded information while processing misleading post-event information, than when the originally encoded information was not reactivated.

Some of the memory conformity studies discussed above adopt the method that mimics how information might be shared between witnesses in real life via a post-event discussion. On the other end of the spectrum are studies that adopt less ecologically valid methods, however, they have the advantage of increased experimental control, which permits the more precise manipulation of a variety of important moderator variables. Researchers interested in memory conformity should select the method best suited to their particular research objectives and the level of experimental control appropriate to address their research questions.

THEORETICAL ACCOUNTS OF WHY MEMORY CONFORMITY OCCURS

A person might conform to another person's memory report rather than reporting their own recollections for a number of different reasons: (1) they might not want to seem to be in disagreement with the other person (normative motivations to conform); or (2) they might believe the other person is actually correct (informational motivations to conform). Deutsch and Gerard (1955) initially explored the distinction between 'normative' or 'informational' motivations to conform. This distinction was expanded on by Cialdini and Goldstein (2004) in a comprehensive review of the conformity literature. Alternatively, 3) they might have constructed a (false) memory based on what the other person has said – perhaps through a source-monitoring error whereby the post-event information is remembered but the source of this information has been forgotten.

Normative motivations to conform often reflect an individual's need for social approval, and manifest as public declarations of agreement despite private disagreement. In this way, a person might outwardly agree with another person's recollected version of events, but not privately believe that this is what actually happened. Thus, normative influence is most often observed when participants are tested together and responses are given publicly rather than privately, and when costs of disagreeing are high (see Allan & Gabbert, 2008; Schneider & Watkins, 1996; Shaw *et al.*, 1997). Under these conditions, participants engaging in a collaborative retrieval task may seem to be conforming in agreement with each other, when in fact this behaviour reveals little about social influences on memory, and more about social desirability motivations to increase social acceptance and to appear more likeable (see Tajfel & Turner, 1986). For example, Baron, Vandello, and Brunsman (1996) conducted an eyewitness identification study and found that participants knowingly gave an errant response so as not to disagree with a confederate when they were told the results were of little importance (that their responses would be used as pilot data), but were less likely to conform when they were told the results were important (that their responses would be used by police and courts).

Informational motivations to conform reflect an individual's desire to be accurate. Here, individuals choose to report the post-event information encountered from a co-witness at test if it is thought to be correct. Informational motivations to conform are often evident in situations where an individual doubts the accuracy of their own memory or when the information encountered from another individual convinces them that their initial judgement might be wrong, and that the other person's recollections are likely to be correct. For

Box 4.1 Framework for investigating memory conformity

The model below presents a framework for investigating memory conformity, adapted with permission from Wright *et al.* (2010). It illustrates how predictions can be made about a person's probability of responding with their own memory, versus that of their partner's, based upon normative and informational influence. The top, normative route, emphasizes the social aspects that can lead to memory conformity, for example, when a person compares the cost of disagreeing with the cost of making an error. The bottom, informational route, emphasizes the cognitive aspects that underlie memory conformity, for example, a person's belief that they are right.

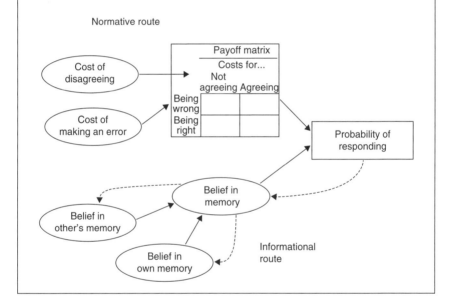

example, the apparent confidence with which individuals make their assertions to each other can operate systematically as a cue that promotes conformity (Allan & Gabbert, 2008; Schneider & Watkins, 1996; Wright *et al.*, 2000).

Box 4.1 shows Wright, London and Waechter's (2010) framework for investigating memory conformity based upon the normative and informational routes to influence discussed above.

As predicted by the informational influence route in Wright *et al.*'s (2010) framework for investigating memory conformity, tendencies to conform can also be increased (or decreased) by manipulating the perceptions of each individual regarding the relative knowledge each has of stimuli they encoded together as a dyad. Gabbert, Memon and Wright (2007) led dyad members to believe that one had viewed slides for twice the length of time as their partner, whereas in reality encoding duration was held constant. Each dyad member encoded different versions of the same slides, and were later asked to provide individual recall statements after discussing their memories together. Despite an instruction about the importance of accuracy, participants who believed that they had seen the slides for less time than their partner were significantly more likely to conform to their partner's memory for items within the slides than those who thought they had viewed the slides for longer. Thus, individuals who believe that they have an inferior memory quality to others are more likely to become influenced by, and subsequently report, items of errant post-event information encountered from another person.

Allan, Midjord, Martin, and Gabbert (2012) replicated and extended the Gabbert *et al.* (2007) study by demonstrating that the perception of another person's memory quality relative to our own does not *always* affect the tendency to conform. Instead, conformity to a person who we believe has a relatively better memory only occurs when our own memory representation is weak. This aspect of conformity was identified by showing participants photos of three household scenes, each for a different encoding duration (one for 30 seconds, one for 60 seconds and one for 120 seconds). Half the participants were told that they would encode each scene for half as long as their partner, while the remaining participants believed they would encode each scene for twice as long as their partner. On a subsequent two-alternative forced-choice memory test, the simulated answer of the partner was shown before participants responded, providing accurate, misleading, or no post-event information. Conformity to the partner's responses was significantly greater for the scene that was viewed for just 30 seconds, versus the scenes viewed for 60 and 120 seconds. This pattern, however, was present *only* in the group who believed that they had encoded each scene for half as long as their partner. Our reliance on other people's memory is therefore dynamically and strategically adjusted according to knowledge of the conditions under which we and other people have acquired different memories (see also French, Garry, & Mori, 2011).

Carlucci, Kieckhaefer, Schwartz, Villalba, and Wright (2011) demonstrated the same effect, but by manipulating perceived memory quality in a more natural way. In their 'South Beach' study, a male confederate approached a group of people at the beach and had a brief interaction. About a minute later a research assistant approached the group and administered a target-absent lineup to each person in the group. Participants were encouraged to make a choice from the lineup, hence all positive identifications were in fact incorrect. Memory conformity was observed: group members often conformed to the identification decision made by the first person to view the lineup. However, bystanders were *twice* as likely to conform to the identification judgement made by the person who had interacted with the confederate, than vice versa. Again, this suggests that people take the perceived accuracy of another person's memory into consideration when deciding on which information to report at test.

Conformity effects driven by informational influence may persist over a delay (Reysen, 2005), and people may report the suggested information in private as well as public (Wright, Gabbert, Memon, & London, 2008), even though they are able to report their own memories if requested to (Corey & Wood, 2002; Meade & Roediger, 2002). Even in situations where it is of utmost importance to provide an accurate and unbiased opinion, research suggests that, in general, individuals who are uncertain will conform to another person's decision (Baron *et al.*, 1996; Betz *et al.*, 1996; Wright *et al.*, 2000). For example, Baron *et al.* (1996) found an interaction between task difficulty and task importance, where participants were more likely to conform on a task that had a meaningful incentive for accuracy, but only when the task was made to be particularly difficult, a manipulation which made participants unconfident in their own judgments.

The more we trust and value the opinion of another, the more we are subject to their influence (Festinger, 1957). In line with this, Hope, Ost, Gabbert, Healey, and Lenton (2008) found that previously acquainted witnesses, in this case, pairs of friends and romantic partners, were significantly more likely to report information obtained from their co-witness than previously unacquainted strangers. These results were replicated in a study by French, Garry, and Mori (2008) who confirmed that participants who discussed an event with their romantic partner (rather than with a stranger) were particularly susceptible to memory conformity.

Further support for informational influence as a cause of susceptibility to memory conformity comes from research demonstrating that social influences on memory can be moderated by person perception factors, such as perceived source credibility. For example, Hoffman, Granhag, Kwong See, and Loftus (2001) conducted a computer-based study where participants heard the name of an object, sometimes accompanied by a picture of the object appearing on a screen immediately following the object name. Other times a blank screen followed the audio stimuli and participants were asked to create a mental image of the object. After a 48-hour delay participants returned for a reality monitoring test, where they were presented with the names of 72 objects and were asked to indicate whether each object had been *seen* before, whether it had been *imagined*, or whether it was a *new* item. Crucially, for some of the objects, participants were presented with an answer that suggested either a correct or incorrect response. Half of the participants were told that this information originated from a previous participant who was a university graduate student (the high-credibility condition). The remaining participants were informed that the response was randomly generated by a computer (the low-credibility condition). In both conditions the participants were asked to make a mark next to the given answer to indicate that they had looked at it before providing their own response. All participants were told that they were free to ignore the information if they wanted to. Hoffman *et al.* (2001) found that when an inaccurate suggested response was associated with a *low-credibility* source, the performance of the participants was not deleteriously affected, and did not differ from baseline performance. In other words, the suggested responses from a low-credibility source were essentially ignored. However, when an inaccurate response was associated with a *high-credibility* source, performance dropped substantially from 62% accuracy (baseline) to only 42% accuracy, demonstrating that the credibility or reliability of the source of the information was taken into account by participants when selecting their own response.

Kwong See, Hoffman and Wood (2001) also manipulated source-credibility to examine the effects of receiving misinformation from one of two individuals that differed in perceived credibility. Participants (young adults) viewed a slide show depicting a theft and were then presented with a narrative summarizing the incident. Depending on experimental condition (high versus low credibility), this narrative was either introduced as being an account of the event as remembered by a 28-year-old, or an 82-year-old. In fact the narratives were the same, each including four items of misinformation. After reading the narrative, participants were asked to provide their impressions of the witness by rating their perceived competence and honesty. The older witness was rated as being less competent, but more honest, than the young witness. This lack of competence associated with the older witness was also associated with higher resistance to memory conformity. Conversely, for the young eyewitness, higher ratings of perceived competence were significantly associated with a larger memory conformity effect.

In summary, when people feel that it is important to report correct information in a recall task, then it is not unusual to look to others, particularly trusted others, as a valid source of information. The studies reported above have shown that informational influence, or the desire to be accurate, underlies many instances of the memory conformity effect. The 'informational route' in Wright *et al.*'s (2010) model (Box 4.1), illustrates how a person's belief in their own memory, versus belief in someone else's memory, can predict whose memory is reported at test.

A third potential explanation for the memory conformity effect is that people are no longer able to distinguish between what they saw themselves and the information encountered subsequently from a co-witness. In other words, a *memory distortion* might account for observed memory conformity effects. To investigate this, Corey and Wood (2002) explored whether participants were able to disregard co-witness information if they were instructed to. In session one, the experimenter sometimes revealed co-witness information to participants while they attempted to answer 18 questions about a witnessed event. In line with previous findings, a significant memory conformity effect was observed for these responses. In session two, one week later, participants received the same 18 items about the event. Here, half of the participants were instructed to work through the questionnaire as accurately as possible. The other half were informed that the co-witness information disclosed by the experimenter a week prior was bogus and should be dismissed. These participants were asked to respond to the questions with information that was remembered from observing the crime event only. Results from session two differed depending on experimental group. The memory conformity effect persisted for those participants who had *not* received a warning about dismissing the co-witness information. In contrast, participants who had been warned about the co-witness information were generally successful in dismissing the bogus information. In this condition the warning served to decrease the use of co-witness information, however, it did not eliminate it entirely. Meade and Roediger (2002) replicated Corey and Wood's (2002) findings that warnings can significantly reduce, but not eliminate the effect.

In contrast, Paterson, Kemp, and Ng (2011) found that warnings do not significantly reduce memory conformity among co-witnesses. Dyad members viewed a mock crime event that was either the same, or slightly different to that of their partner. Following this they discussed their memories together. One week later, half of the participants from each condition were given a warning that they may have been exposed to misinformation from the co-witness with whom they had discussed the event. Following this, participants were individually interviewed about what they had seen in the event. Paterson *et al.* (2009) found that 28% of participants who received a warning reported at least one piece of misinformation in comparison to 32% of those who did not receive a warning. Thus, warning participants about misinformation one week after exposure did not significantly reduce the memory conformity effect.

A second study by Paterson *et al.* (2009) investigated whether warning participants about potential exposure to misinformation immediately after the co-witness discussion was more effective than giving the warning after a week. A control group received no warning.

Once again, it was found that warning participants that they may have been exposed to misinformation from their co-witness did not significantly reduce the degree of memory conformity. This was true both for warnings provided immediately after the misinformation had been encountered and also for the delayed warning. The authors suggest that the originally encoded information may have been 'over-written' by the misinformation encountered during the co-witness discussion.

An alternative explanation is that the participants have made a source-monitoring error. Misinformation is sometimes errantly reported at test because of a source-confusion, whereby individuals misattribute a memory from one source (e.g. discussion with a co-witness) to another source (the witnessed event). The source-monitoring framework (Johnson, Hashtroudi, & Lindsay, 1993) describes the judgement processes that individuals employ to accurately identify the source of a memory, as well as specifying factors that are likely to promote source-monitoring errors (see also Chapter 2). For example, according to the source-monitoring framework, our memories contain various characteristics that provide clues to their origin. Memories from different sources tend to differ on average in the quantity and quality of the characteristics associated with them. Individuals use these differences in memory characteristics as heuristics to attribute their memories to a particular source. However, there is no single aspect of our memories that specifies the true source without fail and, as a consequence, source misattributions can occur (Johnson et al., 1993). Research on the accuracy of source monitoring has shown that source confusion errors increase when there is an overlap in the memory characteristics from two different sources (Henkel & Franklin, 1998; Markham & Hynes, 1993). This finding is particularly pertinent in the context of memory conformity research, as there is a large amount of contextual overlap between the encoding phase and the misinformation phase within an experiment. Both phases concern the witnessed stimuli, and thus overlap in terms of content. Furthermore, both phases (usually) take place within a limited time frame, and in the same experimental environment, thus overlapping in context. When a real crime has been witnessed, a similar amount of overlap might be expected. For example, co-witnesses are likely to talk about what they have just seen (content overlap), they are likely to do this immediately after the crime event (temporal overlap), and it is likely that this discussion occurs at the scene, while waiting for the police to arrive, rather than at a different location (environmental overlap). The consequences of source-monitoring errors can be very serious in a criminal investigation, as they have the potential to lead to inaccurate testimony, biased evidence, and false corroboration between witnesses.

Some memory conformity research has specifically investigated the extent to which source-confusions are accountable for the memory conformity effect. Gabbert *et al.* (2007) examined whether items of incorrect post-event information that had been encountered from a co-witness were errantly reported at test because of source confusion, or due to a conscious decision to report the post-event information based upon beliefs about which person's memory is most likely to be accurate. Over the course of the experiment, participants engaged in a series of discussions with a co-witness about details featured in slides. Each member of the pair had in fact viewed slightly different versions of the slides – a manipulation which introduced the potential for them to share items of misleading post-event information. Following each discussion they were asked to provide an individual account of what had been seen. At the end of the experiment a source monitoring task was administered where participants were asked to review their free-recall responses and (1) to circle the details that they remembered hearing from their co-witness, but not actually seeing themselves; (2) to leave unmarked the details that they did remember seeing in the pictures; and (3) to underline the details for which they could not remember the source. The data showed that about half of the errantly reported details were correctly categorized as having been encountered in the co-witness discussions. However, about half were incorrectly attributed to having been seen in the original slide presentation.

Similar findings were reported in a study by Paterson *et al.* (2009, Experiment 2). Participants discussed their recollections of a mock crime event with a co-witness who had seen a slightly different version. One week later they were interviewed separately about what they could remember. Following the interview, participants were asked to read through their statements and indicate the source of each item of information by attributing it to one of four sources: video only, discussion only, both the video and discussion, or unsure. If suggested items of information that had been reported at test were attributed to (1) the video, or (2) the video and discussion, then the source-monitoring decision was coded as being inaccurate. Participants frequently reported that they had seen items of post-event information that had in fact only been suggested to them in the co-witness discussion. Accurate source-monitoring judgments were made on only 43% of occasions.

Source-monitoring errors are particularly problematic in a forensic investigation. Thus, the high prevalence of source-monitoring errors following co-witness discussion is worthy of further research attention. Such errors are not inevitable, however, as Bodner *et al.* (2009) found that while participants often reported non-witnessed details that they had encountered via a discussion with a co-witness, they were frequently able to correctly identify the source of the information when asked. Specifically, 63% of participants who discussed an event with a co-witness later reported at least one non-witnessed detail, while only 14% attributed these responses to the incorrect source.

In summary, research suggests that observed memory conformity effects can be caused by source-confusions, and also by normative and informational motivations to conform. These underlying mechanisms have different implications for forensic investigations. Where memory conformity has occurred as a result of informational influence, the research suggests that the co-witness information is selectively reported if it is deemed accurate and can, therefore, be recognized and disregarded if necessary. Alternatively, where memory conformity has occurred as a result of a genuine memory distortion, namely, a source confusion, witnesses may be unable to accurately retrieve the source of the information, and may claim to remember seeing items of information that have actually been encountered from a co-witness (Gabbert *et al.*, 2007; Paterson *et al.*, 2009). The fact that some research has found that source judgements can be wrong, even with deliberate consideration, highlights the fact that being able to recall memories does not guarantee their authenticity. Discrepancies in findings from studies that have employed warnings to disregard information from co-witnesses, or instructions to identify the source of items of information reported at test, reveal that other factors must be taken into consideration when determining when conformity effects are caused by either informational influences or source-monitoring errors.

THE FUTURE OF MEMORY CONFORMITY RESEARCH

One exciting new line of research examines conformity effects in memory for actions that are either self-performed or observed. Wright and Schwartz (2010) found that memories for actions can be affected by information suggested by another person, such that people can be made to report that they have performed actions that they have not, and that they have not performed actions that, in fact, they had. This research has clear forensic implications. For example, in certain types of investigative interview settings, officers sometimes suggest to suspects that they have performed particular actions.

Research also continues to explore which factors can increase, decrease, and possibly eliminate the longer-term effects of conformity upon memory. However, progress in addressing such issues has been hampered by the complexity of the phenomenon itself, due to the inherently dynamic and variable nature of realistic interactions between individuals. Despite this, new paradigms to investigate conformity in eyewitness reports are being developed and refined so that the effects of naturalistic interactions on subsequent memory reports can be investigated with full experimental control.

CONCLUSIONS

The research presented in this chapter has shown that the seemingly innocuous activity of discussing memories with another person can expose individuals to post-event information that can subsequently influence one's original memory for what was actually seen. In summary:

- Participants in memory conformity studies demonstrate that our memories are malleable, and that we often conform to the suggestions and judgements of others. Individuals frequently report items at test that they have encountered during a discussion with a co-witness rather than having perceived themselves.
- When memory conformity occurs in the context of a forensic investigation, there can be serious and costly implications as the evidence obtained from witnesses might not be reliable. This can lead to misdirected lines of enquiry and has the potential to lead to miscarriages of justice.
- Broadly speaking, researchers have adopted three main paradigms in order to investigate memory conformity, including: (1) examining the extent of memory conformity between participants who unwittingly share different information when engaging in collaborative retrieval due to (unbeknownst to them) having viewed different versions of an event; (2) the use of a confederate acting as a co-witness who deliberately reports some incorrect details during a collaborative recall task; and (3) providing participants with information about what other co-witnesses have allegedly said, for example, via the experimenter revealing responses that have been given by another witness.
- Informational motivations to conform sometimes underlie observed memory conformity, whereby participants report any information at test that they believe to be correct, regardless of whether this information can be verified by their own recollections. However, this suggests that witnesses are able to disregard co-witness information if instructed to, whereas some research shows this is not always possible. Furthermore, source-monitoring errors have been found to underlie some memory conformity effects, where suggested items of post-event information are mistakenly believed to be veridical recollections.
- Future research continues to explore which factors can increase, decrease, and possibly eliminate the longer-term effects of conformity upon memory.

FORENSIC IMPLICATIONS OF THE MEMORY
CONFORMITY EFFECT

- *Investigative interviewers should be aware that witnesses who have discussed an incident together might have unintentionally influenced each other's memories.* Witnesses should be asked if they have discussed their memories with anyone because seemingly corroborating statements might instead be contaminated statements. Forensic investigators should be cautious about witness testimony that is highly similar (especially if there is other evidence that disconfirms it) particularly if those witnesses have had an opportunity to talk about the witnessing experience.
- *If witnesses reveal that they have discussed their memories with another witness, the length of time between discussing the event and giving a statement should be considered.* If the length of time is relatively short, then a warning to disregard post-event information from a co-witness or other external source may be effective. At longer delays witnesses often forget the source of the information, and can no longer distinguish between their own memories and post-event information encountered from a co-witness.
- *Co-witnesses who know each-other are more susceptible to memory conformity than strangers.*
- *Forensic investigators should take into consideration the role a person plays in an event when assessing eyewitness evidence.* Based upon Carlucci *et al.*'s (2011) findings, by-standers are more susceptible to memory conformity than witnesses who have been actively involved in an incident.

REFERENCES

Allan, K., & Gabbert, F. (2008). I still think it was a banana: Memorable 'lies' and forgettable 'truths'. *Acta Psychologica, 127,* 299–308.

Allan, K., Midjord, J.P., Martin, D., & Gabbert, F. (2012). Memory conformity and the perceived accuracy of Self versus Other. *Memory & Cognition, 40,* 280–286.

Ayers, M.S., & Reder, L.M. (1998). A theoretical review of the misinformation effect: Predictions from an activation-based memory model. *Psychonomic Bulletin & Review, 5,* 1–21.

Baron, R.S., Vandello, J. A., & Brunsman, B. (1996). The forgotten variable in conformity research: Impact of task importance on social influence, *Journal of Personality and Social Psychology, 71,* 915–927.

Betz, A.L., Skowronski, J.J., & Ostrom, T.M. (1996). Shared realities: Social influence and stimulus memory. *Social Cognition, 14,* 113–140.

Bodner, G.E., Musch, E., & Azad, T. (2009). Re-evaluating the potency of the memory conformity effect. *Memory & Cognition, 37,* 1069–1076.

Carlucci, M.E., Kieckhaefer, J.M., Schwartz, S.L., Villalba, D.K., & Wright, D.B. (2011). The South Beach Study: Bystanders' memories are more malleable. *Applied Cognitive Psychology, 25,* 562–566.

Cathcart, B. (2002). Cover story: A question of identity; the conviction of Barry George for the murder of the TV presenter Jill Dando was one of the biggest stories of last year. But did he really do it? *The Independent,* 11 July.

Ceci, S.J., & Bruck, M. (1993). Suggestibility of the child witness: A historical review and synthesis. *Psychological Bulletin, 113,* 403–439.

Cialdini, R.B., & Goldstein, N.J. (2004). Social influence: Compliance and conformity. *Annual Review of Psychology, 55,* 591–621.

Corey, D., & Wood, J. (March, 2002). Information from co-witnesses can contaminate eyewitness reports. Paper presented at the American Psychology-Law Society, Austin, TX.

Deutsch, M., & Gerard, H.G. (1955). A study of normative and informational social influence upon individual judgement. *Journal of Abnormal and Social Psychology, 59,* 204–209.

Festinger, L. (1957). *A Theory of Cognitive Dissonance,* Stanford, CA: Stanford University Press.

French, L., Garry, M., & Mori, K. (2007). The MORI technique produces memory conformity in western subjects. *Applied Cognitive Psychology, 22,* 431–439.

French, L., Garry, M., & Mori, K. (2011). Relative – not absolute – judgments of credibility affect susceptibility to misinformation conveyed during discussion. *Acta Psychologica, 136,* 119–128.

Gabbert, F., Memon, A., & Allan, K. (2003). Memory conformity: Can eyewitnesses influence each other's memories for an event? *Applied Cognitive Psychology, 17,* 533–543.

Gabbert, F., Memon, A., Allan, K., & Wright, D.B. (2004). Say it to my face: Examining the effects of socially encountered misinformation. *Legal & Criminological Psychology, 9,* 215–227.

Gabbert, F., Memon, A., & Wright, D.B. (2007). I saw it for longer than you: The relationship between perceived encoding duration and memory conformity. *Acta Psychologica, 124,* 319–331.

Granhag, P., Ask, K., & Rebelius, A. (2005). 'I saw the man who killed Anna Lindh': A case study of eyewitness descriptions. Presented at 15th European Conference on Psychology & Law, Vilnius, Lithuania, June.

Henkel, L.A., & Franklin, N. (1998). Reality monitoring of physically similar and conceptually related objects. *Memory and Cognition, 26,* 659–673.

Hoffman, H.G., Granhag, P.A., Kwong See, S.T., & Loftus, E.F. (2001). Social influences on reality-monitoring decisions. *Memory and Cognition, 29,* 394–404.

Hollin, C.R., & Clifford, B.R. (1983). Eyewitness testimony – the effects of discussion on recall accuracy and agreement. *Journal of Applied Social Psychology, 13,* 234–244.

Hope, L., Ost, J., Gabbert, F., Healey, S., & Lenton, E. (2008). "With a little help from my friends...": The role of co-witness relationship in susceptibility to misinformation. *Acta Psychologica, 127,* 476–484.

Johnson, M.K., Hashtroudi, S., & Lindsay, D.S. (1993). Source monitoring. *Psychological Bulletin, 114,* 3–28.

Kwong See, S.T., Hoffman, H.G., & Wood, T. (2001). Perceptions of an elderly eyewitness: Is the older eyewitness believable? *Psychology and Aging, 16,* 346–350.

Loftus, E.F., Miller, D.G., & Burns, H.J. (1978). Semantic integration of verbal information into a visual memory. *Journal of Experimental Psychology: Human Learning & Memory, 4,* 19–31.

Markham, R., & Hynes, L. (1993). The effect of vividness of imagery on reality monitoring. *Journal of Mental Imagery, 17,* 159–170.

Meade, M.L., & Roediger, H.L., III. (2002). Explorations in the social contagion of memory. *Memory & Cognition, 30,* 995–1009.

Memon, A., & Wright, D.B. (1999). Eyewitness testimony and the Oklahoma bombing. *The Psychologist, 12,* 292–295.

Paterson, H.M., & Kemp, R.I. (2006). Comparing methods of encountering post-event information: The power of co-witness suggestion. *Applied Cognitive Psychology, 20,* 1083–1099.

Paterson, H.M., Kemp, R.I., & Forgas, J.P. (2009). Co-witnesses, confederates, and conformity: Effects of discussion and delay on eyewitness memory. *Psychiatry, Psychology and Law, 16,* 112–124.

Paterson, H.M., Kemp, R.I., & Ng, J.R. (2011). Combating co-witness contamination: Attempting to decrease the negative effects of discussion on eyewitness memory. *Applied Cognitive Psychology, 25,* 43–52.

Payne, D.G., Toglia, M.P., & Anastasi, J.S. (1994). Recognition performance-level and the magnitude of the misinformation effect in eyewitness memory. *Psychonomic Bulletin and Review, 1,* 376–382.

Reysen, M.B. (2005). The effects of conformity on recognition judgements. *Memory, 13,* 87–94.

Schacter, D.L. (2001). *The Seven Sins of Memory (How the Mind Forgets and Remembers).* New York: Houghton Mifflin Company.

Schneider, D.M., & Watkins, M.J. (1996). Response conformity in recognition testing. *Psychonomic Bulletin and Review, 3,* 481–485.

Shaw, J.S., Garven, S., & Wood, J.M. (1997). Co-witness information can have immediate effects on eyewitness memory reports. *Law and Human Behaviour, 21,* 503–523.

Skagerberg, E.M., & Wright, D.B. (2008). The prevalence of co-witnesses and co-witness discussions in real eyewitnesses. *Psychology, Crime, & Law, 14,* 513–521.

Tajfel, H., & Turner, J.C. (1986). The social identity theory of inter-group behaviour. In S. Worchel, & W.G. Austin (Eds), *Psychology of Inter-group Relations* (2nd edn, pp. 7–24). Chicago: Nelson-Hall.

Valentine, T., Pickering, A., & Darling, S. (2003). Characteristics of eyewitness identification that predict the outcome of real lineups. *Applied Cognitive Psychology, 17,* 969–993.

Wright, D.B., & McDaid, A.T. (1996). Comparing system and estimator variables using data from real line-ups. *Applied Cognitive Psychology, 10,* 75–84.

Wright, D.B., London, K., & Waechter, M. (2010). Social anxiety moderates memory conformity in adolescents. *Applied Cognitive Psychology, 24,* 1034–1045.

Wright, D.B., Gabbert, F., Memon, A., & London, K. (2008). Changing the criterion for memory conformity in free recall and recognition. *Memory, 16,* 137–148.

Wright, D.B., Self, G., & Justice, C. (2000). Memory conformity: Exploring misinformation effects when presented by another person. *British Journal of Psychology, 91,* 189–202.

Wright, D.B., & Schwartz, S.L. (2010). Conformity effects in memory for actions. *Memory & Cognition, 38,* 1077–1086.

Zaragoza, M.S., & Lane, S.M. (1994). Source misattributions and suggestibility of eyewitness memory. *Journal of Experimental Psychology: Learning, Memory and Cognition, 20,* 934–945.

5

Suggestibility and Individual Differences: Psychosocial and Memory Measures

ANNE M. RIDLEY AND GISLI H. GUDJONSSON

KEY POINTS

- The relationships between immediate and delayed suggestibility and psychosocial variables:
  - ○ Self-esteem
  - ○ Adverse life-events.
- The relationships between immediate and delayed suggestibility, and memory related variables:
  - ○ Memory
  - ○ Memory distrust.
- Contrasting findings from studies of immediate and delayed suggestibility and how they contribute to our understanding of the nature of suggestibility.
- The implications of these individual differences for practitioners conducting interviews with victims, witnesses and suspects.

Suggestibility in Legal Contexts: Psychological Research and Forensic Implications,
First Edition. Edited by Anne M. Ridley, Fiona Gabbert and David J. La Rooy.
© 2013 John Wiley & Sons, Ltd. Published 2013 by John Wiley & Sons, Ltd.

> Experimentalists ... could enrich their models [of suggestibility] by
> exploring how differences in personality and cognitive abilities influ-
> ence the impact of leading questions. (Schooler & Loftus, 1986, p. 105)

'Individual differences' is a term used to describe personality or
cognitive variables that vary from person to person. Since Schooler and
Loftus made the above statement more than 25 years ago, a great deal
of research has taken place to explore how such factors affect suggestibility. There are a number of reasons why such research is important in
legal contexts. First, police and legal professionals need to know the
factors that might increase the suggestibility of witnesses and
suspects. Thorough preparation for suspect interviews (as advocated in
the PEACE model of interviewing; Williamson, 1994) *should* enable
interviewing officers to gain some insight into the vulnerabilities of a
suspect and conduct the interview accordingly. In contrast, in many
investigations, little is known about the vulnerabilities of victims and
witnesses. In their efforts to gain essential information from witnesses,
police officers often need to use specific questions and these may
sometimes be leading (Milne & Bull, 1993). Thorough rapport building
prior to starting a formal interview could provide officers with valuable
clues about the background and possible psychological vulnerabilities
of the witness. This review aims to provide insights into the possible
effects of these vulnerabilities arising from individual differences.
The implications will be highlighted throughout, and summarized at
the end of the chapter. Second, psychologists may be asked to assess
an individual's suggestibility for legal purposes and/or appear in court
as an expert witness and it is therefore important to understand the
effects of individual differences on suggestibility and testimony generally. Finally, from a theoretical perspective, as Schooler and Loftus
(1986) and Eisen, Winograd, and Qin (2002) have clearly stated, the
study of individual differences can help us to understand the mechanisms behind suggestibility.
  To fully explore the mechanisms underlying suggestibility, it is
important to distinguish between *immediate* and *delayed* suggestibility. Schooler and Loftus (1993, see also Eisen *et al.*, 2002) were one of
the first to propose this distinction, specifically, between the *immediate* acceptance of misleading information contained in a leading
question, and *delayed* suggestibility due to exposure to misleading
information that is incorrectly reported in a subsequent test.
Immediate suggestibility is observed in the Yield and Shift measures
of the Gudjonsson Suggestibility Scales (Gudjonsson: GSS 1, 1983,
1984; GSS 2, 1987a; Box 5.1), as well as in studies using leading and
misleading questioning styles. Delayed suggestibility is built in to the
'standard' or 'classic' misinformation studies. In a review, Eisen *et al.*
(2002) reported that imagery ability, field dependence/locus of control

Box 5.1 Methodological Explanations

Most of the studies below that consider *immediate suggestibility* use the Gudjonsson Suggestibility Scales (GSS; 1983, 1984, 1987a; see Chapter 3 for a full explanation).
The various scores from the scales are as follows:

Immediate free recall
Delayed free recall (typically following a 50-minute delay)
Yield 1 – the number of suggestible responses to *leading* questions before any negative feedback about answers has been given. Scores 0–15
Yield 2 – the number of suggestible responses to the same questions as in Yield 1 but *following negative feedback*. Scores 0–15
Shift – the number of answers changed *as a result of negative feedback to any question*. Scores 0–20
Total suggestibility – the combined scores of Yield 1 and Shift.

Studies of *delayed suggestibility* (unless otherwise stated) used the three-stage misinformation paradigm:

Stage 1: Witnessing of event
Stage 2: Exposure to misleading post-event information
Stage 3: A delayed test to see whether the misleading post-event information encountered earlier results in suggestible response(s).

See Chapter 2 for a full explanation.

---

and the tendency to dissociate were related to delayed but not immediate acceptance of misleading information, whereas acquiescence, agreeableness and intelligence were associated with immediate but not delayed suggestibility. Based on these findings, the authors concluded that immediate suggestibility is the result of social pressure while delayed suggestibility is due to confusion between what was actually witnessed and what was suggested; delayed suggestibility is thus theoretically accounted for as a failure of source monitoring (see Chapter 2).

In this chapter we will focus on the relationship between immediate and delayed suggestibility and individual differences not reviewed by Eisen *et al.* (2002), that can be divided into two types: psychosocial (anxiety, self-esteem and negative life events) and memory factors (memory, and memory distrust). We will not attempt to address the vast literature on individual differences and suggestibility in children (although one or two studies will be mentioned where relevant to the topic under discussion). Interested readers are referred to Chapter 7, this volume, and to Bruck and Melnyck (2004) for a review.

SUGGESTIBILITY AND PSYCHOSOCIAL VARIABLES

Anxiety

Victims, witnesses and suspects are likely to experience elevated anxiety and related emotions to varying degrees throughout a crime, its investigation and time in court. Anxiety is generally conceptualized in two ways referred to as 'trait' and 'state' anxiety. Trait anxiety is a relatively stable personality construct that reflects a person's general anxiety. State anxiety, in contrast, reflects how anxious a person is at a given moment in time, and varies depending on the situation. Those high in trait anxiety usually react with a greater increase in state anxiety in stressful situations than those who have low trait anxiety.

A number of studies have examined anxiety using the Spielberger State-Trait Anxiety Inventory (STAI; Spielberger, Gorsuch, Luschene, Vagg, & Jacobs, 1983), which is a simple questionnaire consisting of two 20-item scales. Early studies (e.g. Gudjonsson, 1983), indicated that trait anxiety was not related to measures of the GSS 1. Gudjonsson (1988a) went on to test the relationship between state anxiety (using the STAI) and the GSS. He measured state anxiety both after administration of the first free recall test and again at the very end when participants were asked to state how they felt during the inter-rogation stage (when they were given negative feedback). The results showed that elevated state anxiety was associated with high suggesti-bility scores on the Yield 2 and Shift measures of the GSS when measured *before* the interrogation. Importantly, the relationships for *all* suggestibility measures were significant and considerably stronger when anxiety was measured *after* the interrogation. For example, the correlation between anxiety and shift increased from 0.42 before the interrogation stage to 0.69 afterwards. Thus, in Gudjonsson's studies, there is evidence that state anxiety may be related to suggestibility.

In a German study, Wolfradt and Meyer (1998) found a slightly different pattern of findings. They looked at both state and trait anxiety using the STAI and compared clinically anxious participants with a non-clinical control group. Correlations *within* each group were not significant. In contrast, when they combined that data from both groups, they found strong positive correlations between all suggestibility measures and both state anxiety (0.50, 0.62, 0.63 for Yield 1, Shift and Total Suggestibility respectively) and trait anxiety (0.65, 0.70, 0.76 respectively), even though the STAI was completed before the interrogation. Gudjonsson, Rutter and Clare (1995) also found high anxiety (particularly trait anxiety) was associated with high levels of suggestibility among police detainees. It is worth noting, however, that not all studies have shown significant effects. Smith and Gudjonsson (1995) did not observe any significant correlations between suggestibility and anxiety measured at the interrogation stage of the GSS. On balance, the evidence shows that, for immediate suggestibility, high anxiety is associated with greater numbers of suggestible responses, and this effect is strongest following negative feedback.

A series of studies were conducted by Ridley and her colleagues to investigate whether anxiety was related to delayed suggestibility. In the first study (Ridley, Clifford, & Keogh, 2002), 9- and 10-year-old children watched a minor car accident on video, and then completed a questionnaire about the film. Five of the questions contained misleading details. After completing the state anxiety measure from a children's version of the STAI (Spielberger, Edwards, Luschene, Montouri, & Platzek, 1970), the participants completed a second questionnaire about the accident that included five critical questions testing suggestibility for the misleading details. There was a negative relationship between anxiety and suggestibility (−0.33). Children with higher anxiety scores tended to give *fewer* suggestible responses.

In a further study by Ridley and Clifford (2006), a source identification/ attribution methodology was used (this is a variant of the standard suggestibility paradigm in which participants are asked to identify *where* they encountered the misleading information – in the event or in subsequent questions – rather than being tested for recall of it). The source identification test was completed by participants who were warned they had been exposed to incorrect details about the film of a burglary and car chase they had previously seen. This design aimed to reduce possible demand characteristics and interpersonal aspects of suggestibility. Analysis showed that state and trait anxiety and the interaction between them accounted for 26% of the variance in suggestibility (as measured by misleading post-event information incorrectly attributed to the witnessed event). *Higher* levels of state anxiety were associated with *lower* levels of suggestibility. In contrast, there was a positive relationship between trait anxiety and suggestibility. This indicates a complex relationship between suggestibility and state and trait anxiety that is worth investigation in future studies.

The two previous studies investigated the effect of anxiety in baseline conditions that were made as non-stressful as possible by using self-completed questionnaires throughout, and using a standardized measure of anxiety. To enhance ecological validity, Ridley and Clifford (2004) also investigated the effect of state anxiety increased by an experimental manipulation, that aimed to simulate, as far as possible, a situation that might arise in a legal setting. Participants were videotaped as they were questioned about the to-be-remembered event. In addition, they could see themselves 'giving evidence' via a feedback loop. The participants were 160 undergraduate students. Following a brief film of a baby being kidnapped from a hospital ward, misleading information was presented in 5 out of 19 questions in an initial interview, and suggestibility was later tested in a second interview. The timing of the anxiety manipulation varied between experimental groups, so that it was either (i) when participants encountered the misleading post-event information; (ii) when their suggestibility was tested; (iii) at both encoding and retrieval; or (iv) not at all. A manipulation check indicated that the anxiety induction was generally successful. The results showed that all three groups who had their anxiety manipulated were significantly *less* suggestible than the control group who did not experience the anxiety manipulation.

To summarize, these three studies of delayed suggestibility have all shown that higher levels of state anxiety are associated with *lower* levels of suggestibility. This is in direct contrast to the studies of immediate suggestibility in which anxiety was associated with *higher* levels of suggestibility. This is strong support for the notion that different mechanisms underpin immediate and delayed suggestibility.

Ridley and colleagues (Ridley & Clifford, 2004, 2006; Ridley *et al.*, 2002) provide a possible theoretical explanation for this pattern of results. They argued that the reduced suggestibility associated with anxiety in delayed suggestibility studies can be explained by a theory of cognition and emotion. According to processing efficiency theory (Eysenck & Calvo, 1992), anxious individuals worry, and this limits their cognitive processing capacity. However, if processing limits have not been reached and the task in question is not too cognitively demanding, fear of failure means that those high in state anxiety are likely to *put greater effort into performing well* than those with lower anxiety levels. This could explain the reduced suggestibility in the delayed paradigm through more thorough processing of misleading post-event information and correct rejection of it. In contrast, in the case of immediate suggestibility, leading questions, particularly *after* negative feedback (as in Shift), increase worry in those high in state anxiety, to the extent that it limits their processing resources and results in increased suggestibility. Furthermore, if negative feedback within the social interaction of the interview is perceived as the cause of an individual's heightened state anxiety and worry, the resulting behavioural response might be to give the suggested answer in order to reduce the negative feelings associated with anxiety, a finding that would be predicted based on Gudjonsson's Model of Interrogative Suggestibility

(Gudjonsson & Clark, 1986; see also Chapter 9 on emotional factors that reduce the effectiveness of self-regulation in interrogations).

Summary and Forensic Implications for Anxiety and Suggestibility
Although anxiety is associated with reduced suggestibility in the misinformation paradigm (delayed suggestibility), in police investigations it is unlikely that interviewers will know whether a witness has had previous exposure to misleading or incorrect information. Even if this were the case, it is not advocated that they should deliberately resort to increasing the anxiety levels of witnesses to reduce the effects of suggestibility! The most important point for practitioners to note is that the combination of elevated anxiety caused by being the victim of crime, and/or the social interaction of the interview, plus the presence of leading or misleading questions (immediate suggestibility), may combine to create high levels of suggestible responding in some individuals.

Self-esteem

Self-esteem may well become diminished in victims of crime – particularly crimes of violence or violation. This, coupled with the fact that people with low self-esteem might not cope well with the demands of suspect or witness interviews, makes research into the relationship between self-esteem and suggestibility of particular interest.

In a series of studies using the GSS, Bain, Baxter, Boon, and colleagues, examined self-esteem and suggestibility in conjunction with interviewer demeanour. As Gudjonsson and Clark's (1986) model indicates, interrogative suggestibility is a complex phenomenon embedded in a social interaction, therefore the behaviour of the interviewer is an important consideration. In two studies (Baxter, Jackson, & Bain, 2003; Bain, Baxter, & Fellowes, 2004) the demeanour of the interviewer was either abrupt or friendly. In the 2003 study, all suggestibility measures were significantly higher for those with low self-esteem compared to those with high self-esteem (as measured by the Battle Self-esteem Inventory: Battle, 1981). For example, the mean Total Suggestibility score for those in the low self-esteem group was almost twice that found in the high self-esteem group. An abrupt interview manner also had an effect, but only among participants with low self-esteem, resulting in higher levels of suggestibility for this group. In contrast to the above study, Bain *et al.* (2004) observed a smaller but significant relationship between self-esteem and suggestibility as measured by Shift. Participants in the group with the 'abrupt' interviewer were significantly more suggestible on Yield 1 and Total Suggestibility measures than those with the 'friendly' interviewer. In an earlier study, Gudjonsson and Lister (1984) found that the behaviour of the interviewer affected self-esteem. The experimenters concluded that interview techniques that reduce self-esteem and confidence lead to greater suggestibility.

Not all studies have observed a significant relationship between self-esteem and suggestibility as measured by the GSS. Drake, Bull, and Boon (2008) observed negative but not significant relationships with the various suggestibility measures. Peiffer and Trull (2000) used the Self-perception Profile for College Students (Neeman & Harter, 1986), which measures competence and social aspects of self-esteem. They found that competence predicted suggestibility as measured by Shift, but social esteem did not. Using a different methodology, McGroarty and Baxter (2009) conducted a study in which participants viewed a filmed event and then answered a series of closed and open questions. This was followed by negative feedback and a second interview. Although participants exposed to a friendly interview manner changed fewer responses than those exposed to an abrupt one, there was no effect of self-esteem on suggestibility.

To our knowledge there are no published studies that have reported a relationship between self-esteem and the misinformation paradigm. If one looks at the literature relating to children for clues to the likely relationship, there are only a limited number of studies to draw upon. In a review of individual differences in children's suggestibility, Bruck and Melnyck (2004) noted that all but two studies of self-esteem examined immediate suggestibility (with findings consistent with those found for adults). Of the two that looked at delayed suggestibility, the findings were contradictory (Murch & Slater, 1996; Melnyck, 2002; both cited in Bruck & Melnyck, 2004). It may simply be, therefore, that self-esteem is not reliably related to delayed suggestibility. However, as studies that have shown null effects are not usually published, research that combines both immediate and delayed suggestibility might shed further light on this point.

Summary and Forensic Implications for Self-esteem and Suggestibility
These findings indicate that low self-esteem is generally associated with *higher* suggestibility scores on the GSS, but this relationship is not always statistically significant. Self-esteem may increase suggestibility through an individual's negative cognitive appraisal of themselves in the interview situation. This, in turn, may result in an increased tendency to accept suggestions made in leading questions, particularly when accompanied by negative feedback from the interviewer. Therefore, as the above research by Baxter *et al.* (2003) and Bain *et al.* (2004) has shown, a positive interview demeanour should, in theory, reduce suggestibility caused by leading questions, particularly for those with low self-esteem.

Life Adversity

A number of large community studies indicate that false confessions obtained during police interviews are linked to negative life events and previous victimization (Gudjonsson, Sigurdsson, Asgeirsdottir & Sigfusdottir, 2007; Gudjonsson, Sigurdsson, & Sigfusdottir, 2009a, b; 2010; Gudjonsson, Sigurdsson, Sigfusdottir, & Asgeirsdottir, 2008; Gudjonsson, Sigurdsson, Sigfusdottir, & Young, 2012). The Gudjonsson *et al.* (2012) study investigated whether negative life events, attention deficit hyperactive disorder (ADHD), and conduct disorder predicted self-reported false confessions among 16- to 24-year-old students in Iceland. After controlling for gender, age and emotional lability, it was found that all three factors predicted false confessions. This relationship may be mediated by interrogative suggestibility and compliance. It is therefore important to understand the relationship between such negative life events and suggestibility itself (for a review of ADHD and suggestibility and compliance, see Chapter 3).

Kim Drake has carried out a number of studies exploring the relationship between life adversity and interrogative suggestibility. According to Drake (2011b) the type of negative life event most relevant to forensic interviews in terms of heightened suggestibility are interpersonal ones such as workplace and family difficulties, whereas Gudjonsson *et al.* (2009b, 2010) found that being the victim of physical or sexual abuse, childhood bullying by siblings, peers or carers, and peer-group bullying in adolescence, were particularly powerful in relation to a reported history of making false confessions during police questioning. As Drake (2011b) reports, it has also been established that negative life events predispose some individuals to psychological distress such as elevated anxiety and depression, which may bring about vulnerability to suggestive influence. Findings have indeed shown this to be the case as outlined in the section on anxiety.

In an effort to advance understanding of suggestibility in vulnerable witnesses or suspects, Drake has conducted a number of studies that have looked at the relationships between either the number or intensity (or both) of negative life events (NLE measured by Life Events Questionnaire; Norbeck, 1984) in conjunction with a number of other vulnerability factors (Drake 2010a,b, 2011a; Drake & Bull, 2011; Drake *et al.*, 2008).

The statistical analyses required to examine the effects of so many individual factors at once are somewhat complex. In essence, a significant relationship was found between the number of reported negative life events and, in particular, their intensity with Yield 1, Yield 2, Shift and Total Suggestibility. The effects sizes are typically low for Yield 1 (see also Drake, 2011a), but tend to be higher for Shift, reaching medium to large effect sizes (Drake, 2010a,b). Drake also used structured equation modelling to investigate the inter-relationships between interrogative suggestibility, negative life events, and other psychosocial variables. For example, in Drake (2010b), adult attachment style was analysed. The notion of adult attachment has developed from Bowlby's (1988) theory about the psychological import-ance of the quality of the emotional bond between a child and their primary caregiver(s). It is proposed that the resulting internal working models of attachment affect expectations of relationships throughout life. Therefore, secure attachment in childhood is argued to provide resilience in relationships in adulthood. In contrast, a negative attach-ment in childhood can lead to a fearful avoidant attachment style that renders individuals vulnerable in interpersonal relationships. Drake (2010b) found that a fearful avoidant attachment style indirectly affects Shift through the intensity of negative life events. It is argued that this is due to the combination of vulnerability factors resulting in a negative mindset and increased sensitivity to negative feedback in the context of the interview relationship. Using similar analysis, Drake (2010a) found that neuroticism, compliance and intensity of negative life events all exerted a positive direct effect on Shift. This suggests that Shift is more influenced by social factors and anxiety processes than Yield 1, which supports the Gudjonsson and Clark (1986) model of interrogative suggestibility.

Summary and Forensic Implications for Life Adversity and Suggestibility Drake (2011b) points out that this work is in its infancy and, as such, no firm conclusions can yet be reached about the interac-tions between the vulnerability variables she has investigated. No studies to date have examined the relationship between life adversity and delayed suggestibility. The implications for practitioners are that negative life events may be an indicator of psychological vulnerability generally and predispose a witness or suspect to give suggestible responses to leading questions, particularly if the interviewer provides negative feedback.

Conclusions: Suggestibility and Psychosocial Variables

Overall, this review of psychosocial variables indicates that although effect sizes vary, negative psychological states are associated with increased vulnerability to immediate suggestibility, particularly in the presence of negative feedback and/or an abrupt interviewer manner. Based on the very limited research on anxiety, this does not seem to be the case for delayed suggestibility. What is evident is that there is little published research into psychosocial variables using delayed suggestibility paradigms, certainly among adults. It is difficult to know whether this is because none has been conducted, or whether such studies have found null results and were thus not reported by researchers. Research that combines both immediate and delayed suggestibility may help to resolve this important issue.

SUGGESTIBILITY AND MEMORY FACTORS

The evidence reviewed so far indicates that psychosocial factors are more reliably associated with immediate than delayed suggestibility. We now move on to review a number of studies that have looked at factors related to memory. First, we consider the relationship between suggestibility and measures of memory itself. Second, we briefly outline an emerging area of research that looks at the relationship between suggestibility and memory distrust. Contrasting findings for immediate and delayed suggestibility will be highlighted.

Memory

Studies that have examined the relationship between memory and suggestibility frequently use measures for both that derive from the same experimental stimuli and questionnaires. In the majority of studies using the misinformation paradigm, memory is measured as the recall of details of the to-be-remembered event that have *not* been the subject of misleading post-event information. Therefore, the memory and suggestibility measures should be reasonably independent of each other. By contrast, Schooler and Loftus (1986) stated that because of the design of the GSS, it is not possible to eliminate items that might have been freely recalled from the content of the leading questions. To test for this possibility, Gudjonsson (1987b) carried out a study using both the GSS 1 and GSS 2, which use different narratives for the to-be-remembered information. He found that memory (free recall) in the GSS 1 was related to suggestibility on the GSS 2 and vice versa. Furthermore, the correlations were similar to those between memory and suggestibility *within* both the GSS 1 and GSS 2. Gudjonsson therefore argues that exploring the relationships between the free recall and the suggestibility measures within the GSS 1 and GSS 2 is valid.

In these studies, poor memory was associated with higher suggestibility levels. This finding has also been observed in other studies by Gudjonsson (1983, GSS1; 1988b, GSS 2). For example, in Gudjonsson (1983), both immediate and delayed recall were significantly correlated with all suggestibility measures (correlations ranged from −0.44 to −0.58). Polczyk (2005) tested students using Polish translations of both the GSS 1 and 2. Significant correlations were observed for both versions between immediate recall and all suggestibility measures. However, the correlations were generally weaker than Gudjonsson (1983) ranging from −0.18 (for Shift) to −0.38 (for Yield 2) in the GSS 1. By contrast, in a similar study of 76 female undergraduate students, Howard and Chaiwutikornwanich (2006) found that although both immediate and delayed free recall on the GSS were significantly and positively correlated with the Yield 1 (−0.51 and −0.40, respectively) and Total Suggestibility (−0.39 and −0.27, respectively), there was no significant relationship between free recall and Shift. From these studies, it can be concluded that free recall is more reliably associated with Yield 1 than with suggestibility that results from negative feedback. In studies that also included measures of intelligence, it was found that the association between memory and suggestibility was strongest at lower levels of intelligence (Gudjonsson, 1983, 1988b). In other words, for individuals with a low IQ, the negative effect of poor memory on suggestibility was particularly severe.

An alternative way of investigating the relationship between memory and suggestibility is to use memory measures that are completely independent of the target event. Polczyk *et al.* (2004), investigated the relationship between memory measured by the Wechsler Memory Scale (WMS: Wechsler, 1945) and the GSS 2. This early version of the WMS consists of a number of different memory measures including digit span (recall of a random series of numbers), visual memory (memory for objects presented in pictures) and verbal paired associates (presentation of pairs of words followed by a memory test in which the first word is repeated and the participant has to remember the second, associated word). Participants comprised a group of 66 young adults (mean age 22.3, SD 3.3) and a group of 43 older adults (mean age 64.1, SD 9.5). In the young adult group there were significant correlations between immediate and delayed free recall on the GSS and Yield 1 and between delayed free recall and both Yield 1 and Yield 2 measures. However, no relationships were observed between memory measures on the WMS and any of the suggestibility measures. In contrast, in the older adult group poorer memory as measured by the GSS immediate and delayed free recall was associated with higher scores on *all* suggestibility measures, and all correlations were considerably stronger than for the young adult group. The WMS score was also associated with higher levels of suggestibility as measured by the Yield 1 (−0.55), Yield 2 (−0.37) and Total suggestibility (−0.45) scores. However, the WMS score was not related to Shift. Overall, this study shows that poor memory, whether measured by free recall or the WMS, has a greater effect on the suggestibility of older adults than younger adults.

There are three conclusions to be drawn from the research reviewed in this section so far. First, the balance of evidence shows that poor memory is associated with increased suggestibility (particularly for Yield 1) in studies of immediate suggestibility. The pattern of generally strong relationships between memory and Yield 1 accompanied by absent or weak relationships between memory and Shift is the reverse of the trend noted in the review of psychosocial variables. This supports the notion that even within the GSS, there are two 'types' of suggestibility, with Yield 1 related more to memory and Shift related to psychosocial factors (Gudjonsson, 2003). Second, there is evidence to indicate that poor cognitive function, whether due to advancing age or lower intelligence, mediates the relationship between memory and suggestibility as measured by the GSS. Third, standardized memory measures are not reliably related to either immediate or delayed suggestibility.

In delayed suggestibility paradigms, predicting the relationship between memory and suggestibility is more complex. Schooler and Loftus (1993) argued that a positive relationship between the two is possible because individuals with good memory are also more likely to remember misleading post-event information. An alternative prediction is that if memory for the event is poor, the (usually) more recent misleading information will be more readily accessible in memory. Thus, either good or poor memory could result in high levels of suggestibility!

A comprehensive study conducted by Lee (2004) among children and adolescents aged 7–17 years, examined suggestibility measured in three different ways: first using the GSS; second, using a standard misinformation paradigm; and third, using source identification. Thus, both immediate and delayed suggestibility were investigated in the one study. The 'event' was a home burglary depicted in a slide sequence. Suggestibility using the 'standard' methodology was measured by a recognition test in which participants had to select either correct information from the slides or the misleading post-event information. The source identification task involved participants identifying *where* they had encountered the misleading information. Aspects of memory were measured using a battery of neuropsychological measures including a backwards digit span test and a verbal paired associates test from the Children's Memory Scale (Cohen, 1997). Differences between the two age-groups were generally not significant, so the correlation analysis reported was for all participants combined. There were no significant correlations between any of the memory measures and either the (delayed) suggestibility recognition test or the GSS scores. Source identification was weakly but significantly correlated with the verbal paired associate scores such that a high memory score was associated with a high suggestibility score. Regression analysis, however, produced additional significant effects: the relationship between the GSS and the verbal paired associate scores was positive with elevated suggestibility being associated with poorer memory. In contrast, for the delayed tests, 'participants with better memories ... were more likely to select the misinformation in the recognition test and to misattribute the misinformation in the source memory test' (Lee, 2004, p. 1012). Lee argues that the different pattern across the methodologies may be due to the timing of the misleading information and test, providing support for the idea advanced throughout this chapter that immediate and delayed suggestibility are underpinned by different psychological processes.

Three studies of delayed suggestibility using the misinformation paradigm were conducted by Ridley (2003). The witnessed crime was a non-violent abduction of a baby from a hospital ward presented by video. The memory measure was the number of correct responses to 14 cued recall questions about the event contained in the first of two sets of questions about the abduction. The same set of questions also contained five further questions containing misleading post-event information. Suggestibility was tested through five cued recall prompts which formed part of a second questionnaire about the crime. The relationship between memory accuracy and suggestibility was not consistent across the three studies. In two out of three cases no significant relationship was observed, but in the third, there was a significant negative correlation (−0.34) between memory accuracy and suggestibility indicating that poorer memory was associated with higher levels of suggestibility. The inconsistent findings between these three studies may be in part because in the study with the significant correlation, memory accuracy was somewhat better than in the other two studies, and this may have underpinned the correlation. It is important to point out that these studies also investigated the effects of manipulated anxiety on both memory and suggestibility (see earlier section on anxiety). In the study where the significant correlation was observed, the group who had their anxiety manipulated had higher memory accuracy scores compared to the control group, but this was not the case in the other two studies. Thus the differences between studies may be due to a complex inter-relationship between anxiety and memory.

Other studies have also reported that delayed suggestibility and memory are not reliably related to each other. Loftus, Levidow, and Duensing (1992) carried out a study with 1989 participants of all ages (5–75 years) who visited a science museum and viewed a section from a film depicting events at a tense political rally. The hypothesis was that poorer memory for the event would be associated with elevated suggestibility. Approximately half of the participants were exposed to two items of misleading information and later in the same questionnaire were tested for acceptance of it. While the hypothesis was supported among children and older participants, the findings among the remaining participants were puzzling. For example, participants were asked to state their occupations, and it was found that artists and architects had good memory accuracy scores, but were also highly suggestible.

The authors argued that this finding might be due to the imagery skills of these occupational groups. Correlation analysis would have helped assess these relationships more directly.

Summary and Forensic Implications for Memory and Suggestibility
Overall, these studies of memory and suggestibility demonstrate a complicated relationship. With immediate suggestibility, poorer memory (particularly when measured by GSS free recall) is generally associated with higher levels of suggestible responding, particularly for Yield 1. In the delayed suggestibility studies reviewed, relationships have been variously absent, negative or positive. However, from a theoretical perspective, as outlined at the beginning of this section, this outcome for delayed suggestibility is not entirely unexpected: a good memory can apply to both details of an event *and* to misleading post-event information (Schooler & Loftus, 1993). This, coupled with the absence of strong social cues of the expected answer (e.g. negative feedback), and possible confusion about the *source* of misleading information, provide a possible explanation for the different outcomes. In addition, some of the variability is doubtless due to methodological differences between studies. To unpick the complex relationship between delayed suggestibility and memory, further research is required.

For practitioners, it is important to bear in mind that poor memory may result in suggestible responses to leading questions. Paradoxically, even though a witness with a good memory is therefore less likely to succumb to leading questions, that same witness is not necessarily immune to the effects of misleading post-event information (however encountered) on their subsequent reports of events.

Memory Distrust

Memory distrust (Gudjonsson & MacKeith, 1982) is defined as 'a condition where people develop profound distrust of their memory recollections as a result of which they are particularly susceptible to relying on external cues and suggestions' (Gudjonsson, 2003, p. 196). Memory distrust is not confined to people with a generally poor memory, although this may increase susceptibility, particularly if combined with amnesia, alcohol intoxication, or interview techniques that undermine an individual's confidence in their recollections (Gudjonsson, 2003).

Until recently, few studies have directly explored the relationship between memory distrust and suggestibility, although its presence has been used to explain certain patterns in the relationship between memory and immediate suggestibility (e.g. Gudjonsson, 1983; Howard & Chaiwutikornwanich, 2006), and it is also believed to be a contributory factor in false confessions (Henkel & Coffman, 2004).

To explore this relationship directly, Van Bergen and her colleagues have investigated the relationship between memory distrust and suggestibility as measured both by the GSS and a variation of the misinformation paradigm. Memory distrust was measured using the Squire Subjective Memory Questionnaire (SSMQ: Squire, Wetzel, & Slater, 1979; Van Bergen, Brands, Jelicic, & Merckelbach, 2010). Somewhat surprisingly, Van Bergen, Jelicic, and Merckelbach (2009) found that memory distrust was not related to the suggestibility measures of the GSS, although those with high memory distrust also had higher scores on the Gudjonsson Compliance Scales (Gudjonsson, 1989).

In a second study using a delayed paradigm, Van Bergen, Horselenberg, Merckelbach, Jelicic, and Beckers (2010) recruited two groups (each with 40 adult participants aged 18–49 years) by asking them to evaluate their memory on a 10-point scale ('very poor' to 'excellent'). The resulting 'memory distrust' and 'memory confidence' groupings were subsequently justified by significant differences on the SSMQ. All participants watched an event and then provided a free recall account that was transcribed and presented back to them either after a day, or 2 weeks later. Five items of incorrect (misleading) information had been added to these transcripts. For both groups, accurate recognition of the false items was poorer as a result of the 2-week delay. With respect to memory distrust, compared to the memory confidence group, participants in the memory distrust group were less likely to recognize the incorrect details as false. In other words they were more suggestible. However, this effect was not significant when free recall and age were statistically controlled. The authors propose that this is because good memory aids accurate *discrepancy detection* (Schooler & Loftus, 1993), whereas poor memory fuels negative memory evaluations and thereby increases acceptance of misleading information. However, this does not explain the moderating effect of age, and it could be argued that (as age and free recall were not significant covariates) this effect may have simply been due to statistical anomalies.

It is interesting to note that when comparing participants with attention deficit hyperactivity disorder (ADHD) to a normal control group, Gudjonsson, Young, and Bramham (2007) found that the ADHD group had poorer free recall on the GSS2 but were no more suggestible, giving 'don't know' responses instead. The authors argued that this tendency to provide 'don't know' responses may indicate memory distrust. The design of the Van Bergen *et al.* (2010) study was such that 'don't know' responses were unlikely. Further research using a cued recall rather than a recognition task might provide further insights into the relationship between memory distrust and the acceptance of misinformation, and this would also permit 'don't know' responses.

Summary and Forensic Implications for Memory Distrust and Suggestibility The research directly exploring memory distrust and suggestibility is in its infancy and it is therefore difficult to make recommendations for practitioners. Van Bergen's work indicates that memory distrust is not related to immediate suggestibility, but it is modestly related to delayed acceptance of misinformation. Further research into both immediate and delayed suggestibility with a particular focus on 'don't know' responses would be valuable. As Quas, Qin, Schaaf, and Goodman (1997, p. 378) stated:

> Adults and possibly children who have overly positive perceptions of their ability to remember information … may be more likely to rely on suggestions rather than appear as though they have poor memories. In contrast, adults and children who do not perceive themselves as having especially good memories would not expect themselves to remember information and thus need not rely on suggested information.

Conclusions for Suggestibility and Memory Factors

Immediate suggestibility measures (particularly Yield 1) and free recall on the GSS are related, but the relationships between independent memory measures and suggestibility scores from the GSS are less robust. The relationship between delayed suggestibility and memory accuracy is inconsistent, possibly due to the complex relationship between memory for the event and memory for the misleading post-event information which can be explained by source monitoring theory (see Chapter 2), in other words, the ability to correctly identify where one encountered any misleading post-event information. Memory distrust has been shown to be related to delayed suggestibility although further research is required to assess this relationship further.

OVERALL CONCLUSIONS

- Psychosocial factors and suggestibility:
  - Anxiety is related to suggestibility in a complex way. High state anxiety is associated with elevated immediate suggestibility, whereas low state anxiety is associated with elevated delayed suggestibility.
  - Low self-esteem is associated with higher immediate suggestibility, but there is no evidence of a relationship with delayed suggestibility.
  - Adverse life-events may predispose an individual to be suggestible, although the precise mechanism is, as yet, poorly understood.

- Overall, psychosocial vulnerability is associated with higher levels of immediate suggestibility with little evidence of such a relationship with delayed suggestibility. This pattern of findings indicates that suggestibility measured in these different ways involves separate processes: interpersonal aspects of forensic interviews and interrogations interact with vulnerability to increase immediate but not delayed suggestibility.
- Memory related factors and suggestibility:
  - Memory: the relationship between memory and suggestibility is also complex. Poor free recall about an event is related to elevated immediate suggestibility, particularly in the absence of negative feedback. In delayed suggestibility there is little evidence of a systematic relationship and we have argued that this is because memory processes can affect both memory for the to-be-remembered event *and* misleading post-event information in complex ways.
  - Memory distrust: this new area of research has produced somewhat counterintuitive findings showing no relationship between MDS and immediate suggestibility, and only a modest relationship with delayed suggestibility.
- The findings from the memory-related factors reviewed here are less conclusive than those for psychosocial variables in helping us to discriminate the mechanisms of immediate versus delayed suggestibility. However, memory distrust and its counterpart, overconfidence, provide promising areas for further research.
- Overall, this review has provided further support for the notion expressed by Eisen *et al.* (2002) that suggestibility is not a 'unified construct' (p. 227). This is interesting from a theoretical perspective but, frustratingly, we are no closer now than we were in 2002 to being able to identify precisely who will and who will not be suggestible in interviews and court appearances. Nevertheless, this area of research can and should continue to inform investigative interview practice.

FORENSIC IMPLICATIONS OF INDIVIDUAL DIFFERENCES IN SUGGESTIBILITY

- *Interviewers in legal settings may not always know whether the victim, witness or suspect has low self-esteem, high anxiety, a background of life adversity, poor memory or memory distrust.* Thorough preparation and rapport building prior to the interview may help to provide insights into these psychological states. Even in the absence of such knowledge it would be prudent to assume that the situation alone will predispose witnesses to anxiety and activate any psychological vulnerabilities or memory deficits they may have.

- *Psychological vulnerability and poor memory can increase suggestible responses to leading questions.* Practitioners should avoid such questions as much as possible.
- *Negative feedback may increase suggestibility in vulnerable witnesses.* Interviewers should be careful not to give negative feedback either explicitly or implicitly (e.g. through obvious impatience or frustration) and maintain a positive demeanour to help keep suggestible responses to a minimum.

ACKNOWLEDGEMENTS

The authors thank Dr Laura Crane for the assistance she provided sourcing literature for this review and Dr Janice Brown and Detective Sergeant Gary Pankhurst, MSc, of the Metropolitan Police for their comments on a previous draft of this chapter.

REFERENCES

Bain, S.A., Baxter, J.S., & Fellowes, V. (2004). Interacting influences on interrogative suggestibility. *Legal and Criminological Psychology, 9,* 239–252.

Battle, J. (1981). *Culture-free SEI: Self-esteem Inventories for Children and Adults.* Seattle, WA: Special Child.

Baxter, J.S., Jackson, M., & Bain, S.A. (2003). Interrogative suggestibility: Interactions between interviewees' self-esteem and interviewer style. *Personality and Individual Differences, 35,* 1285–1292.

Bowlby, J. (1988). *A Secure Base: Parent-child Attachment and Healthy Human Development.* New York, NY: Basic Books.

Bruck, M., & Melnyk, L. (2004). Individual differences in children's suggestibility: A review and synthesis. *Applied Cognitive Psychology, 18,* 947–996.

Cohen, M. (1997). *Children's Memory Scale.* San Antonio, TX: The Psychological Corporation.

Drake, K.E. (2010a). Interrogative suggestibility: Life adversity, neuroticism and compliance. *Personality and Individual Differences, 48,* 493–498.

Drake, K.E. (2010b). The psychology of interrogative suggestibility: A vulnerability during interview. *Personality and Individual Differences, 49,* 683–688.

Drake, K.E. (2011a). Further insights into the relationship between the experience of life adversity, and interrogative suggestibility. *Personality and Individual Differences, 51,* 1056–1058.

Drake, K.E. (2011b). Why might innocents make false confessions? *The Psychologist, 24,* 752–755.

Drake, K.E., & Bull, R. (2011). Life adversity and field-dependence: Individual differences in interrogative suggestibility. *Psychology, Crime and Law, 17,* 677–687.

Drake, K.E., Bull, R., & Boon, J.C.W. (2008). Interrogative suggestibility, self-esteem, and the influence of negative life events. *Legal and Criminological Psychology, 13,* 299–310.

Eisen, M.L., Winograd, E., & Qin, J. (2002). Individual differences in adults' suggestibility and memory performance. In M.L. Eisen, J.A. Quas, & G.S. Goodman (Eds), *Memory and Suggestibility in the Forensic Interview* (pp. 205–233). Mahwah, NJ: Lawrence Erlbaum.

Eysenck, M.W., & Calvo, M.G. (1992). Anxiety and performance: The processing efficiency theory. *Cognition and Emotion, 6,* 409–434.

Gudjonsson, G.H. (1983). Suggestibility, intelligence, memory recall and personality: An experimental study. *British Journal of Psychiatry, 142,* 35–37.

Gudjonsson, G.H. (1984). A new scale of interrogative suggestibility. *Personality and Individual Difference, 5,* 303–314.

Gudjonsson, G.H. (1987a). A parallel form of the Gudjonsson Suggestibility Scale. *British Journal of Clinical Psychology, 26,* 215–221.

Gudjonsson, G.H. (1987b). The relationship between memory and suggestibility. *Social Behaviour, 2,* 29–33.

Gudjonsson, G.H. (1988a). Interrogative suggestibility: Its relationship with assertiveness, social-evaluative anxiety, state anxiety and method of coping. *British Journal of Clinical Psychology, 26,* 215–221.

Gudjonsson, G.H. (1988b). The relationship of intelligence and memory to interrogative suggestibility: The importance of range effects. *British Journal of Clinical Psychology, 27,* 185–187.

Gudjonsson, G.H. (1989). Compliance in an interrogation situation: A new scale. *Personality and Individual Differences, 10,* 535–540.

Gudjonsson, G.H. (2003). *The Psychology of Interrogations, Confessions, and Testimony: A Handbook.* Chichester: John Wiley & Sons, Ltd.

Gudjonsson, G.H., & Clark, N.K. (1986). Suggestibility in police interrogation: a social psychological model. *Social Behaviour, 1,* 83–104.

Gudjonsson, G.H., & Lister, S. (1984). Interrogative suggestibility and its relationship with perceptions of self-concept and control. *Journal of the Forensic Science Society, 24,* 99–110.

Gudjonsson, G.H., & MacKeith, J.A.C. (1982). False confessions. Psychological effects of interrogation. A discussion paper. In A. Trankell (Ed.), *Reconstructing the Past: The Role of Psychologists in Criminal Trial* (pp. 253–269). Deventer, The Netherlands: Kluwer.

Gudjonsson, G.H., Rutter, S.C., & Clare, I.C.H. (1995). The relationship between suggestibility and anxiety among suspects detained at police stations. *Psychological Medicine, 25,* 875–878.

Gudjonsson, G.H., Sigurdsson, J.F., Asgeirsdottir, B.B., & Sigfusdottir, I.D. (2007). Custodial interrogation. What are the background factors associated with claimed false confessions? *The Journal of Forensic Psychiatry and Psychology, 18,* 266–275.

Gudjonsson, G.H., Sigurdsson, J.F., & Sigfusdottir, I.D. (2009a). Interrogations and false confessions among adolescents in seven countries in Europe. What background and psychological factors best discriminate between false confessors and non-false confessors? *Psychology, Crime and Law, 15,* 711–728.

Gudjonsson, G.H., Sigurdsson, J.F., & Sigfusdottir, I.D. (2009b). False confessions among 15 and 16 year olds in compulsory education and their relationship with adverse life events. *Journal of Forensic Psychiatry and Psychology, 20,* 950–963.

Gudjonsson, G.H., Sigurdsson, J.F., & Sigfusdottir, I.D. (2010). Interrogation and false confessions among adolescents: Differences between bullies and victims. *Journal of Psychiatry and Law, 38,* 57–76.

Gudjonsson, G.H., Sigurdsson, J.F., Sigfusdottir, I.D., & Asgeirsdottir, B.B (2008). False confessions and individual differences. The importance of victimization among youth. *Personality and Individual Differences, 45,* 801–805.

Gudjonsson, G.H., Sigurdsson, J.F., Sigfusdottir, I.D., & Young, S. (2012). False confessions to police and their relationship with conduct disorder, ADHD, and life adversity. *Personality and Individual Differences, 52,* 696–701. doi: 10.1016/j.paid.2011.12.025.

Gudjonsson, G.H., Young, S., & Bramham, J. (2007). Interrogative suggestibility in adults diagnosed with attention-deficit hyperactivity disorder (ADHD). A potential vulnerability during police questioning. *Personality and Individual Differences, 43,* 737–745.

Henkel, L.A., & Coffman, K.J. (2004). Memory distortions in coerced false confessions: A source monitoring framework. *Applied Cognitive Psychology, 18,* 567–588.

Howard, R.C., & Chaiwutikornwanich, A. (2006). The relationship of interrogative suggestibility to memory and attention: An electrophysiological study. *Journal of Psychophysiology, 20,* 79–93.

Lee, K. (2004). Age, neuropsychological, and social cognitive measures as predictors of individual differences in susceptibility to the misinformation effect. *Applied Cognitive Psychology, 18,* 997–1019.

Loftus, E.F., Levidow, B., & Duensing, S. (1992). Who remembers best? Individual difference in memory for events that occurred in a science museum. *Applied Cognitive Psychology, 6,* 93–107.

McGroarty, A., & Baxter, J.S. (2009). Interviewer behaviour, interviewee self-esteem and response change in simulated forensic interviews. *Personality and Individual Differences, 47,* 642–646.

Milne, R., & Bull, R. (1993). Interviewing by the police. In J. Carson, & R. Bull (Eds), *Handbook of Psychology in Legal Contexts* (2nd edn). Chichester: John Wiley & Sons, Ltd.

Neeman, J., & Harter, S. (1986). *Manual for the Self-Perception Profile for College Students.* Denver, CO: University of Denver, Department of Psychology.

Norbeck, J.S. (1984). Modification of life event questionnaires for use with female respondents. *Research in Nursing Health, 7,* 61–71.

Peiffer, L.C., & Trull, T.J., (2000). Predictors of suggestibility and false-memory production in young adult women. *Journal of Personality Assessment, 74,* 384–399.

Polczyk, R. (2005). Interrogative suggestibility: Cross-cultural stability of psychometric and correlational properties of the Gudjonsson Suggestibility Scales. *Personality and Individual Differences, 38,* 177–186.

Polczyk, R., Wesolowska, B., Gabarczyk, A., Minakowska, I., Supska, M., & Bomba, E. (2004). Age differences in interrogative suggestibility: A comparison between young and older adults. *Applied Cognitive Psychology, 18,* 1097–1107.

Quas, J.A., Qin, J., Schaaf, J., & Goodman, G.S. (1997). Individual differences in children's and adults' suggestibility and false event memory. *Learning and Individual Differences, 9,* 359–390.

Ridley, A.M. (2003). The effect of anxiety on eyewitness testimony. Unpublished doctoral thesis. University of East London, United Kingdom.

Ridley, A.M., & Clifford, B.R. (2004). The effects of anxious mood induction on suggestibility to misleading post-event information. *Applied Cognitive Psychology, 18,* 233–244.

Ridley, A.M., & Clifford, B.R. (2006). Suggestibility and state anxiety: How the two concepts relate in a source identification paradigm. *Memory, 14,* 37–45.

Ridley, A.M., Clifford, B.R., & Keogh, E. (2002). The effects of state anxiety on the suggestibility and accuracy of child eye-witnesses. *Applied Cognitive Psychology, 16,* 547–558.

Schooler, J. W., & Loftus, E. F. (1986). Individual differences and experimentation: Complementary approaches to interrogative suggestibility. *Social Behaviour, 1,* 105–112.

Schooler, J.W., & Loftus E.F. (1993). Multiple mechanisms mediate individual differences in eyewitness accuracy and suggestibility. In J.M. Pucket, & H.W. Reese (Eds), *Mechanisms of Everyday Cognition* (pp. 177–204). Hillsdale, NJ: Laurence Erlbaum Associates.

Smith, P., & Gudjonsson, G.H. (1995). Confabulation among forensic inpatients and its relationship with memory, suggestibility, compliance, anxiety and self-esteem. *Personality and Individual Differences, 19,* 517–523.

Spielberger, C.D., Edwards, C.D., Luschene, R., Montouri, J., & Platzek, D. (1970). *How I Feel Questionnaire.* CA: Consulting and Psychologists Press Inc.

Spielberger, C.D., Gorsuch, R.L., Luschene, R., Vagg, P.R., & Jacobs, G.A. (1983). *State-Trait Anxiety Inventory for Adults.* CA: Mind Garden.

Squire, L.R., Wetzel, C.D., & Slater, P.C. (1979). Memory complaint after electroconvulsive therapy: Assessment with a new self-rating instrument. *Biological Psychiatry, 14,* 791–801.

Van Bergen, S., Brands, I., Jelicic, M., & Merckelbach, H. (2010). Assessing trait memory distrust: Psychometric properties of the Squire Subjective Memory Questionnaire. *Legal and Criminological Psychology, 15,* 373–384.

Van Bergen, S., Horselenberg, R., Merckelbach, H., Jelicic, M., & Beckers, R. (2010). Memory distrust and acceptance of misinformation. *Applied Cognitive Psychology, 24,* 885–896.

Van Bergen, S., Jelicic, M., & Merckelbach, H. (2009). Are subjective memory problems related to suggestibility, compliance, false memories, and objective memory performance? *American Journal of Psychology, 122,* 249–257.

Wechsler, D. (1945). *The Wechsler Memory Scale.* San Antonio, TX: The Psychological Corporation.

Williamson, T. M. (1994). Reflections on current police practice. In D. Morgan & G. Stephenson (Eds.), *Suspicion and Silence: The Rights of Silence in Criminal Investigations.* London: Blackstone Press.

Wolfradt, U., & Meyer, T. (1998). Interrogative suggestibility, anxiety and dissociation among anxious patients and normal controls. *Personality and Individual Differences, 25,* 425–432.

6

Recovered Memories and Suggestibility for Entire Events

JAMES OST

KEY POINTS

- The extent to which recovered memory experiences can be explained by relatively ordinary processes of remembering and forgetting.
- The importance of distinguishing between false memories and false beliefs.
- The difference between naturally occurring and suggestion-dependent false memories.
- The extent to which laboratory-generated false memories have relevance outside the laboratory.

In 2005, at the age of 40, Anna sought therapy to help her deal with depression following the loss of her job. At the start of therapy Anna had no memories of being sexually abused in childhood. When that course of therapy ended, Anna sent a letter to her mother claiming that she had remembered being sexually assaulted as a child. In that letter she accused her father of sexually abusing her when she was 9 years old – and that the abuse was responsible for her depression. After a short break, Anna started a course of therapy to help her deal with having been a victim of childhood sexual abuse. Over the following 2 years more details emerged,

Suggestibility in Legal Contexts: Psychological Research and Forensic Implications,
First Edition. Edited by Anne M. Ridley, Fiona Gabbert and David J. La Rooy.
© 2013 John Wiley & Sons, Ltd. Published 2013 by John Wiley & Sons, Ltd.

including sexual abuse perpetrated by her brother and a local civic leader. Her sister, whom Anna claimed was also abused by the same perpetrators, denied any knowledge of the events Anna said she now remembered.[1] Anna decided to bring criminal charges against her father. The key issue for psychologists, the police and legal professionals is whether these memories are genuine and relate to events that actually occurred, or whether they are false beliefs and memories, perhaps generated as a result of suggestive therapy.

Some adults who were sexually abused as children may never disclose that abuse to anyone. Some may not disclose until years after the alleged abuse occurred, some may disclose after a period of psychological therapy, others may disclose and then retract their disclosures, and others still may disclose after a period where they claimed to have been unaware that they had been abused.[2] Each type of disclosure presents its own unique challenges for therapeutic and law enforcement professionals. The consequences of such disclosures can be incredibly high, both for the person making the disclosure and those accused as a result. If legal and therapeutic systems get it wrong, there are equally tragic consequences. Either a genuine victim of abuse is not believed, or someone is falsely accused (Conway, 1997; Pezdek & Banks, 1996). Thus, the goal of psychological research is to improve diagnosticity in these cases – how to increase the detection of genuine cases (i.e. hits), without also increasing the number of false allegations (i.e. false alarms). As a result, a significant body of scientific research has developed over the past 20 years in an attempt to inform therapeutic and legal decision-making in such cases. Still, it remains a controversial issue (Freyd, Putnam, Lyon *et al.*, 2005 and replies).

DIFFERENT TYPES OF 'RECOVERED MEMORY' EXPERIENCE

Anna is not alone. Many individuals claim to have suddenly 'remembered' episodes of childhood abuse of which they were previously unaware – referred to in the literature as 'discontinuous memories' (McNally & Geraerts, 2009). Some argue that individuals might have 'discontinuous' memories because their minds had blocked out the memories of the trauma they had suffered until it was safe for them to remember, years later (e.g. Blume, 1990).[3] However, there is no

---

[1] This vignette is based on an actual case that was reported to UK police. The names and any identifying details have been changed.

[2] For the literature concerning disclosure by child victims, the reader is referred to Pipe, Lamb, Orbach, and Cederborg (2007).

[3] Blume (1990) writes that: 'With the help of blocking, denial, etc., the incest survivor grows into adulthood relieved of the burden of her memories' (p. 95) and that 'Flashbacks often "wait" to occur in a climate of safety, such as in the therapeutic environment or support group' (p. 101).

evidence that the mind is capable of repressing, dissociating, or otherwise 'blocking out' memories of traumatic events, only for them to resurface years later in pristine form (Clancy & McNally, 2005/2006; Hayne, Garry, & Loftus, 2006; Kihlstrom, 2002; McNally, 2003, 2007; Pope, Poliakoff, Parker, Boynes, & Hudson, 2007). Although these ideas continue to have considerable influence in legal (Piper, Lillevik, & Kritzer, 2008) and psychological contexts (Ost, Wright, Easton, Hope, & French, 2010; Yapko, 1994), there are a number of plausible alternatives to repression or dissociation that could account for an apparently 'discontinuous' memory of abuse. McNally and Geraerts (2009) outline several possibilities.

The first alternative interpretation proposed by McNally and Geraerts is that the abuse was not traumatic (or experienced as traumatic) at the time it occurred. It may be in adulthood that a person comes to realize or understand what it was that they experienced (Clancy, 2009; Clancy & McNally, 2005/2006). In this case, it is not that the person has repressed and then recovered a traumatic memory, rather events that have always been remembered, but not fully understood at the time, are interpreted in a very different light (or 're-perceived'; Payne & Blackwell, 1998). There is evidence that this can be very distressing (Clancy & McNally, 2005/2006), but it is clearly not the same as claiming the person had blocked out the traumatic memory. A second possibility is that reminders of the abuse were absent. In other words, memories of abuse are as likely as other memories to fade over time if not cued. If, for example, the person subsequently moved away from the area where the abuse occurred, or the perpetrator died, then there would be few reminders that would cue recall. In addition, due to the often secretive nature of childhood sexual abuse, it is very unlikely that other people would provide memory cues, unless the child had disclosed the abuse at, or near to, the time it occurred. A third possibility raised by McNally and Geraerts (2009) is that people may deliberately try to avoid thinking about the abuse. However, as intentionally trying *not* to think about a particular memory or event is not a particularly effective technique ('don't think about a white bear'; Wegner, Schneider, Carter, & White, 1987), people may avoid thinking about the abuse by distracting themselves, or focusing on other thoughts instead (but see Dalgleish, Hauer, & Kuyken, 2008; Goodman, Quas, & Ogle, 2010). A final possibility is that some individuals may have forgotten that they had previously remembered the abusive episodes. This is termed the 'forgot-it-all-along' (FIA) effect and originates from a series of case studies published by Schooler and colleagues (Schooler, Bendiksen, & Ambadar, 1997; Shobe & Schooler, 2001). Schooler *et al.* (1997) found that some people who claimed to have suddenly 'remembered' forgotten episodes of childhood abuse had, in fact, previously disclosed that abuse to other people (e.g. spouses). The issue then is not that they had forgotten, repressed or dissociated their memories of abuse – rather they had forgotten that they had previously remembered it. Put another way, they had underestimated their previous successful recall of those events. Experimental analogues have provided support for the FIA effect and argued that it is caused by changes in the recall context (Arnold & Lindsay, 2002; Merckelbach *et al.*, 2006).

In summary, the evidence is that some discontinuous abuse memories (i.e. those reported to have been recalled after a period of non-awareness) do indeed seem to be genuine (or at least the events to which they refer can be corroborated at some level). What is less clear is what it is that is responsible for the 'period of non-awareness'. There is no evidence for any kind of mechanism that 'banishes' swathes of traumatic memories from conscious awareness, although this still remains a powerful theory in some contexts.[4] The weight of the evidence suggests that these 'periods of non-awareness' can be accounted for more parsimoniously by reasonably ordinary and mundane processes of forgetting (Clancy & McNally, 2005/2006; Goodman *et al.*, 2003; McNally, 2003).

The implications of this for a client in therapy are as follows: if gentle questioning does not lead an adult client to disclose a history of childhood trauma, then there is no justification for aggressively digging for memories of childhood trauma on the assumption that they must be lying in some dormant part of the client's unconscious mind. Such digging may be particularly problematic for two reasons. First, surveys have shown that the idea that it is possible to forget childhood abuse, and that such forgotten abuse can cause longstanding emotional problems, is perceived as a plausible one in the general population (Pezdek & Blandon-Gitlin, 2008; Rubin & Berntsen, 2007). Furthermore, Rubin and Boals (2010) found a linear relationship between participants' estimates of the likelihood of entering psychotherapy, and their estimates of the likelihood of remembering previously unrecalled memories of childhood trauma. Put another way, 'people who expect to enter therapy also believe that it is more likely that they have forgotten memories of trauma and abuse' (Rubin & Boals, 2010, p. 561). In addition to clients entering therapy being already primed to expect to recall previously unremembered trauma, the second reason for not digging for long-lost memories is that research shows that this runs the risk, in some cases, of creating false beliefs and false memories about events that never occurred. Before outlining this research, it is important to note a distinction in the literature between false beliefs and false memories.

---

[4] Seventy-five percent of a sample of psychological therapists 'strongly agreed' with the statement that 'The mind is capable of unconsciously "blocking out" memories of traumatic events' (Ost *et al.*, 2010).

FALSE BELIEFS VERSUS FALSE MEMORIES

Just because an adult discloses that they were the victim of childhood sexual abuse it does not necessarily follow that they are making that claim on the basis of being able to clearly *remember* such abuse occurring. One respondent in a study by Ost, Costall, and Bull (2001, 2002) who had reported being a victim of childhood sexual abuse, and later retracted that report, said that she had never 'remembered' any abuse occurring to her. Her initial report of having been abused was based solely on a strongly held *belief* that such abuse had occurred (Ost, 2003). In this case there was a strong belief *without* an accompanying memory. This, in itself, is not unusual of course. Many of us *believe* that we have experienced events that we do not *remember* (e.g. that we were fed during the first few days of life; Mazzoni & Kirsch, 2002; Mazzoni & Memon, 2003). Thus a distinction is usually drawn between autobiographical belief (with or without an accompanying memory) and autobiographical memory (remembering an event, including perceptual details, and so on) (Gudjonsson, 1997; Lindsay & Read, 1994; Scoboria, Lynn, Hessen, & Fisico, 2007; Scoboria, Mazzoni, Kirsch, & Relyea, 2004).

In an interesting twist, Mazzoni, Scoboria, and Harvey (2010) recently reported that 20% of an undergraduate student sample recounted at least one event that they could *remember* but which they did not *believe* had happened to them. In some cases they had been told that the event they remembered had, in fact, happened to someone else (see also Sheen, Kemp, & Rubin, 2001, 2006). In other cases the remembered event was impossible (e.g. seeing a living dinosaur). In a final set of cases, there was contradictory evidence that the event occurred. This distinction between autobiographical belief and autobiographical memory is important because research has shown that certain suggestive techniques (e.g. imaginative procedures) can lead people to develop false beliefs, without them necessarily developing false memories (Scoboria *et al.*, 2007; but see also Mazzoni & Memon, 2003).

FALSE BELIEFS AND MEMORIES IN THE WILD

Outside of the laboratory, psychologists have documented compelling evidence of false beliefs and memories. Taken at face value, this evidence shows that people can and do come to falsely believe and report that they remember a variety of traumatic and abusive events. For example, some individuals, referred to as 'retractors', claim to remember having been sexually abused, only later to repudiate those claims (Lief & Fetkewicz, 1995; de Rivera, 1997; Ost *et al.*, 2001, 2002;

Ost & Nunkoosing, 2010; Woodiwiss, 2010). In a survey of 20 retractors from the UK and North America, Ost *et al.* (2001) found that descriptions of the therapy in which they came to 'remember' the abuse, shared social dynamics not dissimilar to police interviews and interrogations where individuals come to falsely confess to criminal acts (e.g. there was a lengthy and emotional interrogation, they were not able to check with outside sources that might have disconfirmed what they were being led to believe, and so on; Gudjonsson, 2003; Ofshe, 1989). In addition some retractors reported a great deal of social pressure from their therapists, as well as from other clients, to 'recall' episodes of abuse (Ost *et al.*, 2001).

The idea that therapy itself might have contributed in some way to individuals 'remembering' events that did not occur is also supported by the emergence in the United States, during the mid-1980s, of cases of alleged satanic ritual abuse (Bottoms & Davis, 1997; Mulhern, 1994). In these cases individuals, usually as a result of participating in some kind of therapy, claimed to have been abused as children in satanic cults, where they were forced to witness horrific events (e.g. the sacrifice of foetuses) and to participate in horrific acts (e.g. being forced to eat faeces; Qin, Goodman, Bottoms, & Shaver, 1998). These acts were supposedly the work of highly organized, trans-generational cults (Bottoms & Davis, 1997). Despite extensive investigations (e.g. Lanning, 1991), no physical evidence of such crimes was ever found. Interestingly, as Bottoms and Davis (1997) note, a large number of these cases seemed to originate from a small number of therapists. A survey of all cases of child abuse in the United Kingdom between 1987 and 1992 where satanic or ritualistic abuse was alleged, was conducted by Professor Jean LaFontaine and reported in her book, published in 1998, entitled *Speak of the Devil*. She found only three cases (of 84) where the abuse occurred in conjunction with some ritual activities, and in these 'the rituals represented a ragbag of elements invented to further the abuse, having no similarity either to occultism or, indeed, to the allegations of satanic abuse' (La Fontaine, 1998, p. 188). While there are clearly cases of abuse in which alleged 'satanic' or 'ritualistic' elements are used to coerce or frighten children, the idea that this is widespread and common is not supported by the available evidence. Thus it is somewhat surprising that a recent survey found that over 30% of psychological therapists in the United Kingdom claimed to have seen such a case (Ost, Wright, Easton, Hope, & French, in press).

One final noteworthy category of real-life false beliefs consists of individuals who claim to have been abducted, and in some cases interfered with sexually, by visitors from outer space (Clancy, 2005; Clancy, McNally, Schacter, Lenzenweger, & Pitman, 2002; Holden & French, 2002; McNally *et al.*, 2004). As Holden and French (2002) note, the evidence shows that these individuals are not 'deliberately deceiving others' and 'are almost certainly wrong in thinking that they really have had a close encounter with an alien' (p. 164). How then do such claims arise? Some authors argue that the origins may lie in a phenomenon called sleep paralysis (Holden & French, 2002; McNally & Clancy, 2005). Sleep paralysis occurs during the rapid eye movement (REM) phase of the sleep cycle when the muscles of the body are paralysed. Occasionally, however, people are conscious during this phase and, in addition to an awareness that they are unable to move, they may experience a puzzling (and sometimes frightening) variety of auditory (e.g. heavy footsteps, buzzing) and visual experiences (lights, strange figures; Holden & French, 2002). As Lynn and Kirsch (1996) suggest, someone who is predisposed to accept such puzzling experiences as telltale signs of UFO abduction (perhaps due to widely available UFO abduction scripts that are common in our culture; Clancy, 2005) may well seek out a therapist who is receptive to such ideas, who then reinforces this belief and encourages the individual to try and remember more about the event(s) (French & Santomauro, 2007). Given that the dominant abduction script often (but not always; see Spence, 1996) consists of some kind of sexual experimentation, this may explain why such individuals come to report that they remember experiences like having sperm and eggs removed. Evidence from the psychological laboratory has also shown that there may be important individual differences in the extent to which people develop false beliefs and false memories. For example, people who report recovered memories of alien abduction are also prone to making other kinds of memory errors in laboratory experiments – specifically recall and recognition errors in word list paradigms (Clancy et al., 2002). It is to these laboratory studies of false belief and false memory that we now turn.

FALSE BELIEFS AND MEMORIES IN THE LABORATORY

In carefully controlled laboratory experiments, psychologists have documented a whole variety of memory distortions to which people fall prey. These fall into two distinct categories that Mazzoni (2002) refers to as 'naturally-occurring' and 'suggestion-dependent' memory distortions. Naturally-occurring memory distortions are essentially by-products of remembering and, as such, do not require any special manipulation to induce. For example, in his studies using serial and repeated reproduction, Bartlett (1932) showed how participants filled in missing gaps, generated extra details, transformed existing details, or simply omitted details altogether in an attempt to make sense of the information (e.g. stories and pictorial material) they had been presented with. Here, no direct suggestions or instructions were needed and participants altered their memory reports along schema-consistent lines.[5] They were engaged in an *effort after meaning*. Put another way, they were trying to transform unfamiliar material into something more familiar and, in the process, modifying the original stories in ways that made sense to them (but see also Ost & Costall, 2002). In a recent example, Gerrie, Belcher, and Garry (2006) showed that participants who, having watched video-recorded sequences of everyday events (e.g., making a sandwich) that had some key steps taken out, nevertheless claimed to have seen the missing steps in a later recognition test. In everyday life, then, we are constantly engaged in a process of trying to make sense of events around us. As Mazzoni (2002) notes, this common and regular process of elaboration can distort the content of a memory.

Another kind of naturally-occurring memory distortion is demonstrated by the large body of research showing that participants will erroneously recall and recognize non-presented words (e.g. Anger) as having been presented in an earlier list of semantically-related associates (e.g. Annoy, Mad, Hate). This is referred to as the Deese–Roediger–McDermott effect (or DRM; Roediger & McDermott, 1995), although there is disagreement about whether these kinds of semantic memory errors (or memory illusions; Schacter, Verfaellie, & Pradere, 1996) should be treated as being in the same category as those involving the suggestion and implantation of entirely new autobiographical memories (DePrince, Allard, Oh, & Freyd, 2004; Pezdek & Lam, 2007; Wade *et al.*, 2007; see also Wilkinson & Hyman, 1998). There is also debate about whether these memory errors generalize to cases where individuals allegedly falsely remember entire autobiographical events (Freyd & Gleaves, 1996; and reply by Roediger & McDermott, 1996). However, several experiments have demonstrated that individuals who report experimenter-suggested memories of childhood events (Qin, Ogle, & Goodman, 2008), recovered memories of childhood trauma (Clancy, Schacter, McNally, & Pitman, 2000), of abduction by aliens (Clancy *et al.*, 2002) and of past lives (Meyersburg, Bogdan, Gallo, & McNally, 2009) are also more vulnerable to DRM effect. Thus, Meyersburg *et al.* (2009) note that although DRM errors and false autobiographical memories may not be equivalent, 'elevated false memory rates in the DRM paradigm may identify individuals likely to develop false memories outside the laboratory' (p. 403; see also Gallo, 2010).

The second class of memory distortions are those that Mazzoni (2002) referred to as 'suggestion-dependent'. In this class of studies, suggestions of various kinds are used to lead a participant to believe that they

---

[5] Although subsequent work showed that just asking participants to be 'accurate' in their reproductions of the material drastically reduced the extent of the reconstruction (Gauld & Stephenson, 1967).

witnessed a particular detail of an event (see also, Wright, Loftus, & Hall, 2001; Roos af Hjelmsäter, Granhag, Strömwall, & Memon, 2008, for experiments on inhibition or omission of details). We know, for example, that some eyewitnesses, following exposure to misleading post-event information, will incorporate those incorrect details into their own accounts of witnessed events (e.g. Chapter 2 of this book; Ayers & Reder, 1998; Loftus & Hoffman, 1989). Another line of research, referred to as the 'crashing memories method', shows that suggestion can lead participants to report false details about highly charged public events that they did *not* directly witness (e.g. Crombag, Wagenaar, & van Koppen, 1996; Ost, Vrij, Costall, & Bull, 2002; Sjödén, Granhag, Ost, & Roos af Hjelmsäter, 2009; Wilson & French, 2006). In one study, nearly 40% of people claimed to have seen CCTV footage of the explosion of the No. 30 bus in Tavistock Square, London, United Kingdom, on 7 July 2005 and a subsample provided dramatic descriptions of what they claimed to have seen (Ost, Granhag, Udell, & Roos af Hjelmsäter, 2008). In line with the classic work on the interaction of language and memory on eyewitness reports (e.g. Loftus & Palmer, 1974), the extent of this effect can be modified by subtle changes in wording. Smeets *et al.* (2006) found that fewer participants endorsed an item asking them 'Did you see *a* film of ...?' compared to participants who were asked 'Did you see *the* film of ...?'. Interestingly, and in line with the Paradoxical Negative Emotion hypothesis (PNE), which proposes that negative emotion generally facilitates memory but also heightens susceptibility to false memories (Porter & Peace, 2007), participants are more likely to endorse having seen non-existent footage of negative, as opposed to positive, events (Porter, Taylor, & ten Brinke, 2008).

Participants' responses in the crashing memories method are also susceptible to relatively subtle confederate influence. Granhag, Strömwall, and Billings (2003) asked participants to complete a questionnaire about their memory of the (non-existent) footage of when the *Estonia* ferry sank. Participants completed the questionnaire in the presence of a confederate who either claimed to have seen the non-existent film ('*Estonia* – I remember that film') or claimed not to have seen it ('*Estonia* – I do not remember that film'). Granhag *et al.* (2003) found that participants either increased, or decreased their levels of false reporting in line with the social influence exerted by the confederate. When the confederate claimed to have seen the film, the number of participants also claiming to have seen the film increased, and vice versa (see Ost, Hogbin, & Granhag, 2006, for a replication). This implies that when we are not sure how to respond in a particular situation we often look to other sources to help guide our behaviour (Bless, Strack, & Walther, 2001). In other words, social psychological processes, in addition to the usual cognitive judgments, come into play when participants make decisions about whether or not to report misinformation that has, deliberately, or inadvertently, been suggested to them (see Blank, 1998, 2009).

A similar effect can also occur in co-witness discussions where participants are not deliberately being misled. This is referred to as memory conformity and can occur when eyewitnesses discuss events they have seen with another witness (Paterson & Kemp, 2006). Some witnesses will incorporate details that they did not see – but were exposed to in their discussion with a co-witness – into their own eye-witness accounts (Gabbert, Memon, & Allan, 2003; Kanematsu, Mori, & Mori, 2003; Schneider & Watkins, 1996). Experimental analogues of this effect have shown that participants will falsely report witnessing criminal events (e.g. a theft) after discussion with a co-witness who did witness a theft. Furthermore, this effect is more pronounced when the co-witnesses are acquaintances, rather than strangers (French, Garry, & Mori, 2008; Hope, Ost, Gabbert, Healey, & Lenton, 2008). Typically, however, the studies mentioned so far examine the effects of suggestion on memory for event details (i.e. a theft, some CCTV footage; see Chapter 4 of this book). What about memory for entire events?

In fact, laboratory experiments have shown that a range of suggestive techniques (e.g. direct suggestion, exposure to doctored photographs) can lead adults to report that they remember entirely fictitious events from their childhood (Loftus, 2004). Across a number of experiments, 37% of participants have reported images or memories for false childhood events (Wade, Garry, Nash, & Harper, 2010). These studies in particular have been designed to mimic, as far as is ethically possible, the dynamics of counselling and therapy (i.e. repeated interviews over a number of weeks, encouragements to 'try and remember'). Participants in these experiments have reported false memories of: being lost in a shopping mall (Loftus & Pickrell, 1995); having spilt a punch bowl over the bride at a wedding (Hyman, Husband, & Billings, 1995); being attacked by a dog (Porter, Yuille, & Lehman, 1999); being hospitalized overnight for an ear infection (Ost, Foster, Costall, & Bull, 2005); taking a ride in a hot-air balloon (Wade, Garry, Read, & Lindsay, 2002); and playing a prank on a teacher (Desjardins & Scoboria, 2007; Lindsay, Hagen, Read, Wade, & Garry, 2004). There are, of course, important caveats in the extent to which these kinds of studies can inform us about cases like Anna's (see Ost, 2010). One of these caveats is that we can never be sure that the suggested events, or ones very similar to them, did not occur to participants. Yet, as Loftus (1997a) argues, the important point is not that participants might be able to construct a general narrative of such an event, but that they report specific details suggested by the experimenter. Referring to her 'lost in the shopping mall' experiment, Loftus argued that participants 'were not asked about ANY experience of being lost. They were asked to remember being lost around the age of five, in a particular location, with particular people present, being frightened, and ultimately being rescued by an elderly person' (Loftus, 1997a, p. 180). Furthermore, research has shown that suggestive techniques (in this case false information incorporated into an advert) can be used to increase participants' confidence that they had experienced an *impossible* event as a child – in this case having shaken hands with Bugs Bunny at Disneyland (Braun, Ellis, & Loftus, 2002).[6] Thus, laboratory research has shown that, as a result of suggestion, people will falsely report that they remember idiosyncratic, positively and negatively charged childhood events. But is there any evidence that these beliefs or memories can have long-lasting effects?

HOW LONG DO LABORATORY-GENERATED FALSE BELIEFS AND MEMORIES LAST?

Outside of the laboratory there is ample evidence of the havoc that can be wrought by persistent false beliefs and false memories (Loftus, 1997b). However, it is difficult to establish whether participants in psychological experiments continue to accept the truth of the implanted beliefs or memories once they have left the laboratory. This is because ethical considerations rightly prevent psychologists from allowing people to leave the laboratory without having reversed the effects of any experimental manipulation. In the case of false memory research, this means that researchers have a duty to point out which memories, or details, had been suggested as part of an experiment. Establishing whether laboratory-generated false beliefs and false memories can have consequences beyond the end of an experiment is therefore a challenging task. Yet it is an important one. So what can laboratory studies say about the consequences of false beliefs and false memories (Bernstein & Loftus, 2009)? There are two strands of research that have attempted to provide answers to this question. The first examines the extent to which individuals change their behaviour as a result of suggestions, and the second examines how long laboratory suggestions persist.

THE CONSEQUENCES OF FALSE BELIEFS AND MEMORIES

One important test of whether a participant has genuinely adopted and internalized a false belief, or a suggested detail of an event suggested in a laboratory experiment is the extent to which they would be prepared to alter their behaviour on the basis of that suggestion

---

[6] Bugs Bunny is a Warner Brothers character and, thus, could not have been at Disneyland.

(e.g. Bernstein & Loftus, 2009; Kassin & Kiechel, 1996; see also Smeets, Merckelbach, Horselenberg, & Jelicic, 2005). Bernstein, Laney, Morris, and Loftus (2005) used a false feedback paradigm to test the extent to which participants would change their behaviour as a result of suggestion. In the false feedback paradigm, participants complete a questionnaire which is then fed into a computer. The computer then provides bogus feedback indicating that, among other things, the participant's responses show clearly that, as a child, they were ill after eating a particular type of food. In Bernstein *et al.*'s (2005) experiment participants were given false feedback that they had become ill as children after having eaten too many eggs or pickles. Next they were given a questionnaire about an imaginary barbecue which asked them to indicate which kinds of food they would be likely to eat. They found participants who believed the false feedback about becoming sick as a child after eating too many eggs or pickles, reported that they would be less likely to choose to eat those foods, than those who did not believe the feedback. Thus, this experiment demonstrated that false feedback about the likelihood of past events influenced self-reported behaviour – at least for those participants who believed the feedback. As Bernstein and Loftus (2009) note, one possible limitation of these findings is that perhaps the manipulation in that study was too obvious – participants may have guessed the true nature of the experiment and responded in what they perceived to be a desirable manner (Orne, 1962).

To overcome this potential limitation, Scoboria, Mazzoni, and Jarry (2008) separated the suggestion context from the measurement context. Scoboria *et al.* (2008) suggested to participants that they had become ill after eating out-of-date peach yoghurt as children. One week later participants were recruited for a separate market research exercise, part of which involved rating peach yoghurt on various dimensions. Those who had received the false feedback were more likely to give low ratings of taste and odour than control participants. Thus, Scoboria *et al.* (2008) provided a further demonstration that suggestions made in one context can carry over into other, ostensibly separate, contexts (see also Mazzoni, Loftus, Seitz, & Lynn, 1999). In a novel twist, Laney, Morris, Bernstein, Wakefield, and Loftus (2008) found that the same kind of false feedback could be used to positive effect to convince participants that, as a child, they really enjoyed eating a healthy food – in this case, asparagus. These effects also carry over from self-reported behaviour into overt behaviour.

In a non-food-related study, Berkowitz, Laney, Morris, Garry, and Loftus (2008) used the false feedback method to expose college students to material which suggested that, as children they had a negative or positive experience at Disneyland. Specifically, participants completed a questionnaire which asked them, among other things, about their feelings and experiences of Disneyland, their preferences for various

Disney characters (including Pluto) and how much they would be prepared to pay for a Pluto stuffed animal. Embedded in this lengthy questionnaire was a critical item which asked participants to rate the likelihood that, while at Disneyland, 'You had your ear licked by Pluto'.

Participants returned to the laboratory one week later and received a faked computer profile – which they were told contained unique and personalized information. In fact, the information was systematically varied. In the negative experience condition participants were given a computer profile which described a number of common childhood fears (e.g. loud noises, public displays of affection) and were provided with an excerpt of a newspaper article which they were told might be relevant to them. This newspaper excerpt described a Pluto character that abused hallucinogenic drugs and had a habit of inappropriately licking the ears of many young visitors to Disneyland with his large fabric tongue. In the positive experience condition, participants were given a personalized profile that emphasized enjoyable childhood activities (e.g. playing with friends, watching cartoons), and were given a newspaper excerpt describing a lovable Pluto character who had delighted children by licking their ears with his tongue. A control group of participants were provided with a profile that emphasized current aspects of their personality and read a newspaper article that did not mention Pluto. All participants then completed the same preferences questionnaire from the previous week. Berkowitz et al. (2008) found that, relative to controls, participants in both the negative and positive experiences conditions had become more confident that Pluto had licked their ear. In addition, relative to participants in the positive experience condition, those in the negative experiences condition (and who believed that they had experienced the negative ear licking event), were not willing to pay as much money for the stuffed Pluto toy as they had been one week previously.

Taken together, this body of literature shows that some participants who are given false feedback about their childhood food preferences, or childhood experiences, will alter their behaviour accordingly (but see Pezdek & Freyd, 2009 who urge caution in generalizing from the food studies). But how long do these false beliefs and false memories persist?

THE PERSISTENCE OF FALSE BELIEFS AND FALSE MEMORIES

Smeets, Telgen, Ost, Jelicic, and Merckelbach (2009) conducted an experiment, using the crashing memories method, in which they suggested to participants that they had seen non-existent film of the moment Pim Fortuyn, a controversial Dutch politician, was assassinated. In line with similar experiments (e.g. Crombag et al., 1996), they found that two-thirds (66%) of their participants claimed to have seen the film. In order to examine the persistence of these false reports, Smeets *et al.* (2009) then conducted extensive post-experiment interviews with their participants. They told participants that there was, in fact, no footage of the moment of the shooting and were asked to indicate why they claimed to have seen it. Of those who had claimed to have seen the film, most (81%) reported that they had assumed that the question referred to the aftermath of the shooting and not the actual shooting itself. One participant claimed that they had seen so many images of the assassination that it was difficult to disentangle what they had seen from what they had read about. Three participants admitted that they had answered the question in the affirmative because they wanted to help the experimenters. Finally six participants (10%) reported that they truly 'remembered' seeing the film of the moment of the shooting. All 58 participants were asked to answer the critical question again ('Have you seen footage of the moment Pim Fortuyn was shot?'). All, bar the six participants who claimed to still remember seeing the film, changed their answers from 'yes' to 'no' or 'not sure'. The 10% who reported that they 'remembered' seeing the non-existent film stuck to their original answer (i.e. answered 'yes'). The fact that 10% of participants were willing to answer in the affirmative – even knowing that no film existed – suggests that, for some people, memory errors may be particularly compelling.

In summary, the psychological literature is replete with examples of memory errors. From relatively inconsequential memory errors (Roediger & McDermott, 1995), to dramatic examples of false autobiographical memories (Clancy, 2005), it is beyond question that (i) our memories are error prone; and (ii) that such errors can persist and lead people to change their behaviour. A note of caution must be sounded, however. As Koriat, Goldsmith, and Pansky (2000) argued over 10 years ago, 'the interest in memory illusions and false memories, spurred perhaps by real life problems, has led researchers to selectively focus on the dark side of memory, resulting in a somewhat biased picture' (p. 522). At this point in time, however, it is clear that in the controlled world of the psychological experiment, memory errors of varying levels of complexity and persistence are relatively easy to demonstrate.

WHERE NEXT?

Our understanding of recovered memory and false memory experiences has advanced rapidly over the past 20 years. One ongoing challenge is to find out whether there is a type of person who is susceptible to different memory errors – either the error of remembering something that didn't occur, or the error of remembering something as if for the first time. Recent work points to the importance of metacognitive processes in understanding these kinds of memory illusions (Koriat & Goldsmith, 1996; see Mazzoni & Kirsch, 2002; Merckelbach *et al.*, 2006; Nash, Wade, & Brewer, 2009). For example, Raymaekers, Peters, Smeets, Abidi, and Merckelbach (2011) conducted two studies investigating the relationship between performance on the DRM task and the FIA task and found that the two were unrelated. This suggests that these two kinds of memory errors may be being driven by different cognitive (or metacognitive) mechanisms. Furthermore, they found that cognitive efficiency (as measured by the self-report Cognitive Failures Questionnaire; Broadbent, Cooper, Fitzgerald, & Parkes, 1982) was related to both DRM and FIA performance. Raymaekers *et al.* (2011) suggest that a relative lack of cognitive efficiency might somehow immunize against these kind of memory errors although the correlational nature of their analyses precluded a causal interpretation. This highlights the need for continuing research into individual differences and the metacognitive underpinnings of recovered memory experiences.

CONCLUSIONS AND FORENSIC IMPLICATIONS

- What seem to be newly remembered (i.e. recovered) memories of past trauma are sometimes accurate, sometimes inaccurate, and sometimes a mixture of accuracy and inaccuracy (Wright, Ost, & French, 2006).
- There is no convincing evidence that individuals can repress, dissociate or otherwise selectively 'block out' memories of traumatic experiences – not *disclosing* a history of trauma is different from not *remembering* a history of trauma (McNally, 2003).
- There is evidence that individuals will come to believe, remember and, in some cases, act on events that were suggested to them as part of psychological experiments (Laney *et al.*, 2008).
- In the absence of independent corroboration, reports of past trauma based on recovered memories are not reliable enough to be the sole basis for legal decisions.

REFERENCES

Arnold, M.M., & Lindsay, D.S. (2002). Remembering remembering. *Journal of Experimental Psychology: Learning, Memory, & Cognition, 28*, 521–529.

Ayers, M.S., & Reder, L.M. (1998). A theoretical review of the misinformation effect: Predictions from an activation-based memory model. *Psychonomic Bulletin & Review, 5*, 1–21.

Bartlett, F.C. (1932). *Remembering: A Study in Experimental and Social Psychology*. Cambridge: Cambridge University Press.

Berkowitz, S.R., Laney, C., Morris, E.K., Garry, M., & Loftus, E.F. (2008). Pluto behaving badly: False beliefs and their consequences. *American Journal of Psychology, 121,* 643–660.

Bernstein, D.M., Laney, C., Morris, E.K., & Loftus, E.F. (2005). False memories about food can produce food avoidance. *Social Cognition, 23,* 11–34.

Bernstein, D.M., & Loftus, E.F. (2009). The consequences of false memory for food preferences and choices. *Perspectives on Psychological Science, 4,* 135–139.

Blank, H. (1998). Memory states and memory tasks: An integrative framework for eyewitness memory and suggestibility. *Memory, 6,* 481–529.

Blank, H. (2009). Remembering: A theoretical interface between memory and social psychology. *Social Psychology, 40,* 164–175.

Bless, H., Strack, F., & Walther, E. (2001). Memory as a target of social influence? Memory distortions as a function of social influence and metacognitive knowledge. In J.P. Forgas, & K.D. Williams (Eds), *Social Influence: Direct and Indirect Processes*. Philadelphia, PA: Psychology Press.

Blume, E.S. (1990). *Secret Survivors: Uncovering Incest and its Aftereffects in Women*. New York: Ballantine Books.

Bottoms, B.L., & Davis, S.L. (1997). The creation of satanic ritual abuse. *Journal of Social and Clinical Psychology, 16,* 112–132.

Braun, K.A., Ellis, R., & Loftus, E.F. (2002). Make my memory: How advertising can change our memories of the past. *Psychology and Marketing, 19,* 1–23.

Broadbent, D.E., Cooper, P.F., Fitzgerald, P., & Parkes, L.R. (1982). The cognitive failures questionnaire (CFQ) and its correlates. *British Journal of Clinical Psychology, 21,* 1–16.

Clancy, S.A. (2005). *Abducted: How People Come to Believe They Were Kidnapped by Aliens*. Cambridge, MA: Harvard University Press.

Clancy, S.A. (2009). *The Trauma Myth: The Truth About the Sexual Abuse of Children – and its Aftermath*. New York: Basic Books.

Clancy, S.A., & McNally, R.J. (2005/2006). Who needs repression? Normal memory processes can explain "forgetting" of childhood sexual abuse. *Scientific Review of Mental Health Practice, 4,* 66–73.

Clancy, S.A., McNally, R.J., Schacter, D.L., Lenzenweger, M.F., & Pitman, R.K. (2002). Memory distortion in people reporting abduction by aliens. *Journal of Abnormal Psychology, 111,* 455–461.

Clancy, S.A., Schacter, D.L., McNally, R.J., & Pitman, R.K. (2000). False recognition in women reporting recovered memories of sexual abuse. *Psychological Science, 11,* 26–31.

Conway, M.A. (1997). *Recovered Memories and False Memories*. Oxford: Oxford University Press.

Crombag, H.F.M., Wagenaar W.A., & van Koppen, P.J. (1996). Crashing memories and the problem of 'source monitoring'. *Applied Cognitive Psychology, 10,* 95–104.

Dalgleish, T., Hauer, B., & Kuyken, W. (2008). The mental regulation of autobiographical recollection in the aftermath of trauma. *Current Directions in Psychological Science, 17,* 259–263.

DePrince, A.P., Allard, C.B., Oh, H., & Freyd, J.J. (2004). What's in a name for memory errors? Implications and ethical issues arising from the use of the term "false memory" for errors in memory for details. *Ethics & Behavior, 14,* 201–233.

de Rivera, J. (1997). The construction of false memory syndrome: The experience of retractors. *Psychological Inquiry, 8,* 271–292.

Desjardins, T., & Scoboria, A. (2007). 'You and your best friend Suzy put Slime in Ms. Smollett's desk': Producing false memories with self-relevant details. *Psychonomic Bulletin and Review, 14,* 1090–1095.

French, C.C., & Santomauro, J. (2007). Something wicked this way comes. Causes and interpretations of sleep paralysis. In S. Della Sala (Ed.), *Tall Tales about the Mind and Brain: Separating Fact from Fiction* (pp. 380–398). Oxford: Oxford University Press.

French, L., Garry, M., & Mori, K. (2008). You say tomato? Collaborative remembering leads to more false memories for intimate couples than for strangers. *Memory, 16,* 262–273.

Freyd, J.J., & Gleaves, D.H. (1996). "Remembering" words not presented in lists: Relevance to the current recovered/false memory controversy. *Journal of Experimental Psychology: Learning, Memory, and Cognition, 22,* 811–813.

Freyd, J.J., Putnam, F.W., Lyon, T.D., Becker-Blease, K.A., Cheit, R.E., Siegel, N.B., & Pezdek, K. (2005). The science of child sexual abuse. *Science, 308,* 501.

Gabbert, F., Memon, A., & Allan, K. (2003). Memory conformity: Can eyewitnesses influence each other's memories for an event? *Applied Cognitive Psychology, 17,* 533–543.

Gallo, D. A. (2010). False memories and fantastic beliefs: 15 years of the DRM illusion. *Memory & Cognition, 38,* 833–848.

Gauld, A., & Stephenson, G.M. (1967). Some experiments relating to Bartlett's theory of remembering. *British Journal of Psychology, 58,* 39–50.

Gerrie, M.P., Belcher, L.E., & Garry, M. (2006). 'Mind the gap': False memories for missing aspects of an event. *Applied Cognitive Psychology, 20,* 689–696.

Goodman, G.S., Ghetti, S., Quas, J.A., Edelstein, R.S., Alexander, K.W., Redlich, A.D., Cordon, I.M., & Jones, D.P.H. (2003). A prospective study of memory for child sexual abuse: New findings relevant to the repressed-memory controversy. *Psychological Science, 14,* 113–118.

Goodman, G.S., Quas, J., & Ogle, C.M. (2010). Child maltreatment and memory. *Annual Review of Psychology, 61,* 325–351.

Granhag, P.-A., Strömwall, L., & Billings, F.J. (2003). 'I'll never forget the sinking ferry': How social influence makes false memories surface. In M. Vanderhallen, G. Vervaeke, P. J. van Koppen, & J. Goethals (Eds), *Much Ado About Crime: Chapters on Psychology and Law* (pp. 129–140). Belgium: Uitgeverij Politeia.

Gudjonsson, G.H. (1997). False memory syndrome and the retractors: Methodological and theoretical issues. *Psychological Inquiry, 8,* 296–299.

Gudjonsson, G.H. (2003). *The Psychology of Interrogations and Confessions: A Handbook.* Chichester, UK: John Wiley & Sons, Ltd.

Hayne, H., Garry, M., & Loftus, E.F. (2006). On the continuing lack of evidence for repressed memories. *Behavioral and Brain Sciences, 29,* 521–522.

Holden, K.J., & French, C.C. (2002). Alien abduction experiences: Some clues from Neuropsychology and Neuropsychiatry. *Cognitive Neuropsychiatry, 7,* 163–178.

Hope, L., Ost, J., Gabbert, F., Healey, S., & Lenton, E. (2008). "With a little help from my friends...": The role of co-witness relationship in susceptibility to misinformation. *Acta Psychologica, 127,* 476–484.

Hyman, I.E., Jr., Husband, T.H., & Billings, F.J. (1995). False memories of childhood experiences. *Applied Cognitive Psychology, 9,* 181–197.

Kanematsu, H., Mori, K., & Mori, H. (2003). Memory distortion in eyewitness pairs who observed nonconforming events and discussed them. *Journal of the Faculty of Education, Shinshu University, 109,* 75–84.

Kassin, S.M., & Kiechel, K.L. (1996). The social psychology of false confessions: Compliance, internalization, and confabulation. *Psychological Science, 7,* 125–128.

Kihlstrom, J.F. (2002). No need for repression. *Trends in Cognitive Sciences, 6,* 502.

Koriat, A., & Goldsmith, M. (1996). Monitoring and control processes in the strategic regulation of memory accuracy. *Psychological Review, 103,* 490–517.

Koriat, A., Goldsmith, M., & Pansky, A. (2000). Toward a psychology of memory accuracy. *Annual Review of Psychology, 51,* 481–537.

La Fontaine, J.S. (1998). *Speak of the Devil: Tales of Satanic Abuse in Contemporary England.* Cambridge: Cambridge University Press.

Laney, C., Morris, E.K., Bernstein, D.M., Wakefield, B.M., & Loftus, E.F. (2008). Asparagus, a love story: Healthier eating could be just a false memory away. *Experimental Psychology, 55,* 291–300.

Lanning, K.V. (1991). Ritual abuse: A law enforcement view or perspective. *Child Abuse and Neglect, 15,* 171–173.

Lief, H., & Fetkewicz, J. (1995). Retractors of false memories: The evolution of pseudo-memories. *The Journal of Psychiatry and Law, 23,* 411–436.

Lindsay, D.S., Hagen, L., Read, J.D., Wade, K.A., & Garry, M. (2004). True photographs and false memories. *Psychological Science, 15,* 149–154.

Lindsay, D.S., & Read, J.D. (1994). Psychotherapy and memories of childhood sexual abuse: A cognitive perspective. *Applied Cognitive Psychology, 8,* 281–338.

Loftus, E.F. (1997a). Dispatches from the (un)civil memory wars. In J.D. Read, & D.S. Lindsay (Eds), *Recollections of Trauma: Scientific Evidence and Clinical Practice* (pp. 171–194). New York: Plenum Press.

Loftus, E.F. (1997b). Repressed memory accusations: Devastated families and devastated patients. *Applied Cognitive Psychology, 11,* 25–30.

Loftus, E.F. (2004). Memories of things unseen. *Current Directions in Psychological Science, 13,* 145–147.

Loftus, E.F., & Hoffman, H.G. (1989). Misinformation and memory: The creation of new memories. *Journal of Experimental Psychology: General, 118,* 100–104.

Loftus, E.F., & Palmer, J.C. (1974). Reconstruction of automobile destruction: An example of the interaction between language and memory. *Journal of Verbal Learning and Verbal Behavior, 13,* 585–589.

Loftus, E.F., & Pickrell, J.E. (1995). The formation of false memories. *Psychiatric Annals, 25,* 720–725.

Lynn, S.J., & Kirsch, I. (1996). Alleged alien abductions: False memories, hypnosis, and fantasy proneness. *Psychological Inquiry, 7,* 151–155.

Mazzoni, G. (2002). Naturally-occurring and suggestion-dependent memory distortions. *European Psychologist, 7,* 17–30.

Mazzoni, G., & Kirsch, I. (2002). Autobiographical memories and beliefs: A preliminary metacognitive model. In T. Perfect, & B. Schwartz (Eds), *Applied Metacognition* (pp. 121–145). Cambridge, UK: Cambridge University Press.

Mazzoni, G., Loftus, E.F., Seitz, A., & Lynn, S.J. (1999). Changing beliefs and memories through dream interpretation. *Applied Cognitive Psychology, 13,* 125–144.

Mazzoni, G., & Memon, A. (2003). Imagination can create false autobiographical memories. *Psychological Science, 14,* 186–188.

Mazzoni, G., Scoboria, A., & Harvey, L. (2010). Non-believed memories. *Psychological Science, 21,* 1334–1340.

McNally, R.J. (2003). *Remembering Trauma.* Cambridge, MA: Harvard University Press.

McNally, R.J. (2007). Betrayal trauma theory: A critical appraisal. *Memory, 15,* 280–294.

McNally, R.J., & Clancy, S.A. (2005). Sleep paralysis in adults reporting repressed, recovered, or continuous memories of childhood sexual abuse. *Journal of Anxiety Disorders, 19,* 595–602.

McNally, R.J., & Geraerts, E. (2009). A new solution to the recovered memory debate. *Perspectives on Psychological Science, 4,* 126–134.

McNally, R.J., Lasko, N.B., Clancy, S.A., Macklin, M.L., Pitman, R.K., & Orr, S.P. (2004). Psychophysiological responding during script-driven imagery in people reporting abduction by space aliens. *Psychological Science, 15,* 493–497.

Merckelbach, H., Smeets, T., Geraerts, E., Jelicic, M., Bouwen, A., & Smeets, E. (2006). I haven't thought about this for years! Dating recent recalls of vivid memories. *Applied Cognitive Psychology, 20,* 33–42.

Meyersburg, C.A., Bogdan, R., Gallo, D.A., & McNally, R.J. (2009). False memory propensity in people reporting recovered memories of past lives. *Journal of Abnormal Psychology, 118,* 399–404.

Mulhern, S. (1994). Satanism, ritual abuse, and multiple personality disorder. *International Journal of Clinical and Experimental Hypnosis, 42,* 265–288.

Nash, R.A., Wade, K.A., & Brewer, R.J. (2009). Why do doctored images distort memory? *Consciousness & Cognition, 18,* 773–780.

Ofshe, R. (1989). Coerced confessions: The logic of seemingly irrational action. *Cultic Studies Journal, 6,* 1–15.

Orne, M.T. (1962). On the social psychology of the psychological experiment: With particular reference to demand characteristics and their implications. *American Psychologist, 17,* 776–783.

Ost, J. (2003). Essay review: Seeking the middle ground in the 'memory wars'. *British Journal of Psychology, 94,* 125–139.

Ost, J. (2010). Recovered memories. In T. Williamson, T. Valentine, & R. Bull (Eds), *Handbook of Psychology of Investigative Interviewing: Current Developments and Future Directions* (pp. 181–204). Chichester, UK: John Wiley & Sons, Ltd.

Ost, J., & Costall, A. (2002). Misremembering Bartlett: a study in serial reproduction. *British Journal of Psychology, 93,* 243–255.

Ost, J., Costall, A., & Bull, R. (2001). False confessions and false memories? A model for understanding retractors' experiences? *The Journal of Forensic Psychiatry, 12,* 549–579.

Ost, J., Costall, A., & Bull, R. (2002). A perfect symmetry? A study of retractors' experiences of making and repudiating claims of early sexual abuse. *Psychology, Crime & Law, 8,* 155–181.

Ost, J., Foster, S., Costall, A., & Bull, R. (2005). False reports of childhood events in appropriate interviews. *Memory, 13,* 700–710.

Ost, J., Granhag, P.-A., Udell, J., & Roos af Hjelmsäter, E. (2008). Familiarity breeds distortion: The effects of media exposure on false reports concerning the media coverage of the terrorist attacks in London on 7th July 2005. *Memory, 16,* 76–85.

Ost, J., Hogbin, I., & Granhag, P.-A. (2006). Altering false reports via confederate influence. *Social Influence, 1,* 105–116.

Ost, J., & Nunkoosing, K. (2010). Reconstructing Bartlett and revisiting the 'false memory' controversy. In J. Haaken, & P. Reavey (Eds), *Memory Matters: Understanding Contexts for Recollecting Child Sexual Abuse* (pp. 41–62). London: Routledge.

Ost, J., Vrij, A., Costall, A., & Bull, R. (2002). Crashing memories and reality monitoring: distinguishing between perceptions, imaginings and false memories. *Applied Cognitive Psychology, 16,* 125–134.

Ost, J., Wright, D., Easton, S., Hope, L., & French, C.C. (2010). Recovered memories, satanic abuse, dissociative identity disorder and false memories in the United Kingdom: A survey of Chartered Clinical Psychologists and Hypnotherapists' (and students') beliefs. Paper presented at the 20th conference of the European Association of Psychology and Law, 15–18 June, 2010, Göteborg, Sweden.

Ost, J., Wright, D.B., Easton, S., Hope, L., & French, C.C. (in press). Recovered memories, satanic abuse, dissociative identity disorder and false memories in the United Kingdom: A survey of Clinical Psychologists and Hypno-therapists. *Psychology, Crime & Law.*

Paterson, H.M., & Kemp, R.I. (2006). Co-witnesses talk: A survey of eyewitness discussion. *Psychology Crime & Law, 12,* 181–191.

Payne, D.G., & Blackwell, J.M. (1998). Truth in memory: Caveat emptor. In S.J. Lynn, & K.M. McConkey (Eds), *Truth in Memory* (pp. 32–61). New York: Guilford Press.

Pezdek, K., & Banks, W.P. (1996). Preface. In K. Pezdek, & W.P. Banks (Eds), *The Recovered Memory/False Memory Debate* (pp. xi–xv). San Diego: Academic Press.

Pezdek, K., & Blandon-Gitlin, I. (2008). Planting false memories for childhood sexual abuse only happens to emotionally disturbed people … not me or my friends. *Applied Cognitive Psychology, 23,* 162–169.

Pezdek, K., & Freyd, J.J. (2009). The fallacy of generalizing from egg salad in false belief research. *Analyses of Social Issues and Public Policy, 9,* 177–183.

Pezdek, K., & Lam, S. (2007). What research paradigms have cognitive psychologists used to study "false memory," and what are the implications of these choices? *Consciousness & Cognition, 16,* 2–17.

Pipe, M.-E., Lamb, M.E., Orbach, Y., & Cederborg, A.-C. (Eds) (2007). *Child Sexual Abuse: Disclosure, Delay, and Denial.* New York: Routledge.

Piper, A., Lillevik, L., & Kritzer, R. (2008). What's wrong with believing in repression? A review for legal professionals. *Psychology, Public Policy, and Law, 14,* 223–242.

Pope, H.G., Jr., Poliakoff, M.B., Parker, M.P., Boynes, M., & Hudson, J.I. (2007). Is dissociative amnesia a culture-bound syndrome? Findings from a survey of historical literature. *Psychological Medicine, 37,* 225–233.

Porter, S., & Peace, K. (2007). The scars of memory: A prospective, longitudinal investigation of the consistency of traumatic and positive emotional memories in adulthood. *Psychological Science, 18,* 435–441.

Porter, S., Taylor, K., & ten Brinke, L. (2008). Memory for media: Investigation of false memories for negatively and positively charged public events. *Memory, 16,* 658–666.

Porter, S., Yuille, J.C., & Lehman, D.R. (1999). The nature of real, implanted, and fabricated memories for emotional childhood events: Implications for the recovered memory debate. *Law and Human Behavior, 23,* 517–537.

Qin, J., Goodman, G.S., Bottoms, B.L., & Shaver, P.R. (1998). Repressed memories of ritualistic and religion-related child abuse. In S. J. Lynn, & K. M. McConkey (Eds.), *Truth in Memory* (pp. 260–283). New York: Guilford Press.

Qin, J., Ogle, C. M., & Goodman, G. S. (2008). Adults' memories of childhood: True and false reports. *Journal of Experimental Psychology: Applied, 14,* 373–391.

Raymaekers, L., Peters, M.J.V., Smeets, T., Abidi, L., & Merckelbach, H. (2011). Underestimation of prior remembering and susceptibility to false memories: Two sides of the same coin? *Consciousness and Cognition, 20,* 1144–1153.

Roediger, H.L., & McDermott, K.B. (1995). Creating false memories: Remembering words not presented in lists. *Journal of Experimental Psychology: Learning, Memory, and Cognition, 21,* 803–814.

Roediger, H.L., & McDermott, K.B. (1996). False perceptions of false memories. *Journal of Experimental Psychology: Learning, Memory, and Cognition, 22,* 814–816.

Roos af Hjelmsäter, E., Granhag, P.A., Strömwall, L.A., & Memon, A. (2008). The effects of social influence on children's memory reports: The omission and commission error asymmetry. *Scandinavian Journal of Psychology, 49,* 507–513.

Rubin, D.C., & Berntsen, D. (2007). People believe it is plausible to have forgotten memories of childhood sexual abuse. *Psychonomic Bulletin & Review, 14,* 776–778.

Rubin, D.C., & Boals, A. (2010). People who expect to enter psychotherapy are prone to believing that they have forgotten memories of childhood trauma and abuse. *Memory, 18,* 556–562.

Schacter, D.L., Verfaellie, M., & Pradere, D. (1996). The neuropsychology of memory illusions: False recall and recognition in Amnesic patients. *Journal of Memory and Language, 35,* 319–334.

Schneider, D.M., & Watkins, M.J. (1996). Response conformity in recognition testing. *Psychonomic Bulletin & Review, 3,* 481–485.

Schooler, J.W., Bendiksen, M., & Ambadar, Z. (1997). Taking the middle line: Can we accommodate both fabricated and recovered memories of sexual abuse? In M.A. Conway (Ed.), *Recovered Memories and False Memories* (pp. 251–292). Oxford: Oxford University Press.

Scoboria, A., Lynn, S.J., Hessen, J., & Fisico, S. (2007). So that is why I don't remember: Normalizing forgetting of childhood events influences false autobiographical beliefs but not memories. *Memory, 15,* 801–813.

Scoboria, A., Mazzoni, G., & Jarry, J. (2008). Suggesting childhood food illness results in reduced eating behavior. *Acta Psychologica, 128,* 304–309.

Scoboria, A., Mazzoni, G., Kirsch, I., & Relyea, M. (2004). Plausibility and belief in autobiographical memory. *Applied Cognitive Psychology, 18,* 791–807.

Sheen, M., Kemp, S., & Rubin, D. (2001). Twins dispute memory ownership: A new false memory phenomenon. *Memory & Cognition, 29,* 779–788.

Sheen, M., Kemp, S., & Rubin, D. (2006). Disputes over memory ownership: What memories are disputed? *Genes, Brain and Behavior, 5,* 9–13.

Shobe, K.K., & Schooler, J.W. (2001). Discovering fact and fiction: Case-based analyses of authentic and fabricated discovered memories of abuse. In G.M. Davies, & T. Dalgleish (Eds), *Recovered Memories: Seeking the Middle Ground* (pp. 95–151). Chichester: John Wiley & Sons, Ltd.

Sjödén, B., Granhag, P.-A., Ost, J., & Roos af Hjelmsäter, E. (2009). Is the truth in the detail? Extended narratives help distinguishing false "memories" from false "reports". *Scandinavian Journal of Psychology, 50,* 203–210.

Smeets, T., Jelicic, M., Peters, M.J.V., Candel, I., Horselenberg, R., & Merckelbach, H. (2006). "Of course I remember seeing that film!" – How ambiguous questions generate crashing memories. *Applied Cognitive Psychology, 20,* 779–789.

Smeets, T., Merckelbach, H., Horselenberg, R., & Jelicic, M. (2005). Trying to recollect past events: Confidence, beliefs, and memories. *Clinical Psychology Review, 25,* 917–934.

Smeets, T., Telgen, S., Ost, J., Jelicic, M., & Merckelbach, H. (2009). What's behind crashing memories? Plausibility, belief, and memory of reports of having seen non-existent images. *Applied Cognitive Psychology, 23,* 1333–1341.

Spence, D. P. (1996). Abduction tales as metaphors. *Psychological Inquiry, 7,* 177–179.

Wade, K.A., Garry, M., Nash, R.A., & Harper, D.N. (2010). Anchoring effects in the development of false childhood memories. *Psychonomic Bulletin & Review, 17,* 66–72.

Wade, K.A., Garry, M., Read, J.D., & Lindsay, D.S. (2002). A picture is worth a thousand lies: Using false photographs to create false childhood memories. *Psychonomic Bulletin and Review, 9,* 597–603.

Wade, K.A., Sharman, S.J., Garry, M., Memon, A., Mazzoni, G., Merckelbach, H., & Loftus, E.F. (2007). False claims about false memory research. *Consciousness & Cognition, 16,* 18–28.

Wegner, D.M., Schneider, D.J., Carter, S., & White, T. (1987). Paradoxical effects of thought suppression. *Journal of Personality and Social Psychology, 53,* 5–13.

Wilkinson, C., & Hyman, I.E. (1998). Individual differences related to two types of memory errors: Word lists may not generalize to autobiographical memory. *Applied Cognitive Psychology, 12,* 29–46.

Wilson, K., & French, C.C. (2006). The relationship between susceptibility to false memories, dissociativity, and paranormal belief and experience. *Personality and Individual Differences, 41,* 1493–1502.

Woodiwiss, J. (2010). 'Alternative memories' and the construction of a sexual abuse narrative. In J. Haaken, & P. Reavey (Eds), *Memory Matters: Understanding Contexts for Recollecting Child Sexual Abuse* (pp. 105–127). London: Routledge.

Wright, D.B., Loftus, E.F., & Hall, M. (2001). Now you see it; now you don't: Inhibiting recall and recognition of scenes. *Applied Cognitive Psychology, 15,* 471–482.

Wright, D.B., Ost, J., & French, C.C. (2006). Ten years after: What we know now that we didn't know then about recovered and false memories. *The Psychologist, 19,* 352–355.

Yapko, M. (1994). Suggestibility and repressed memories of abuse: A survey of psychotherapists' beliefs. *American Journal of Clinical Hypnosis, 36,* 163–171.

7

Suggestibility and Individual Differences in Typically Developing and Intellectually Disabled Children*

KAMALA LONDON, LUCY A. HENRY, TRAVIS CONRADT
AND RYAN CORSER

KEY POINTS

- Children's ability to form coherent and detailed narratives about their experiences sometimes facilitates their event memories. Strong narratives can provide an organizational structure and increase memory strength.
- Providing narratives about a past event is a very social experience. Children who provide rich narratives may at times be *more* susceptible to changing their reports to go along with their conversational partner.
- Individual difference variables including theory of mind and executive functioning have been shown to play a role in children's suggestibility. Such cognitive skills may help children resist misleading questions.

*Our chapter is dedicated to the memory of Sarah Kulkofsky. Sarah passed away on January 13, 2011 at the age of 30. Sarah's work made a unique contribution to developmental psychology, and she will be greatly missed.

Suggestibility in Legal Contexts: Psychological Research and Forensic Implications,
First Edition. Edited by Anne M. Ridley, Fiona Gabbert and David J. La Rooy.
© 2013 John Wiley & Sons, Ltd. Published 2013 by John Wiley & Sons, Ltd.

- The existing scientific literature regarding the effect of emotions on children's memory has mainly focused on varying levels of arousal (high versus low stress) in negative events. This work has been very mixed. A new body of work is emerging that takes a more multidimensional view towards emotion by considering valence (positive versus negative events) and resulting discrete emotions. Such work may help reconcile the past mixed research findings on memory and emotion.
- Children with intellectual disabilities (IDs) generally perform similar to their mental age. However, work is needed to tease apart how different aetiologies of ID affect children's forensic reports.

In their seminal and award-winning 1993 book, *Jeopardy in the Courtroom*, Ceci and Bruck wrote that '... the incidence of sexual abuse is very large and must never be minimized' (p. iv). They also opined that '... much of the time children's statements are reliable and credible ...' However, they further cautioned that there are circumstances which run a high risk of tainting children's forensic reports. In the two decades since their book was published, a flurry of research activity has helped developmental psychologists better understand the development of event memory as well as the factors that influence suggestibility.

One of the most replicated findings in the suggestibility literature is that preschool-aged children are generally more suggestible than older children (for reviews, see Bruck & Ceci, 1999; Bruck, Ceci, & Principe, 2006; London & Kulkofsky, 2010). A number of researchers, though, recently have demonstrated that school-aged children can sometimes be equally or even more suggestible than preschoolers (e.g. Bruck, London, Landa, & Goodman, 2007; Ceci, Kulkofsky, Klemfuss, Sweeney, & Bruck, 2007; Finnillä, Mahlberga, Santtilaa, Sandnabbaa, & Niemib, 2003; Principe, Guiliano, & Root, 2008; see Brainerd, Reyna, & Ceci, 2008, for a review). Of course, age does not account for individual differences and developmental shifts in suggestibility. Rather, developmental differences and shifts in suggestibility reflect some underlying cognitive, physical, and social factors. Key to better understanding memory suggestibility, then, is elucidating these individual difference and contextual variables. In this chapter, we review contemporary research findings regarding several variables that underlie suggestibility in children. In the first section, we review the literature on memory suggestibility in typically developing children. We pay particular attention to two individual difference variables that relate to suggestibility: narrative ability and theory of mind. We also review the literature on one contextual variable related to suggestibility: emotional states. In the second section of the chapter, we review research findings regarding memory and suggestibility in children with intellectual disabilities.

SUGGESTIBILITY IN TYPICALLY DEVELOPING CHILDREN: THE ROLE OF NARRATIVE ABILITY, THEORY OF MIND, AND EMOTIONAL STATES

Previous research on suggestibility shows that adults and children are not only susceptible to assenting to false information about an event, but also to incorporating that information into their memory (for reviews, see Ceci & Bruck, 1993; Zaragoza, Belli, & Payment, 2006). Importantly, though, there are individuals in suggestibility studies who do not yield to suggestion, leaving open the possibility that some individual difference or contextual variables may be contributing to this resistance to suggestion.

Suggestibility and Narrative Abilities

Studies have only recently begun to investigate the role of narrative ability in suggestibility. Narrative ability refers to children's skills at conveying cohesive and detailed information about an event. There are two bodies of literature that lead to the hypothesis that narrative ability may play a role in suggestibility. First, there is some evidence indicating verbal ability and suggestibility are related. Second, narrative ability has been shown to play an important role in the development of autobiographical memory.

Bruck and Melnyk (2004) reviewed twelve studies of verbal abilities and suggestibility, mostly involving preschoolers. They reported two major findings. Of six studies to investigate vocabulary, only one (Danielsdottir, Sigurgeirsdottir, Einarsdottir, & Haraldsson, 1993) found an association with suggestibility, and even then, only one of eight correlations reported in that study was significant. While vocabulary alone did not relate robustly to suggestibility, four studies gave comprehensive language batteries and reported children with higher expressive and productive language abilities were more resistant to suggestions. However, language ability was not shown to be associated with suggestibility when single measures of language were used. See Bruck and Melnyk (2004, Table 5) for a further review. A handful of studies published subsequent to the Bruck and Melnyk (2004) review have reported that increased language abilities are associated with reduced error on misleading questions (Chae & Ceci, 2005; Kulkofsky & Klemfuss, 2008; Roebers & Schneider, 2005).

A second area of research regarding autobiographical memory points to a possible relationship between narrative ability and suggestibility. Narrative ability is important to the development of autobiographical memory (Fivush & Reese, 1992; Nelson, 2003; Nelson & Fivush, 2004).

Children who engage in more elaborate conversations with their care-givers tend to give more detailed accounts of experienced events (Haden, Haine, & Fivush, 1997; Harley & Reese, 1999; Reese, Haden, & Fivush, 1993). Therefore, narrative ability may influence memory and suggestibility.

Kulkofsky and colleagues (2008, 2010) hypothesized a complex relationship between narrative ability and suggestibility whereby narrative ability is at times related to *increased* suggestibility and at other times related to *decreased* suggestibility. They reasoned that narrative quality should be associated with the underlying memory representation for an event. Weaker memories should be reflected in sparse narratives; memories that are couched in rich elaborate narratives should reflect stronger memories. Kulkofsky and Klemfuss (2008) wrote:

> ... a child's ability to produce a high-quality narrative of a previously experienced event may indicate that the child also has a well-structured, elaborate, and inter-connected representation of the event. Thus, narrative ability may be related to lower levels of sug-gestibility because narrative ability reflects a stronger memory trace of the original event. (p. 1443)

Kulkofsky and Klemfuss (2008) further put forth the seemingly coun-terintuitive hypothesis that general narrative ability may, at times, be related to *increased* suggestibility. Narrative ability is a very social con-struct (Fivush & Reese, 1992). Kulkofsky and Klemfuss hypothesized that children with more advanced narrative abilities may more readily recognize that conversing about an event is a shared experience. Children with more advanced narrative skills may be more sensitive to the cues provided by their conversational partner and hence may more readily succumb to pressure to change their answers.

In two studies, Kulkofsky and Klemfuss (2008) took comprehensive measures of narrative ability. They defined narrative quality by a combined variable representing '... the amount of information that is provided, both overall and within each statement, the descriptiveness of that information, and the degree to which that information is con-nected linguistically' (p. 1454). In Study 1, Kulkofsky and Klemfuss (2008) staged an event for children in their classroom. Following the event, children were asked misleading questions about the event once a week for four weeks. If children did not assent to a misleading ques-tion, they were given increasingly leading prompts. A week after the last suggestive interview, a novel interviewer asked children the same misleading questions. Findings revealed that children who provided better narratives about the event were less suggestible when ques-tioned about that event.

In Study 2, Kulkofsky and Klemfuss (2008) replicated findings from Study 1, again demonstrating that increased event narratives predicted reductions in children's tendency to assent to misleading questions (during a single interview session) regarding the staged event. However, in Study 2, Kulkofsky and Klemfuss also gave children an autobiographical memory survey, where they asked children to report on recent events such as 'What did you do before bed last night?' Kulkofsky and Klemfuss found that increased narrative abilities on the autobiographical survey were associated with *higher* suggestibility levels. Specifically, children with better overall narrative skills (as measured in the autobiographical memory survey) were more apt to change their responses from initial denials of false events to assents during increasingly leading questions.

Taken as a whole, children's developing narrative abilities likely confer some resistance to suggestibility by helping them provide coherent structure and stronger memory traces of the specific event. At the same time, children who produce high-quality narratives may at times be more suggestible, particularly with regard to shifting initial denials to false assents.

There are two ways the legal system can capitalize on the research findings showing a relationship between narrative ability and suggestibility. First, researchers have already found that a top-down approach of using child-centred, simple language facilitates children's eyewitness memory performance (Lamb & Brown, 2006; Shapiro & Purdy, 2005). A second implication is that a bottom-up approach of providing children with narrative training might help to bolster their abilities to resist suggestive influences. Three recently published studies provide evidence that training young children to provide rich narratives promotes their recall quality and quantity (Brown & Pipe, 2003a, 2003b; Kulkofsky, 2010) and reduces errors to directed and misleading questions (Kulkofsky, 2010). Hence, future research needs to explore whether narrative training might reduce children's suggestibility during investigative interviews.

Theory of Mind and Suggestibility

Another individual difference variable that has been investigated in the suggestibility literature is children's ability to reason about their own and other's mental states. This working understanding of mental states, such as beliefs, desires, and intentions, is referred to as *theory of mind* (ToM). Between the ages of 3 and 6 years, children show marked improvements in ToM; for example, they come to appreciate that two people can have conflicting representations of reality, one of which is a false-belief, and they can predict each person's behaviour accordingly (Perner, Leekam, & Wimmer, 1987; Wellman, Cross, & Watson, 2001).

Applied to the context of a forensic interview, children who have an appreciation for false-beliefs may understand that they do not have to adopt a false-belief held by an interviewer and, consequently, may be less suggestible (Scullin & Bonner, 2006).

Empirical support for a relationship between ToM and suggestibility has been mixed. Bruck and Melnyk (2004, Table 7) reviewed 11 studies examining this topic and noted five studies which found that increases in ToM performance predicted reductions in suggestibility. In contrast, two studies showed that ToM and suggestibility were positively correlated (e.g. Templeton & Wilcox, 2000) and four studies found no relationship between the two variables (e.g. Quas & Schaaf, 2002). The next section provides a summary of studies reviewed by Bruck and Melnyk (2004) as well as new research to help elucidate the relationship between ToM and suggestibility.

Studies examining the relationship between ToM and suggestibility in a misinformation paradigm have usually reported negative correlations between these variables, although some exceptions exist. In one of the initial studies on this topic, Welch-Ross, Diecidue, and Miller (1997) found that performance on a battery of ToM measures negatively correlated with suggestibility among 3- to 5-year-olds. Furthermore, this relationship remained significant even after controlling for age and general memory ability. In subsequent studies, Welch-Ross (1999a, b) only partially replicated her initial results. In one study, increases in ToM performance only helped children with poor event memory (Welch-Ross, 1999a); while in another study, improvement in ToM performance was associated with reduced suggestibility only among children who were interviewed by an ignorant interviewer as opposed to a knowledgeable interviewer who knew the details of the event in question (Welch-Ross, 1999b). In fact, in the knowledgeable interviewer condition, children passing false-belief tasks were *more* suggestible than children who failed the false-belief tasks (also see Templeton & Wilcox, 2000). To explain this reversal, Welch-Ross (1999b) argued that children passing ToM tasks quickly dismissed the suggestions made by naïve interviewers because they knew the interviewer was absent for the story and, thus, could be mistaken about some of the details. In contrast, these children may have taken longer to dismiss the misinformation presented by the knowledgeable interviewer because they expected the interviewer to know the correct details since she was present for the story. As a result, the children may have processed this conflicting information more deeply, and upon retrieval, this information might have interfered with the correct information.

More recently, Bright-Paul, Jarrold, and Wright (2008) showed that, among 3- to 6-year-olds, increases in ToM performance predicted significant reductions in suggestibility even after controlling for age and verbal ability. They also found that individual differences in source monitoring mediated the relationship between ToM performance and suggestibility. Thus, in the context of the misinformation paradigm, ToM interacts with other cognitive abilities that develop during early childhood – an issue that we will return to shortly.

As well as examining how individual differences in ToM might attenuate suggestibility in the misinformation paradigm, others have investigated how ToM ability might help children resist misleading questions. Consistent with this hypothesis, two studies demonstrated that children performing well on ToM tasks were less likely to assent to false information during an interview (Scullin & Bonner, 2006; Thomsen & Bernsten, 2005). These results, however, should be interpreted in the light of several other studies which have found no relationship between suggestibility and theory of mind (see Bruck & Melnyk, 2004, Table 7).

Although there is some evidence supporting a relationship between ToM and suggestibility, more recent studies cast further doubt on this relationship. For example, individual differences in executive functioning are more predictive of suggestibility than is ToM (Karpinski & Scullin, 2009; Melinder, Endestad, & Magnussen, 2006). Melinder *et al.* (2006) found that while inhibitory control (i.e. the ability to inhibit an incorrect immediate response) and age accounted for a significant proportion of the variance in suggestibility scores (i.e. the number of assents to false information during an interview), ToM was not a significant predictor. Similarly, Karpinski and Scullin (2009) found that when controlling for age, ToM skills played a limited role in children's suggestibility regarding both a staged event and during a general assessment of suggestibility (the Video Suggestibility Scale). The Video Suggestibility Scale (Scullin & Ceci, 2001) measures individual differences in preschoolers' tendency to assent to misleading questions. Advanced ToM skills only led to reductions in suggestibility under high-pressured interview conditions. Moreover, this benefit was only observed for older children (more than 54 months) and not younger children. In contrast, executive function measures were more predictive of suggestibility in low- and high-pressure interview conditions.

In the above studies, ToM and inhibitory control were positively correlated, and they were both negatively correlated with suggestibility. It is plausible that the negative correlation between ToM and suggestibility could be driven by the executive function component of ToM. Thus, the mixed results obtained in other studies could be due to the ToM tasks measuring inhibitory control albeit imprecisely. Bright-Paul *et al.* (2008) provide a discussion on how executive function, ToM, and source monitoring may work together to drive individual differences in suggestibility.

The literature reviewed here suggests that the relationship between theory of mind and suggestibility is complex and varies with other cognitive abilities (e.g. source monitoring and executive function) and situational variables (e.g. pressured versus unpressured interviews) influencing the relationship. Furthermore, the relationship also seems to depend upon how the constructs of suggestibility and theory of mind are measured (Bruck & Melnyk, 2004).

Future studies should try to disentangle some of the above variables to understand individual differences in suggestibility. These studies can also aim to test whether individual differences in ToM influence suggestibility among older populations greater than age six. Previous critics have argued that ToM has limited explanatory power because it does not account for suggestibility effects found among adults (Bruck & Melnyk, 2004; Quas, Qin, Schaaf, & Goodman, 1997). Although important ToM milestones are reached early in development, an individual's ability to reason about mental states continues to undergo changes during childhood and even adulthood (e.g. Bartsch & London, 2000; Happe, Winner, & Brownell, 1998; LaLonde & Chandler, 2002) and this may, in turn, explain differences in suggestibility.

Children's Suggestibility for Emotional Events

In an effort to boost ecological validity, many suggestibility researchers have examined children's suggestibility for negative emotional events that approximate events of forensic interest. However, much of the research examining children's suggestibility for emotional events has concentrated on one aspect of emotion, namely negative emotional arousal (i.e. stress) or the intensity of children's negative emotional reaction (Davis, Quas, & Levine, 2008). Emotional arousal as it pertains to memory refers to the affective intensity the experienced event elicits, ranging from relaxed to highly excitable. Empirical work examining the effects of emotion on children's memory and suggestibility has primarily construed emotion as arousal, specifically focusing on children's memory for negative emotionally arousing events (for review, see Paz-Alonso, Larson, Castelli, Alley, & Goodman, 2009). Bruck and Melnyk (2004) evaluated 15 studies that examined the effect of children's emotional arousal during the to-be-remembered event on their subsequent suggestibility. Eight of the 15 studies revealed a significant relationship between emotional arousal and suggestibility, half showing greater suggestibility with increased emotional arousal and the other half showing lower suggestibility with increased emotional arousal. Thus, findings vary considerably.

One reason for the mixed findings in the extant literature may be that different studies have used many different types of events when assessing the effects of emotions on memory. However, even when similar events are compared, the findings vary. Additionally, mixed findings could be a result of differences in the way arousal was measured and the ages of children included in the studies (Quas, Carrick, Alkon, Goldstein, & Boyce, 2006). Moreover, the inconclusive findings may be a result of the simplified construal of emotion as arousal without consideration for differences in emotional valence or the specific emotional states associated with the negative event (Davis *et al.*, 2008; Levine & Pizzaro, 2006). The relationship between emotion and memory/suggestibility may be better clarified by further dividing emotions into discrete emotions.

Discrete Emotions and Suggestibility In accordance with cognitive appraisal theories, Stein and colleagues (Stein & Levine, 1989, 1990; Stein & Liwag, 1997; Stein, Liwag, & Wade, 1996) hold that the elicitation of discrete emotions depends on how one appraises an event in correspondence to certain goal contingencies. Happiness, anger, sadness and fear are differentiated by the goal–outcome relationships in conjunction with beliefs about reinstating or maintaining a goal (Stein & Liwag, 1997). Once an emotion is evoked, it directs present cognitions, behaviours and responses accordingly to fit the demands of the person's present emotional state (Davis *et al.*, 2008).

According to Levine and Pizarro (2004, 2006), discrete emotions such as happiness, anger, sadness and fear which are associated with different appraised goal outcomes have specific implications for memory. Levine, Burgess and Laney (2008) conducted two studies examining the effects of happy, angry and sad discrete emotional states on the suggestibility of 4- to 6-year-old children. Levine *et al.* (2008) showed that children in a sad emotional state were more suggestible than children in a happy or angry emotional state. Additionally, children in the sad condition were more likely to assent to misleading questions and incorporate false information into later reports. Levine *et al.* (2008) contend that children in a sad emotional state may turn to adults, understanding that their own resources are inadequate to cope with the present outcome. This greater reliance leads to heightened suggestibility. Contrarily, children in a happy or angry emotional state have greater feelings of self-efficacy allowing them to resist complying with false information.

The study by Levine *et al.* (2008) provides a snapshot across a small developmental window of the effects that discrete emotions have on children's suggestibility. Further research needs to examine whether older children display similar patterns of suggestibility in discrete emotional states because older children would be less likely to rely on others' assistance in understanding emotional events, but may be more prone to making cognitively based memory errors in certain contexts (Brainerd *et al.*, 2008). Further investigation on discrete emotions and memory might provide important insight regarding the mixed findings in extant research. Such investigation could improve our theoretical understanding of memory as well help formulate forensic guidelines.

CHILDREN WITH INTELLECTUAL DISABILITIES

The remaining part of this chapter addresses suggestibility in children with intellectual disabilities (ID). The scope of discussion will be more limited than it was for typical children as there is relatively little evidence in relation to individual differences, suggestibility and intellectual disabilities.

Intellectual disabilities refer to cognitive and adaptive difficulties that have their onset early in life (Harris, 2006). The simplest definition of ID is based around a low level of cognitive functioning, or IQ. Those with an IQ of less than 70 would fall into the intellectually disabled range. However, most definitions also require that there is some impairment in social adaptation (e.g. daily living skills, communication, socialization, motor skills). Our discussion will be restricted to those with mild to moderate ID (IQ of approximately 55–69 and 40–54, respectively). ID represent 'the most common developmental disorder and the most handicapping of the disorders beginning in childhood' (Harris, 2006, p. 79), with prevalence levels of around 1–3%. Many regard ID as limiting participation in society more than any other disorder (Harris, 2006).

Children with intellectual and other disabilities are more vulnerable than typically developing children to maltreatment, abuse and sexual violence (Hershkowitz, Lamb & Horowitz, 2007; Lin, Yen, Kuo, Wu, & Lin, 2009; Sullivan & Knutson, 2000; Westcott, 1991). Increased severity of disability seems to be linked with increased severity of abuse (Hershkowitz et al., 2007; Williams, 1995; Wilson & Brewer, 1992), but cases rarely lead to prosecution or other punishment (Mencap, 1999; Sharp, 2001). It is, therefore, imperative to help children with ID fully participate in the legal system. The question of whether or not children with ID show heightened levels of *suggestibility* is one of the key factors to consider in relation to forensic interviewing.

Gudjonsson and Clark (1986) presented a model of interrogative suggestibility, which outlines why individuals with ID might show heightened levels of suggestibility (see Chapter 3, this volume). Children with ID tend to show memory deficits in a range of remembering tasks (e.g. Weiss, Weisz, & Bromfield, 1986), which means they are likely to have weaker event memories. This may make them more susceptible to suggestive questioning (particularly leading or misleading prompts). Additionally, individuals with ID are less able to cope with stressful and unfamiliar demands, which, again, may increase suggestibility.

We will now consider research evidence concerning whether children with ID are more suggestible than would be expected based on their *chronological age (CA)* or *mental age (MA)*. Before this, it is worth outlining two methods of assessing suggestibility. The first is to show children a real event (live or via a video) and then carry out a suggestibility manipulation: either (a) assents to misleading questions, or (b) misinformation effects. The second method of measuring suggestibility is to use specially designed scales (e.g. Gudjonsson Suggestibility Scales; Gudjonsson, 1997), some of which have been modified for use in those with ID (e.g. Milne, Clare, & Bull, 2002).

Are there Suggestibility Differences between Children with ID and Typical Children?

Bruck and Melnyk's (2004) comprehensive review explicitly considered whether children with ID showed greater levels of suggestibility than typical children matched for CA. In most of the studies they considered, the method of assessing suggestibility was to prompt children by asking misleading questions. The findings were clear. Children with ID were more likely to assent to misleading prompts than children of the same CA. Similarly, Gudjonsson and Henry (2003), using the Gudjonsson Suggestibility Scale 2 (GSS 2), found that children with ID were more likely to 'yield' to misleading prompts and to change their answers in response to negative feedback ('shift') than typical children of the same CA.

However, many would argue that typical children of comparable developmental level represent a more revealing comparison group for children with ID. Such 'mental age matched' comparison groups assess whether suggestibility is at mental age level, even if a child with ID would not be expected to reach CA-appropriate performance levels.

Henry and Gudjonsson (1999, 2003) examined this issue by presenting a staged live event to 11- and 12-year-old children with mild and moderate ID and assessing suggestibility 1 day later (1999 study: mean IQ 60, mean MA 7 years; 2003 study: mild ID, mean IQ 66, mean MA 8 years; moderate ID, mean IQ 45, mean MA 6 years). Two types of misleading prompts were used: those with an open-ended format ('What colour was the lady's coat?' when she did not wear one) and those with a closed yes/no format ('You saw that lady on television before, didn't you?'). In both studies, suggestibility levels were never below MA level in children with ID, although differences between children with ID and CA comparison groups were found.

Similar results were reported by Gordon, Jens, Hollings, and Watson (1994), comparing 8- to 13-year-olds with mild/moderate ID to children matched for MA (mean MA 6½ years, mean IQ 57). Children participated in activities with an experimenter and were later interviewed.

Embedded in the interview were 12 misleading prompts. Children with ID did not differ from the MA group in their ability to respond accurately to misleading prompts either immediately or after a delay of 6 weeks (see also Jens, Gordon, & Shaddock, 1990).

In a further relevant study, Michel, Gordon, Ornstein, and Simpson (2000) administered a simulated health check to 9- to 14-year-olds with ID (mean verbal IQ 58, mean MA 6 years). Subsequent interviews immediately after the health check and 6 weeks later included 12 prompts that were misleading, phrased in a yes/no format ('The woman checked your private parts, didn't she?'). There were no suggestibility differences between children with ID and typical comparisons of the same MA (although the usual CA group advantage was observed).

Agnew and Powell (2004) used a method involving a separate biasing interview (followed by cued-recall prompts) to investigate suggestibility in 9- to 12-year-old children with mild or moderate ID. All children participated in a magic show and received a biasing interview 3 days later (suggested details about the event that were either true or false were presented), followed by a second interview the next day. Children with ID were no more likely to report 'false interviewer suggestions' from the biasing interview than typical children of the same MA or CA. Miles, Powell, Gignac, and Thomson (2007), using a similar biasing interview method, replicated this finding in relation to a CA-matched comparison group.

Overall, these findings imply that suggestibility in children with ID is broadly in line with MA level, although it is higher than typical peers of the same CA. Another important question concerns whether suggestibility might be higher in those with ID compared to CA peers because children with ID do not recall the event as accurately in the first place. This was an issue considered by Henry and Gudjonsson (1999, 2003). They found that, even when controlling statistically for how well children with ID could recall the event during 'free recall', those with ID still showed higher levels of suggestibility in comparison to CA peers.

Therefore, although suggestibility is higher in those with ID than typical peers of the same CA, this may not be related to weaker recall for the event. Gudjonsson and Henry (2003) also put forward the view that 'yield', as measured by the GSS, may be more related to cognitive variables such as memory for the event, whereas GSS 'shift' may be more related to social and interpersonal factors. We will return to this point in the next section.

Are There Any Variables That Predict Suggestibility in Children with ID? In practical and theoretical terms, it is of interest to establish the types of variables that are related to suggestibility. Bruck and Melnyk (2004) drew a distinction between cognitive variables such as IQ and memory ability, as opposed to psychosocial variables such as self-concept, shyness or compliance. We will now consider the relevant research on these variables where available.

As already discussed, children with ID show greater levels of suggestibility than peers of the same CA. However, this does not necessarily mean that IQ will be a good predictor of suggestibility *within* a population of children with ID. Gudjonsson (1988) found that intelligence was related to standardized measures of suggestibility in adults with IQ levels below 100, and we will now consider relevant research on children with ID.

Henry and Gudjonsson (1999) reported a correlation between IQ and suggestibility among children with ID: those with higher IQs were better at resisting misleading prompts about a staged event ($r=0.42$, $n=28$). In a separate sample of 47 children with mild and moderate ID, Henry and Gudjonsson (2003) found the same relationship (even when controlling for small variations in age within the sample; $r=0.43$). A further replication study using a video-presented event found that verbal IQ was related to suggestibility in children with mild to moderate ID ($r=0.44$, $n=34$), whereas non-verbal IQ was not (Henry & Gudjonsson, 2007).

These significant but rather modest correlations indicate that IQ may account for less than 20% of the total variation in suggestibility among children with ID. However, these relationships were only found for prompts phrased using a 'closed' yes/no format. In none of these studies was suggestibility, as measured using open-ended misleading prompts, ever significantly related to IQ. In fact, IQ group differences on open-ended misleading prompts (typical, mild ID, moderate ID; Henry & Gudjonsson, 2003) were not significant either, implying that such questions are not handled any better or worse by children with ID than typical children. Children with ID seem particularly vulnerable to yes/no closed questions, showing an elevated tendency to agree with the questioner (see also Heal & Sigelman, 1995).

Another variable that has been examined is general memory ability. Henry and Gudjonsson (2003) included assessments of verbal and non-verbal memory, using subtests from the Test of Memory and Learning (Reynolds & Bigler, 1994). For children with ID, verbal and non-verbal memory measures were significantly related to suggestibility ($r=0.42$, $r=0.38$, respectively). Again, these relationships emerged for 'yes/no' closed misleading prompts, but not for open-ended misleading prompts. There was evidence that *verbal* memory was the more powerful predictor of suggestibility: in multiple regressions, it accounted for significant amounts of variance whereas non-verbal memory did not.

Other variables that have been considered include speed of information processing and chronological age. No convincing evidence has been reported linking speed of information processing with suggestibility in children with ID (Henry & Gudjonsson, 2007). In relation to chronological age, Miles *et al*. (2007) reported a small correlation between age and reports of false-interviewer suggestions about a magic show after a biasing interview ($r = 0.23$), but age was not related to performance on misleading prompts in a further study (Henry & Gudjonsson, 2007).

A handful of studies have examined suggestibility as measured using the Gudjonsson Suggestibility Scale 2 (GSS 2; Gudjonsson, 1997; see Chapter 3, this volume, for methodology). For example, Young, Powell, and Dudgeon (2003) examined relationships between suggestibility, age, IQ, communication skills and shyness. These authors assessed 6- to 13-year-olds with ID (mean IQ 62, $n = 75$), finding that higher GSS 2 'Yield' scores (assenting to misleading prompts) were related to lower IQ ($r = -0.30$) and communication skills ($r = -0.34$). The other measure of GSS 2 suggestibility, namely 'Shift', was unrelated to any variable (also see Miles *et al*., 2007).

Overall, consistent evidence for relationships between suggestibility and IQ has emerged, but such relationships have not been present for all suggestibility measures. There is limited evidence that verbal memory, communication skills and recall accuracy are related to suggestibility. However, the literature in this area is sparse and requires replication and extension, particularly in relation to psychosocial variables. It might be valuable to compare different methodologies by assessing suggestibility in children with ID using misleading prompts as well as biasing interviews (the misinformation paradigm). Further research is also needed to determine whether different ID aetiologies produce different patterns of suggestibility. For example, individuals with Down syndrome show different cognitive and social strengths and weaknesses compared to individuals with Autism Spectrum Disorder (Henry, Bettenay, & Carney, 2011). Learning more about such patterns may help forensic investigators determine how best to tailor interviews according to individuals' strengths and weaknesses.

One of the more interesting issues for future research is to assess whether or not Yield measures of suggestibility are more related to cognitive variables than Shift measures, which may be more related to interpersonal and social variables (Gudjonsson & Henry, 2003). Recent work on the cross-examination of children with ID has indicated that state anxiety after a cross-examination interview is related to the tendency to cede to cross-examination challenges (Bettenay, 2010). Cross-examination procedures place a heavy reliance on techniques that confuse and intimidate the witness into changing aspects of their testimony. It is possible that the mechanisms underlying cross-examination vulnerability may show some parallels to suggestibility in investigative interviews, in terms of Yield and Shift, but further research on this issue will be needed before firm conclusions can be drawn.

CONCLUSIONS

- The complex nature of suggestibility is demonstrated in recent work showing that narrative ability leads to both reductions and increases in suggestibility. Advanced narrative skills may assist children in having stronger memories for an event, which makes them less suggestible; however, more advanced narrative skills also make children more sensitive to social cues, which may cause children to attempt to include the interviewer's (true or false) information into their conversation.
- Theory of mind is an individual difference variable where mixed evidence has emerged in the suggestibility literature. Part of the reason for the mixed relationship is the complex nature of suggestibility, but also the complex nature of ToM. Taken together, extant research suggests sophisticated ToM skills are associated with reductions in suggestibility.
- Past research has yielded mixed findings regarding whether and how the emotional quality of an event affects children's memory and suggestibility. Most research in the area has focused exclusively on negative events, exploring whether the emotional arousal of a negative experience affects memory. Recently, researchers have begun to explore whether the mixed findings in the literature could be accounted for in part by emotional valence. Research is only beginning to emerge examining the role of discrete emotions on memory and suggestibility.
- Children with intellectual disabilities typically show patterns of memory and suggestibility similar to mental-aged matched peers. Additional research on memory and suggestibility in children with IDs is urgently needed given that this population of children is at increased risk for abuse.

FORENSIC IMPLICATIONS

- *Forensic interviewers should be sensitive to the developmental needs of their interviewees*. Interviewers should realize that while older children may be able to provide more complete and coherent narratives about past events, at the same time, older children may be more sensitive to the social cues of the interviewer. Therefore the interviewer needs to be careful to not provide any explicit or implicit cues to the children that might pressure them to change their responses.
- *A developmentally-sensitive interviewer would also recognize that children may not fully understand the role of the interviewer*. Young

children may think the interviewer has the correct answers which may lead to suggestibility. Forensic interviewers can avoid pitfalls associated with immature ToM abilities by explaining to the child that it is their job to provide information and that the interviewer was not present and does not know what happened.

• *When interviewed in a proper context, children can provide accurate reports about both stressful and non-stressful events.* Forensic interviewers should be aware that extant studies have reported very mixed findings regarding whether children remember stressful events better or worse than non-stressful events.

• *At present, research findings suggest children with IDs perform similar to their mental age matched peers.* Interviewers should be aware that if a 15-year-old youth has the mental age of a typical 7-year-old, that youth would be expected to show memory and suggestibility similar to the 7-year-old level.

REFERENCES

Agnew, S.E., & Powell, M.B. (2004). The effect of intellectual disability on children's recall of an event across different question types. *Law and Human Behavior, 28,* 273–294.

Bartsch, K., & London, K. (2000). Children's use of mental state information in persuasion. *Developmental Psychology, 36,* 352–365.

Bettenay, C. (2010). Memory under cross-examination of children with and without intellectual disabilities. Unpublished doctoral dissertation, London South Bank University.

Brainerd, C.J., Reyna, V.F., & Ceci, S.J. (2008). Developmental reversals in false memory: A review of data and theory. *Psychological Bulletin, 134,* 343–382.

Bright-Paul, A., Jarrold, C., & Wright, D.B. (2008). Theory-of-mind development influences suggestibility and source monitoring. *Developmental Psychology, 44,* 1055–1068.

Brown, D.A., & Pipe, M.E. (2003a). Individual differences in children's event memory reports and the narrative elaboration training. *Journal of Applied Psychology, 88,* 195–206.

Brown, D.A., & Pipe, M.E. (2003b). Variations on a technique: Enhancing children's recall through Narrative Elaboration Training. *Applied Cognitive Psychology, 17,* 377–399.

Bruck, M., & Ceci, S.J. (1999). The suggestibility of children's memory. *Annual Review of Psychology, 50,* 419–439.

Bruck, M., Ceci, S.J., & Principe, G.F. (2006). The child and the law. In K.A. Renninger, I.E. Sigel, W. Damon, & R.M. Lerner (Eds), *Handbook of Child Psychology* (6th edn, Vol. 4, pp. 776–816). New York: John Wiley & Sons, Ltd.

Bruck, M., London, K., Landa, R., & Goodman, J. (2007). Autobiographical memory and suggestibility in children with autism spectrum disorder. *Development and Psychopathology, 19,* 73–95.

Bruck, M., & Melnyk, L. (2004). Individual differences in children's suggestibility: A review and synthesis. *Applied Cognitive Psychology, 18,* 947–996.

Ceci, S.J., & Bruck, M. (1993). Suggestibility of the child witness: A historical review and synthesis. *Psychological Bulletin, 113,* 403–439.

Ceci, S.J., Kulkofsky, S., Klemfuss, J.Z., Sweeney, C.D., & Bruck, M. (2007). Unwarranted assumptions about children's testimonial accuracy. *Annual Review of Clinical Psychology, 3,* 311–328.

Chae Y., & Ceci S.J. (2005). Individual differences in children's recall and suggestibility: The effect of intelligence, temperament, and self-perceptions. *Applied Cognitive Psychology, 19,* 383–407.

Danielsdottir, G., Sigurgeirsdottir, S., Einarsdottir, H.R., & Haraldsson, E. (1993). Interrogative suggestibility in children and its relationship with memory and vocabulary. *Personality and Individual Differences, 14,* 499–502.

Davis, E., Quas, J.A., & Levine, L.J. (2008). Children's memory for stressful events: Exploring the role of discrete emotions. In M. Howe, D. Cicchetti, & G. Goodman (Eds), *Stress, Trauma, and Children's Memory Development: Neurobiological, Cognitive, Clinical, and Legal Perspectives* (pp. 236–264). Oxford: Oxford University Press.

Finnillä, K., Mahlberga, N., Santtilaa, P., Sandnabbaa, K., & Niemib, P. (2003). Validity of a test of children's suggestibility for predicting responses to two interview situations differing in their degree of suggestiveness. *Journal of Experimental Child Psychology, 85,* 32–49.

Fivush, R., & Reese, E. (1992). The social construction of autobiographical memory. In M.A. Conway, D.C. Rubin, H. Spinnler, & W.A. Wagenaar (Eds), *Theoretical Perspectives on Autobiographical Memory* (pp. 115–132). Dordrecht, the Netherlands: Kluwer Academic.

Gordon, B.N., Jens, K.G., Hollings, R., & Watson, T.E. (1994). Remembering activities performed versus those imagined: Implications for testimony of children with mental retardation. *Journal of Clinical Child Psychology, 23,* 239–248.

Gudjonsson, G.H. (1988). The relationship of intelligence and memory to interrogative suggestibility: The importance of ranged effects. *British Journal of Clinical Psychology, 27,* 185–187.

Gudjonsson, G.H. (1997). *The Gudjonsson Suggestibility Scales Manual.* London, UK: Psychology Press.

Gudjonsson, G.H., & Clark, N.K. (1986). Suggestibility in police interrogation: A social psychological model. *Social Behaviour, 1,* 83–104.

Gudjonsson, G.H., & Henry, L.A. (2003). Child and adult witnesses with intellectual disability: The importance of suggestibility. *Legal and Criminological Psychology, 8,* 241–252.

Haden, C.A., Haine, R.A., & Fivush, R. (1997). Developing narrative structure in parent–child reminiscing across the preschool years. *Developmental Psychology, 33,* 295–307.

Happe, F.G.E., Winner, E., & Brownell, H. (1998). The getting of wisdom: Theory of mind in old age. *Developmental Psychology, 34,* 358–362.

Harley, K., & Reese, E. (1999). Origins of autobiographical memory. *Developmental Psychology, 35,* 1338–1348.

Harris, J.C. (2006). *Intellectual Disability: Understanding Its Development, Causes, Classification, Evaluation and Treatment.* Oxford: Oxford University Press.

Heal, L.W., & Sigelman, C.K. (1995). Response biases in interviews of individuals with limited mental ability. *Journal of Intellectual Disability Research, 39,* 331–340.

Henry, L.A., & Gudjonsson, G.H. (1999). Eyewitness memory and suggestibility in children with mental retardation. *American Journal on Mental Retardation, 104,* 491–508.

Henry, L.A., & Gudjonsson, G.H. (2003). Eyewitness memory, suggestibility and repeated recall sessions in children with mild and moderate intellectual disabilities. *Law and Human Behavior, 27,* 481–505.

Henry, L.A., & Gudjonsson, G.H. (2007). Individual and developmental differ-
    ences in eyewitness memory and suggestibility in children with intellectual
    disabilities. *Applied Cognitive Psychology, 21,* 361–381.
Henry, L.A., Bettenay, C., & Carney, D.P.J. (2011). Children with intellectual
    disabilities and developmental disorders. In M.E. Lamb, D.J. La Rooy, L.C.
    Malloy, & C. Katz (Eds), *Children's Testimony: A Handbook of Psychological
    Research and Forensic Practice* (2nd edn, pp. 251–283). Chichester: John
    Wiley & Sons, Ltd.
Hershkowitz, I., Lamb, M.E., & Horowitz, D. (2007). Victimisation of children
    with disabilities. *American Journal of Orthopsychiatry, 77* (4), 629–635.
Jens, K.G., Gordon, B.N., & Shaddock, A.J. (1990). Remembering activities per-
    formed versus imagined: A comparison of children with mental retardation
    and children with normal intelligence. *International Journal of Disability,
    Development and Education, 37,* 201–213.
Karpinski, A.C., & Scullin, M.H. (2009). Suggestibility under pressure: Theory
    of mind, executive function and suggestibility in preschoolers. *Journal of
    Applied Developmental Psychology, 30,* 749–763.
Kulkofsky, S. (2010). The effect of verbal labels and vocabulary on memory and
    suggestibility. *Journal of Applied Developmental Psychology, 31,* 460–466.
Kulkofsky, S., & Klemfuss, J.Z. (2008). What the stories children tell can tell
    about their memory: Narrative skill and young children's suggestibility.
    Developmental Psychology, 44, 1442–1456.
Kulkofsky, S., Wang, Q., & Ceci, S.J. (2008). Do better stories make better mem-
    ories? Narrative quality and memory accuracy in preschool children. *Applied
    Cognitive Psychology, 22,* 21–38.
LaLonde, C.E., & Chandler, M.J. (2002). Children's understanding of interpre-
    tation. *New Ideas in Psychology, 20,* 163–198.
Lamb, M.E., & Brown, D.A. (2006). Conversational apprentices: Helping chil-
    dren become competent informants about their own experiences. *British
    Journal of Developmental Psychology, 24,* 215–234.
Levine, L.J., Burgess, S.L., & Laney, C. (2008). Effects of discrete emotions on
    young children's suggestibility. *Child Development, 44,* 681–694.
Levine, L.J., & Pizarro, D.A. (2004). Emotion and memory research: A grumpy
    overview. *Social Cognition, 22,* 530–554.
Levine, L.J., & Pizarro, D.A. (2006). Emotional valence, discrete emotions, and
    memory. In B. Uttl, N. Ohta, & A.L. Siegenthaler (Eds), *Memory and Emotion:
    Interdisciplinary Perspectives.* Oxford: Blackwell Publishing.
Lin, L.-P., Yen, C.-F., Kuo, F.-Y., Wu, J.-L. & Lin, J.-D. (2009). Sexual assault of
    people with disabilities: Results of a 2002–2007 national report in Taiwan.
    Research in Developmental Disabilities, 30, 969–975.
London, K., & Kulkofsky, S. (2010). Factors affecting the reliability of children's
    reports. In G. M. Davies, & D. B. Wright (Eds), *New Frontiers in Applied
    Memory* (pp. 119–141). New York: Psychology Press.
Melinder, A., Endestad, T., & Magnussen, S. (2006). Relations between episodic
    memory, suggestibility, theory of mind, and cognitive inhibition in the pre-
    school child. *Scandinavian Journal of Psychology, 47,* 485–495.
Mencap (1999). *Living in Fear.* London: Mencap.
Michel, M.K., Gordon, B.N., Ornstein, P.A., & Simpson, M.A. (2000). The abili-
    ties of children with mental retardation to remember personal experiences:
    Implications for testimony. *Journal of Clinical Child Psychology, 29,*
    453–463.
Miles, K.L., Powell, M.B., Gignac, G.E., & Thomson, D.M. (2007). How well does
    the Gudjonsson Suggestibility Scale for Children, version 2 predict the recall
    of false details among children with and without intellectual disabilities?
    Legal and Criminological Psychology, 12, 217–232.

Milne, R., Clare, I.C.H., & Bull, R. (2002). Interrogative suggestibility among witnesses with mild intellectual disabilities: The use of an adaptation of the GSS. *Journal of Applied Research in Intellectual Disabilities, 15,* 8–17.

Nelson, K. (2003). Self and social functions: Individual autobiographical memory and collective narrative. *Memory, 11,* 125–136.

Nelson, K. & Fivush, R. (2004). The emergence of autobiographical memory: A social cultural developmental theory. *Psychological Review, 111,* 486–511.

Paz-Alonso, P.M., Larson, R.P., Castelli, P., Alley, D., & Goodman, G.S. (2009). Memory development: emotion, stress, and trauma. In M.L. Courage, & N. Cowan (Eds), *The Development of Memory in Infancy and Childhood* (2nd edn; pp. 197–239). New York: Psychology Press.

Perner, J., Leekam, S.R., & Wimmer, H. (1987). Three-year-olds' difficulty with false belief: The case for a conceptual deficit. *British Journal of Developmental Psychology, 5,* 125–137.

Principe, G.F., Guiliano, S., & Root, C. (2008). Rumor mongering and remembering: How rumors originating in children's inferences can affect memory. *Journal of Experimental Child Psychology, 99,* 135–155.

Quas, J.A., Carrick, N., Alkon, A., Goldstein, L., & Boyce, W.T. (2006). Children's memory for a mild stressor: The role of sympathetic activation and parasympathetic withdrawal. *Developmental Psychobiology, 48,* 686–702.

Quas, J.A., Qin, J., Schaaf, J.M., & Goodman, G.S. (1997). Individual differences in children's and adult's suggestibility and false event memory. *Learning and Individual Differences, 9,* 359–390.

Quas, J.A., & Schaaf, J.M. (2002). Children's memories for experienced and nonexperienced events following repeated interviews. *Journal of Experimental Psychology, 83,* 304–338.

Reese, E., Haden, C.A., & Fivush, R. (1993). Mother–child conversations about the past: Relationships of style and memory over time. *Cognitive Development, 8,* 403–430.

Reynolds, C.R., & Bigler, E.R. (1994). *Test of Memory and Learning (TOMAL).* Austin, TX: Pro-Ed.

Roebers, C.M., & Schneider, W. (2005). Individual differences in young children's suggestibility: Relations to event memory, language abilities, working memory, and executive functioning. *Cognitive Development, 20,* 427–447.

Scullin, M.H., & Bonner, K. (2006). Theory of mind, inhibitory control, and preschool-age children's suggestibility in different interviewing contexts. *Journal of Experimental Child Psychology, 93,* 120–138.

Scullin, M. H., & Ceci, S. J. (2001). A suggestibility scale for children. *Personality and Individual Differences, 30,* 843–856.

Scullin, M.H., Kanaya, T., & Ceci, S.J. (2002). Measurement of individual differences in children's suggestibility across situations. *Journal of Experimental Psychology: Applied, 8,* 233–246.

Shapiro, L.R., & Purdy, T. (2005). Suggestibility and source monitoring errors: Blame the interview style, interviewer consistency, and the child's personality. *Applied Cognitive Psychology, 19,* 489–506.

Sharp, H. (2001). Challenging crime and harassment against people with learning difficulties. *Mental Health Care & Learning Disabilities, 4,* 398–400.

Stein, N.L., & Levine, L.J. (1989). The causal organization of emotional knowledge: A developmental study. *Cognition and Emotion, 3,* 343–378.

Stein, N.L., & Levine, L.J. (1990). Making sense out of emotion: The representation and use of goal-structured knowledge. In N.L. Stein, B. Leventhal, & T. Trabasso (Eds), *Psychological and Biological Approaches to Emotion* (pp. 45–73). Hillsdale, NJ: Erlbaum.

Stein, N.L., & Liwag, M.D. (1997). Children's understanding, evaluation, and memory for emotional events. In P.W. van den Broek, P.J. Bauer, & T. Bourg

(Eds), *Developmental Spans in Event Comprehension and Representation: Bridging Fictional and Actual Events* (pp. 199–235). Hillsdale, NJ: Erlbaum.

Stein, N.L., Liwag, M.D., & Wade, E. (1996). A goal-based approach to memory for emotional events: Implications for theories of understanding and socialization. In R.D. Kavanaugh, B. Zimmerberg, & S. Fein (Eds), *Emotion: Interdisciplinary Perspectives* (pp. 91–118). Mhawah, NJ: Erlbaum.

Sullivan, P.M., & Knutson, J.F. (2000). Maltreatment and disabilities: A population-based epidemiological study. *Child Abuse & Neglect, 24,* 1257–1273.

Templeton, L.M., & Wilcox, S.A. (2000). A tale of two representations: The misinformation effect and children's developing theory of mind. *Child Development, 71,* 402–416.

Thomsen, Y., & Bernsten, D. (2005). Knowing that I didn't know: Preschoolers' understanding of their own false belief is a predictor of assents to fictitious events. *Applied Cognitive Psychology, 19,* 507–527.

Weiss, B., Weisz, J.R., & Bromfield, R. (1986). Performance of retarded and nonretarded persons on information-processing tasks: Further tests of the similar structure hypothesis. *Psychological Bulletin, 100,* 157–175.

Welch-Ross, M.K. (1999a). Preschoolers' understanding of mind: Implications for suggestibility. *Cognitive Development, 14,* 101–131.

Welch-Ross, M.K. (1999b). Interviewer knowledge and preschoolers' reasoning about knowledge states moderate suggestibility. *Cognitive Development, 14,* 423–442.

Welch-Ross, M.K., Diecidue, K., & Miller, S.A. (1997). Young children's understanding of conflicting mental representations predicts suggestibility. *Developmental Psychology, 33,* 43–53.

Wellman, H. M., Cross, D., & Watson, J. (2001). Meta-analysis of theory-of-mind development: The truth about false belief. *Child Development, 72,* 655–684.

Westcott, H. (1991). The abuse of disabled children: A review of the literature. *Child Care Health and Development, 174,* 243–258.

Williams, C. (1995). *Invisible Victims: Crime and Abuse against People with Learning Difficulties.* London: Jessica Kingsley Publishers.

Wilson, C., & Brewer, N. (1992). The incidence of criminal victimisation of individuals with an intellectual disability. *Australian Psychologist, 27,* 114–117.

Young, K., Powell, M.B., & Dudgeon, P. (2003). Individual differences in children's suggestibility: A comparison between intellectually disabled and mainstream sample. *Personality and Individual Differences, 35,* 31–49.

Zaragoza, M.S., Belli, R.S., & Payment, K.E. (2006). Misinformation effects and the suggestibility of eyewitness memory. In M. Garry, & H. Hayne (Eds), *Do Justice and Let the Sky Fall: Elizabeth F. Loftus and Her Contributions to Science, Law, and Academic Freedom* (pp. 35–63). Hillsdale, NJ: Lawrence Erlbaum Associates.

8

Suggestibility in Vulnerable Groups: Witnesses with Intellectual Disability, Autism Spectrum Disorder, and Older People

KATIE L. MARAS AND RACHEL WILCOCK

INTRODUCTION

The term 'vulnerable witnesses' is used to encompass a heterogeneous group of individuals that includes intimidated witnesses, children, witnesses with mental disorders, physical disabilities, intellectual disabilities, and those with autism spectrum disorder (Ministry of Justice, 2011). In this chapter we focus on suggestibility in adult witnesses with intellectual disability, autism spectrum disorder, and older people. We will consider each of these groups in turn.

KEY POINTS

- An overview of the condition and its relevance to the Criminal Justice System.

Suggestibility in Legal Contexts: Psychological Research and Forensic Implications,
First Edition. Edited by Anne M. Ridley, Fiona Gabbert and David J. La Rooy.
© 2013 John Wiley & Sons, Ltd. Published 2013 by John Wiley & Sons, Ltd.

- The factors that increase vulnerability to suggestibility.
- Review of the existing studies that have specifically examined suggestibility in each of these groups.
- Identification of the key findings for practitioners.

INTELLECTUAL DISABILITY

Intellectual Disability and the Criminal Justice System

Intellectual disability (ID) is characterized by significantly sub-average general intellectual functioning, with an IQ of less than 70 (Luckasson, *et al.*, 2002). People with ID can have impairments in a range of areas, including communication, self-care, home living, social/interpersonal skills, self-direction and functional academic skills. They also have abnormalities in cognitive processing, with deficits in areas of attention and memory (American Psychiatric Association, 2000).

Individuals with ID comprise around 1% of the population (Hatton, Emerson, Bromley, & Caine, 1998), but it is likely that a disproportionately higher percentage than this pass through the Criminal Justice System (CJS) as witnesses, victims or suspects. For example, they may be more vulnerable to being exploited by others to commit crimes on their behalf (Perske, 2004) and are often the sole witnesses to crimes (Gudjonsson, Murphy, & Clare, 2000). Moreover, people with ID are at an increased risk of entering into the CJS as victims of physical attacks (Nettelbeck & Wilson, 2002), and sexual attacks and exploitation (Tharinger, Horton, & Millea, 1990). In this context it is important to understand the reliability of the accounts provided by witnesses with ID, as well as how prone they are to suggestive influences.

Why Might People with ID be Vulnerable to Suggestibility?

Cognitive factors including poorer memory in ID can mean difficulties encoding and retrieving memory for an event (see Lifshitz, Shtein, Weiss, & Vakil, 2011, for a meta-analysis). Poorer memory can then lead to increased suggestibility through feelings of uncertainty, at which point social factors also come into play. For example, individuals with ID tend to be more reliant on authority figures for information, and have a greater desire to please (Perske, 2004). This means that they are more likely to acquiesce when they have a poor memory of the event, and perceive themselves to be of low status and the interviewer to be of high status, leading to the perception that 'the interviewer must be right' (Heal & Sigelman, 1995).

Nevertheless, there is consistent evidence demonstrating that the accounts given by individuals with ID are often as accurate as their general population counterparts in response to *free-recall* or *open-ended* prompts, although the information may not be as complete as that provided by non-ID individuals (Cederborg, Hultman, & La Rooy, 2012; Perlman, Ericson, Esses, & Isaacs, 1994). As a result, interviewers may rely on a greater number of closed and specific prompts when interviewing them (Cederborg & Lamb, 2008; Kebbell, Hatton, & Johnson, 2004), which results in more detailed but less accurate information (Cardone & Dent, 1996; Kebbell & Hatton, 1999; Perlman *et al.*, 1994; Sigelman, Budd, Spanhel, & Schoenrock, 1981; Ternes & Yuille, 2008). Kebbell, Milne, and Wagstaff (1999) suggested that this effect is best understood in terms of the different social and cognitive demands associated with different types of question. For example, open prompts elicit details based on what the witness can 'freely' remember, whereas more specific and closed prompts can lead the witness to report what they feel is expected by the interviewer (Clare & Gudjonsson, 1993), rendering individuals with ID vulnerable to suggestive influences.

Cognitive limitations associated with ID can also lead to difficulties in understanding the questions asked by interviewers. For example, individuals with ID often experience difficulties in remembering dates and times (Clements, 1998), which Ericson, Perlman, and Isaacs (1994) propose can lead to increased suggestibility for questions pertaining to numbers, dates and times, and how long an event lasted. Moreover, working memory limitations (Henry, Cornoldi, & Mahler, 2010) can cause difficulties in understanding and answering long or complex questions with multiple parts (Ericson *et al.*, 1994). Difficulties in remembering the reply choices can lead to biased responding to questions by individuals with ID, such as simply selecting the latter option in two false alternative questions (Milne, Clare, & Bull, 2002; Prosser & Bromley, 1998), and 'yea-saying' or 'nay-saying' (Shaw & Budd, 1982). Similarly, questions containing negatives, double negatives, and advanced vocabulary (e.g. 'occluded') are also problematic, yet this sort of language is favoured by lawyers in court (Kebbell *et al.*, 2004).

While individuals with ID are relatively more prone to biased responding than non-ID individuals to closed questions, this does not equate to them actually holding their responses as true accounts of their memory. Gudjonsson (2003) terms this *acquiescence*, which is the tendency of an individual to answer questions in the affirmative irrespective of the content (Cronbach, 1946). Another factor that can influence acquiescence is repeated prompts, where individuals with ID will change around 40% of their responses when asked the same question a second time, because they perceive this to signal that their initial response was unacceptable or incorrect (Cederborg, Danielsson, La Rooy, & Lamb, 2009; Sigelman *et al.*, 1981). Paradoxically, however, witnesses with ID may actually find themselves more likely to be asked repeated questions due to difficulties in understanding what was meant by the question and each of its components. One obvious solution to this problem would be for the interviewer to give shorter and simpler prompts. This is especially important where complex or adult terminology is concerned, for example, that regarding sexuality and sexual abuse. People with ID often have emotional and social insecurities and a lack of education regarding issues of sexuality and sexual abuse (Tharinger *et al.*, 1990), and thus may also be more suggestible to questions pertaining to these issues.

Taken together, the factors just discussed indicate that individuals with ID will be more vulnerable to suggestive questioning styles than their non-ID typical counterparts. Accordingly, interviewer guidelines throughout the world attempt to accommodate the needs of vulnerable witnesses. This guidance is welcome in the light of two studies examining the field data of forensic information with ID individuals, which are summarized next.

Research Exploring Suggestibility in ID Individuals

Kebbell *et al.* (2004) examined the types of questions lawyers asked witnesses with ID in court, and found that despite their well-documented increased susceptibility to suggestive questioning styles, witnesses with ID were questioned in an almost identical manner to witnesses from the general population. In fact, the ID group were actually asked more multiple questions (6% of questions) than were their general population counterparts (3% of questions). Kebbell *et al.* also found that the ID witnesses gave shorter answers (mean=3.53 words) and were more likely to agree with leading questions than their typical counterparts (who responded to leading questions with a mean of 9.60 words).

More recently, Cederborg and Lamb (2008) examined the transcripts of 12 police interviews of alleged victims of crime with ID. They found that police officers used directive questions (focusing attention on details of the incident that the witness had already mentioned) and option-posing utterances (focusing the witness' attention on details the witness has not previously mentioned) equally often. Moreover, police officers questioned all witnesses similarly, regardless of the witnesses' type of disability, and asked a high number of option-posing (32% of questions) and suggestive questions (6% of questions).

As both studies by Cederborg and Lamb (2008) and Kebbell *et al.* (2004) used real-life interviews, it was not possible to ascertain the accuracy of witnesses' responses to these question types. While it should also be noted that this is a largely unexplored area, the available evidence from these two studies, together with empirical findings demonstrating the detrimental effects on accuracy of these question types, suggests that the ways in which individuals with ID are currently interviewed by the police is not ideal.

A widely used measure of suggestibility is the Gudjonsson Suggestibility Scales (GSS), discussed in detail in Chapter 3. Studies that have used the GSS have found that reports of increased suggestibility in ID are consistent with a higher rate of 'Yield' (susceptibility to misleading questions) responses on the GSS (Cardone & Dent, 1996; Clare & Gudjonsson, 1993). Interestingly, however, there is no difference between ID and comparison groups on their 'Shift' scores – that is, their susceptibility to interrogative pressure as measured by changing their responses when asked a second time around following negative feedback (Gudjonsson & Clare, 1995; Gudjonsson *et al.*, 2000; Milne *et al.*, 2002). According to Gudjonsson (2003), Yield scores are influenced by memory processes, while Shift scores are more biased by social and anxiety processes; a conjecture that clearly explains the higher Yield scores in ID, given that poorer memory is associated with ID. However, Shift scores may be unaffected in ID either because people with ID are not more anxious (but see Reid, Smiley, & Cooper, 2011), or because, given that all 20 questions of the GSS are asked in succession before they are repeated, individuals with ID simply cannot remember what their first response was when asked a second time around. If they were inclined to bow to interrogative pressure, this could actually make them more accurate because they would not remember the direction from which to shift.

While it seems that when tested with the GSS, individuals with ID have poorer recall and are more suggestible than the general population, these studies have been criticized for presenting the to-be-remembered event in only one modality – verbally – and that the to-be-remembered narrative bears little resemblance to a personally experienced event (Willner, 2008). This point is particularly pertinent given that low intellectual ability correlates with poor *verbal* recall, and thus with high suggestibility and acquiescence on the GSS (Milne *et al.*, 2002). Experimental work that has modified the presentation of the GSS by using audio-visual material has found improved recall and Yield scores in individuals with ID (Cardone & Dent, 1996), because the dual presentation of the to-be-remembered information in both auditory and visual modalities strengthens the original memory and leads to more resistance to leading questions (Gudjonsson, 1992). Since Shift responses are thought to be more related to mood and personality characteristics and less to memory factors (Gudjonsson, 1992; Sharrock & Gudjonsson, 1993), these are relatively unchanged by the dual presentation of material in visual and verbal modalities (Cardone & Dent, 1996). However, it should be noted that not all research that has modified the GSS to include visual material reports this improvement in Yield scores. Milne *et al.* (2002) adapted the GSS to include questions pertaining to a previously witnessed event recorded on video so that it contained both visual and verbal information, and reported identical findings to those obtained with the GSS.

Beail (2002) has suggested that poor memory for narratives by individuals with ID could make them more suggestible for events that were not actually experienced. Beail's argument is that narrative-based tasks require different memory processes than event-based tasks. This conjecture is supported by evidence from White and Willner (2005) who found that total suggestibility, as measured both by Yield and by Shift scores, was reduced by nearly two-thirds for an event that individuals with ID had personally witnessed compared to the GSS. Since most eye-witness events are both personally experienced and visually perceived, individuals with ID might actually be much less suggestible to misleading forms of questioning than would be predicted by the GSS. Indeed Willner (2011) has gone so far as to say that for these reasons the GSS should not be used to assess the suggestibility of people with ID at all. Nevertheless, this is an area that needs more research.

To summarize, individuals with ID are, on the whole, more suggestible than their non-ID counterparts. They are likely to give shorter answers to questions, are more prone to biased responding (especially to questions that require only an acquiescent 'yes' response) and are particularly vulnerable to misleading questions. However, just because they are more suggestible to certain questioning styles does not mean that they make bad witnesses; even in response to specific misleading questions individuals with ID are still around 84% accurate (Perlman *et al.*, 1994). Further, caution must be exercized in generalising laboratory findings to real-life cases, and it must be emphasised that witnesses with ID are not a homogeneous group and should not be treated as such. While the research reported in this chapter provides insights into the suggestibility of individuals with ID, future work is still needed to explore individual differences in suggestibility in ID in more depth.

AUTISM SPECTRUM DISORDER

Autism Spectrum Disorder (ASD) and the Prevalence of Individuals with ASD in the Criminal Justice System

Autism spectrum disorder (ASD) affects approximately 1% of the population and is around three to four times more common in males than females (Baird, Simonoff, & Pickles, 2006). However, as is the case with ID, a number of risk factors indicate that individuals with ASD may be over-represented within the CJS as witnesses, victims or perpetrators of crime (Hare, Gould, Mills, & Wing, 1999; Petersilia, 2001). For example, their diminished insight into what others are thinking, and their repetitive and stereotyped interests, can render them vulnerable to exploitation or victimization by others (Allen, Evans, Hider, Hawkins, Peckett, & Morgan, 2008; Howlin, 1997).

ASD is clinically characterized by deficits in reciprocal social interaction and communication in the presence of repetitive and stereotyped patterns of behaviour (American Psychiatric Association, 2000). It is often difficult for individuals with ASD to understand complex emotions, and recognize that others' perspectives and knowledge may differ from their own (i.e. 'theory of mind'; Baron-Cohen, 2001). They also demonstrate difficulties with *executive functions*, which are higher-order cognitive operations that allow the flexible shifting of attention, and control and regulation of other abilities and behaviours (Bennetto, Pennington, & Rogers, 1996). Because of the wide variations in its manifestation, it is considered a spectrum disorder with varying degrees of severity. The term 'ASD' is commonly used to include the different variants of the condition, from Kanner's (1943) 'classic' autism that is typically accompanied by learning disabilities with an IQ less than 70 and language delay, to high-functioning autism and Asperger syndrome with the core autistic symptoms but normal or above normal IQ, and in Asperger syndrome without the history of language delay. The ASD population is extremely heterogeneous in terms of general cognitive functioning and language, and while there is still officially a distinction between Asperger syndrome and autism, there is no conclusive evidence for this. For the purposes of the present chapter it is the *DSM-IV-TR* (*Diagnostic and Statistical Manual of Mental Disorders*, American Psychiatric Association, 2000) framework that will be adopted here, and the term ASD will be used to encompass all variants of the condition, although there will be differences between the variants, for example, if ASD is accompanied by severe ID.

Apart from the clinical dysfunctions, ASD is also characterized by a unique cognitive profile including sensory and motor abnormalities (see Dawson & Watling, 2000, for a review), and impairments in selective attention with difficulties in filtering out irrelevant information, which often leads to bombardment with sensory information and over-arousal (Burack, 1994; Ciesielski, Courchesne, & Elmasian, 1990; Remington, Swettenham, Campbell, & Coleman, 2009). Furthermore, as will be discussed in the next section, individuals with ASD have very specific memory impairments, which some have argued may even account for some of the diversity of behavioural features that characterize the disorder (Boucher & Bowler, 2008).

Why Might People with ASD be Vulnerable to Suggestibility?

In contrast to witnesses with ID who tend to have more global deficits, individuals with ASD demonstrate a rather distinctive memory profile of specific strengths and weaknesses. For example, they tend to show intact performance on tests of cued recall (Bennetto *et al.*, 1996; Tager-Flusberg, 1991), recognition (Bennetto *et al.*, 1996; Minshew &

Goldstein, 1993), and memory for facts (Crane & Goddard, 2008). However, they have difficulty with recognizing faces (Blair, Frith, Smith, Abell, & Cipolotti, 2002) and in organizing their memories in a semantically meaningful way (Bowler, Gaigg, & Gardiner, 2008). They also show impairments on tests of episodic memory (Bowler, Gardiner, & Grice, 2000; Crane & Goddard, 2008) and have particular difficulties with recalling events that were *personally experienced* (Crane, Goddard, & Pring, 2009; Klein, Chan, & Loftus, 1999; Millward, Powell, Messer, & Jordan, 2000). Moreover, people with ASD have difficulties monitoring the source of their memories: the *who, what, where,* or *when* (Bowler *et al.*, 2000). These difficulties in source monitoring can, however, be eliminated if more support is provided when their memories are tested, for example, by using cued rather than free recall test procedures (Bowler, Gardiner, & Berthollier, 2004).

Research Exploring Suggestibility in ASD

Despite the memory difficulties outlined above, very few studies have examined suggestibility in adults with ASD from a forensic perspective (see Maras & Bowler, in press, for a review). North, Russell and Gudjonsson (2008) administered the GSS2 and several mental state measures known to correlate with suggestibility to high-functioning individuals with ASD and an IQ-matched typical comparison group. There were no differences between groups on the suggestibility measures for Yield or Shift scores, but consistent with previous work, the ASD group scored higher on depression, anxiety, fear of negative social evaluation and paranoia measures (Cath, Ran, Smit, van Balkom, & Comijs, 2008). North *et al.* suggested that although the ASD participants included in their study were susceptible to many of the risk factors for increased Shift scores (such as anxiety and fear of disapproval), they were not able, or willing (because of their executive function deficits) to shift their responses on the GSS, and thus scored similarly to their typical counterparts. Alternatively, it is also possible that the ASD group simply failed to recognize that the motivations or intentions of the interviewer were to elicit a different response by providing negative feedback. The finding that the ASD group were no more suggestible as measured by Yield scores supports the notion that this measure is influenced by more cognitive factors, as the ASD group in this study had apparently good memory (good recall scores and high IQ that was matched to the comparison group). The ASD group did, however, score higher on the measure of compliance (the Gudjonsson Compliance Scale, GCS) than their typical matched counterparts. This is not surprising, as the above psychological trait measures that the ASD group scored highly on are known to correlate with GCS scores (Gudjonsson, 1988). North and colleagues have interpreted these findings as indicating that individuals with ASD might be more vulnerable in an interrogative interview than people from the general population. However, given the scarcity of this research, any conclusions must be made cautiously, and it will be important for future work to extend these findings using more ecologically valid compliance scenarios.

Maras and Bowler (2011) also found comparable levels of suggestibility between ASD witnesses and their IQ-matched comparison participants using a misinformation paradigm with standard test. They showed participants a slide sequence of photographs depicting a bank robbery. Participants later read an extract from a mock newspaper clipping that contained several details of misinformation, some of which were schema-typical (e.g. that the robbers were carrying a gun), and some of which was schema-atypical (e.g. that the robbers removed their balaclavas). Both groups went on to incorporate more schema-typical misinformation (mean number of intrusions: ASD participants=1.75; comparison participants=1.31), but not the schema-atypical misinformation (mean number of intrusions: ASD participants=0.31; comparison participants=0.25), into their subsequent memory reports. These findings suggest that individuals with ASD are no more susceptible to misinformation than typical individuals, and that both ASD and typical individuals are more suggestible when the misinformation fits with their existing schemas for events of that kind.

Based on this very sparse work, we can cautiously conclude that high-functioning individuals with ASD are as suggestible as their typical counterparts, despite a number of factors predicting that they might differ in this respect. It is worth mentioning, that because some factors predict that they might be *more* suggestible (e.g. memory difficulties and increased desire to please), while other factors predict they might be *less* suggestible (e.g. intact rote memory and local processing style), these factors might simply cancel each other out. On that note, the difference between high and low functioning individuals with ASD in terms of IQ and memory needs to be highlighted. That is, lower functioning individuals experience a double blow as far as potential suggestibility is concerned: they have a broader memory impairment associated with their lower intellectual functioning (Boucher, Mayes, & Bigham, 2008), in addition to their specific memory difficulties. Future work is needed to explore suggestibility in low-functioning people with ASD.

OLDER WITNESSES

Ageing and the Prevalence of Older Witnesses in the Criminal Justice System

Defining when a witness becomes an 'older witness' is fraught with difficulty. However, in the research that will be discussed below, researchers have classified older witnesses as either 60 and over, or 65 and over. In the United Kingdom, by 2020 one in five people will be aged 65 years and over. This means there will be more people over 65 years old than people aged 16 years and under (Allan, 2008). Despite these figures and other figures from developed countries around the world suggesting that we have an ageing population (see, for example, Eurostat, 2010 and Aging in the Americas in the 21st Century), eyewitness researchers have mostly focused on examining the performance of young adult witnesses and child witnesses. Nevertheless, older adults may witness crime (Wilcock, Bull, & Milne, 2008) and be targets for certain types of crime. For example, Thornton *et al.* (2003) suggest that the majority of victims in distraction burglaries are older adults. Furthermore, older adults are consistently the victims of crimes of elder abuse and neglect (Görgen, 2006) and financial scam crimes (Nerenberg, 2000). Thus, there is a need to examine the abilities of older witnesses. The remainder of this chapter will contain a brief discussion of why older adults may be more susceptible to suggestibility, before reviewing the limited literature examining the performance of older adults in terms of their eyewitness suggestibility.

Why Might Older People be Vulnerable to Suggestibility?

There are a number of reasons why older adults may be more prone to suggestibility when compared to younger adults that relate to what happens when we perceive, encode and retrieve information from memory as we age. When perceiving a crime, older adults are immediately at a disadvantage compared to younger adults due to losses in the sensory systems. Changes in the structures of the eye associated with ageing result in less efficient processing of visual stimuli, and half of individuals aged between 75 and 79 years have measurable hearing loss (Schneider & Pichora-Fuller, 2000). To successfully encode information, witnesses must selectively pay attention to the crime event while ignoring other surrounding irrelevant information. Evidence suggests that older adults are more likely to demonstrate attentional deficits (McDowd & Shaw, 2000), meaning that they may not encode information as efficiently as younger adults. With respect to contextual information (items important for making memories distinctive), Rabinowitz, Craik, and Ackerman (1982) found that older adults were less likely to encode specific contextual details. Related to this, according to the Associative Deficit Hypothesis (Navah-Benjamin, 2000), older adults' episodic memory performance declines because they experience difficulties associating or linking individual items of information to form a complete episode. Older adults are also more likely to have difficulty in correctly identifying the source of their memory compared to younger adults. For example, Hashtroudi, Johnson, and Chrosniak (1989) found that older adults were more likely to make mistakes in discriminating between words they said and words they thought, and between words one person said and words a different person said.

The effects of ageing outlined herein could mean that older adults are more susceptible to suggestibility than young adults. For example, if the crime event was not fully attended to and the event was not encoded sufficiently, this will lead to a weaker memory trace and poorer episodic memory. As discussed earlier, suggestibility is likely to be greater for those with poorer episodic memory. Because older adults are likely to have poor source memory, they may be particularly vulnerable to suggestibility. Eyewitnesses may view a crime, and afterwards learn incorrect information about it from other witnesses, the newspaper, or during an interview. However, compared to younger adults, older witnesses may be less successful at monitoring where they learnt such items of incorrect information. This could render them more likely to include these details in their account of the witnessed event, as they may believe it was part of what they witnessed. Because of the known effects of cognitive ageing on memory, older adults may be more suggestible than younger adults, and it is this issue that we now consider.

Research Exploring Suggestibility in Older Witnesses

Research adopting the misinformation paradigm has revealed mixed findings for older adults. Some studies show that older adults are more likely to be suggestible than younger adults. For example, Cohen and Faulkner (1989, experiment two) showed young adults (mean age 35 years) and older adults (mean age 70 years) a video recording and, after a short delay, half of the participants read a correct account of the video, and half read an account containing incorrect information. Following a further short delay, participants completed an 18-item multiple choice recognition test. There was no difference in performance between the two age groups on the non-critical questions (i.e. no misinformation). However, while for both age groups, participants in the misinformation condition were more suggestible for the critical (misinformed) items, the older misinformed participants had a significantly higher proportion of errors (0.57) than their younger counterparts (0.28). Furthermore, older participants were significantly more confident in the accuracy of their incorrect responses to the critical items than younger participants. The authors suggested that because there was no difference between the age groups in their accuracy on the non-critical items, the older adults' increased proneness to misinformation is unlikely to reflect an age deficit in older adults' memory for the to-be-remembered event. Instead, the authors suggested that older participants' greater susceptibility to the misinformation effect may be due to poorer source monitoring ability. Similar results have been found by Loftus, Levidow, and Duensing (1992).

Two further studies which used a source identification task also found older adults to be more suggestible, and examined in greater depth the circumstances that may affect suggestibility in older adults. Karpel, Hoyer, and Toglia (2001) investigated whether a greater opportunity to encode the to-be-remembered event would modify the misinformation effect shown by older adults, but found that even with a second exposure to the event, older participants were more suggestible than younger participants (who had also been exposed to the event twice). Mitchell, Johnson, and Mather (2003) investigated the effect of explicitly identifying different sources of misinformation by explaining that some statements contained information only found in the video, some statements contained information only found in the questions, and some statements did not contain information from either the video or the questions. Furthermore, participants were told to make judgements based on their own memory to help ensure that the researchers were measuring false memory rather than other aspects of suggestibility such as demand characteristics. For misattributions of critical items to the video, it was found that older participants were significantly more likely than younger participants to say they had seen items that had only been suggested to them. Both Karpel *et al.* (2001) and Mitchell *et al.* (2003) investigated the relationship between participants' self-reported ratings of confidence and the accuracy of their answers. Across both studies older adults were significantly more confident in the accuracy of their answers that contained suggested information than were young adults.

A study examining older witnesses' suggestibility for aspects of a live event consisting of a massage of participants' backs, necks and shoulders, showed that overall older adults were more suggestible than younger adults (0.49 and 0.21 for older and younger adults, respectively; Mueller-Johnson & Ceci, 2004). However, there were differences in suggestibility for misinformation that related to different aspects of the event. For example, for suggestions about participant involvement, such as where on their body they had been touched, older adults showed a larger misinformation effect than younger adults. The authors correctly identify this as a worrying finding considering that older adults are likely to be victims of elder abuse (see above). Conversely, for other suggestions including what the massage therapist had been wearing, younger adults were in fact more suggestible than older adults. The authors suggest that possibly neither group of participants effectively encoded details relating to clothing, and then the younger participants had a better memory for the misinformation, thus they were more suggestible for this item than other items. The authors of this study also examined how suggestibility affected participants' self-reported confidence in the accuracy of their answers. Younger adults were less confident in the accuracy of answers which incorporated misinformation than answers that did not contain misinformation, while no such difference was observed with older adults.

Further studies examining older witnesses' suggestibility have focused on the very real problem of what happens after witnesses view a crime and discuss it with fellow witnesses, which can result in memory conformity. Possibly, misinformation encountered in this social manner could be more detrimental than misinformation presented in misinformation paradigm studies. Gabbert, Memon, Allan, and Wright (2004) asked young adults (mean age 20 years) and older adults (mean age 69 years) to view a simulated robbery. Participants either watched the video with a confederate whom participants believed to be a fellow participant or watched the event alone. After a short delay they completed a 20-item cued recall questionnaire. Afterwards, participants who watched the event with the confederate had a discussion during which the confederate either disclosed four pieces of misinformation or disclosed no misinformation. Participants who watched the event alone read a narrative that either contained the same misinformation discussed by the confederate or contained no misinformation. After a further short delay, participants answered the same questionnaire with the instruction to answer it using information from the video. The data showed that both younger and older participants who received socially encountered misinformation reported more misinformation than participants who read the misinformation from the narrative. Despite older participants having poorer recall for the event than younger participants, they reported less misinformation than younger participants. These findings are similar to those reported by Gabbert, Memon, and Allan (2003) who found that although older participants had a poorer memory for the event, they were no more likely to yield to misinformation than younger participants. The authors suggest that young adults may be more susceptible to socially encountered misinformation because of a desire for social approval. However, in both studies the recall tests were completed in private so this may not explain the finding. An alternative explanation the authors put forward was that discussion with a co-witness could equate to environmental support that aids older adults' memory for what they saw versus what they discussed. Related to the discussion above on the effect of age on self-reported confidence ratings, Gabbert *et al.* (2003) examined ratings of confidence in the accuracy of answers that either relied on co-witness information or did not. The authors found that young participants reported lower ratings of confidence in the accuracy of their answers that relied on information provided by a co-witness compared to those that did not rely on co-witness information. However, for older adults there was no difference in ratings of confidence between answers that relied on co-witness information and those that did not, thus replicating the findings of other researchers, mentioned above.

Other studies have also found older adults to be no more suggestible than younger adults. Coxon and Valentine (1997) showed young adults (mean age 17) and older adults (mean age 70) a video followed by 17 questions, four of which contained misinformation. After a short delay participants were given a further 20 questions, four of which pertained to the misleading information. All of the questions required participants to give short recall answers. Older participants were less accurate on the non-critical questions than younger adults, as one would expect bearing in mind a recall task demands active retrieval of information from memory which a recognition task does not. For the critical questions relating to the misinformation, 39% of young adults who received misinformation gave suggestible answers compared to 14% of young adult controls – a statistically significant difference. However, 39% of older adults in the misinformation condition gave suggestible responses compared to 24% in the control condition, which was not significantly different. Thus, in this study, older witnesses were no more suggestible than younger witnesses, however, it must be borne in mind that older participants had poorer memory for the non-critical items than the younger participants, and those older participants in the control condition gave more misled responses than young participants in the control condition.

This tendency for older adults to make false recognitions in the control condition should be taken into account when examining data from studies that have found older adults to be no more suggestible than young adults or indeed young adults to be more suggestible than older adults. If older adults are making errors even though they have not received misinformation, then any suggestibility demonstrated by participants receiving misinformation will be masked. For example, Bornstein, Witt, Cherry, and Greene (2000) found a misinformation effect in young participants and no misinformation effect in older participants. The absence of a misinformation effect in older participants could be attributed to their poor performance in the control condition (80% correct) and this only fell to 75% correct for those in the misinformation condition. Thus, as recommended by Bartlett and Memon (2007), young and old adults need to be matched in the control condition in order to build up a true picture of the suggestibility effect in older adults.

Dodson and Krueger (2006) attempted to address this by testing three groups of participants: a young group (mean age 19 years) and an older group (mean age 68 years) who were both subject to the same conditions, and a further young group (mean age 20 years) who were subject to a 2-day delay prior to completing their test of suggestibility. The data on correct recognition and source memory performance showed, as expected, no significant differences between older participants and young-delay participants and that young participants (not subject to a delay) demonstrated significantly better performance than the other two groups. The authors had therefore been successful in matching 'control' performance between their young and old participants. In terms of suggestibility, the older and young-delay groups were more suggestible than the young group and there were no differences in suggestibility between the older and young-delay groups. Consistent with the research reported above, the authors found that older adults were more likely to be extremely confident in the accuracy of their suggestible responses while younger adults lacked confidence in the accuracy of their suggestible responses.

Only one study has compared the performance of young and old adults on interrogative suggestibility as measured by the GSS. Polczyk *et al.* (2004) found that older participants were more likely to be suggestible as measured by Yield 1, Yield 2, and total suggestibility compared to younger participants. However, there was no significant difference between younger and older participants with regard to Shift. In addition, the authors tested participants on the Wechsler Memory Scale and a self-assessment of memory. They found that memory was poorer in older participants than younger participants and suggested that older participants compared to younger participants had a higher suggestibility score because of poorer memory. In contrast, on the Shift score, older participants resisted the negative feedback because they were more self-confident and less susceptible to social influences. Furthermore, the age range for the older participants was very wide and a few were considerably below the normal threshold that would be considered an older age (60 years). In light of this, further research needs to be conducted using the GSS with older adults before any firm conclusions can be reached.

On the basis of the limited research undertaken examining suggestibility in older adults, the balance of evidence indicates that they may be more prone to suggestibility than younger adults, possibly because of the effect of cognitive ageing on memory. Furthermore, it seems that older witnesses have significantly greater confidence in the accuracy of their suggestible answers compared to young adults. This has implications for the courtroom, bearing in mind the weight that jurors attach to confident witnesses (Cutler, Penrod, & Stuve, 1988) and possibly for police officers who may also be affected by witness confidence. However, two things must be borne in mind when assessing the accuracy of older witnesses who may have been exposed to misleading information. First, the research reviewed above is based on laboratory studies. It is, therefore, unclear how these findings will translate into a real-life crime situation. Second, although older adults generally have poorer memory than younger adults, the effects of ageing on memory are not uniform. Thus, we must acknowledge the role of individual differences. By no means will all older adults be susceptible to suggestibility.

As discussed above, Gabbert *et al.* (2003, 2004) found that although older adults had poorer event memory than younger adults, they were no more suggestible. The authors argued this could be because their older participants may not have been overly representative of the older adult population in that they were active and willing to travel to a university to engage in the research.

In conclusion, older witnesses tend to be more suggestible as a group and it is therefore important to reduce the opportunities for misinformation to occur by using good interviewing practice. If older witnesses do report misinformation, it is likely that they will be confident in the accuracy of their answers. Further investigation of the circumstances under which older adults may or may not be suggestible, and the role that individual differences play in suggestibility in older witnesses is warranted.

CONCLUSIONS

In this chapter we have considered witnesses with intellectual disability (ID), autism spectrum disorder (ASD), and older witnesses. Each of these vulnerable groups has a number of 'risk' factors that might make them more vulnerable to suggestibility. However, these predisposing features do not always equate to increased suggestibility in practice. To summarize:

- Witnesses with ID may be more suggestible to misleading questions. However, they are no more susceptible to interrogative pressure as measured by the 'Shift' component of the GSS.
- The limited work to date that has examined suggestibility in witnesses with ASD shows that high-functioning people with the disorder they are no more suggestible than their typical counterparts. However, future research is needed to extend this work to lower functioning individuals with ASD, who have broader memory impairments in addition to delayed or impaired language development.
- While older witnesses tend to be more suggestible and more confident about their responses, there are individual differences and it should be borne in mind that some will be resistant to suggestive influences.

FORENSIC IMPLICATIONS

- *Witnesses with ID find long and multiple-part questions difficult, and they are also particularly prone to biased responding.* Therefore, interviewers should phrase their questions using as few words as possible, while being careful not to rely on closed questions.

- *Investigative interviewers should be aware that witnesses with ASD may, under certain circumstances, be more compliant.* That is, while they are no more suggestible than their typical counterparts, people with ASD may be more likely to go along with suggestions even if they do not actually hold them as being a true account of events.
- *Interviewers should be particularly mindful that older witnesses and those with ID may be more suggestible under certain circumstances.* They should therefore avoid adopting a suggestive questioning style.
- *At present, investigative professionals know relatively little about how best to interview each of these vulnerable groups.* It will be important for these and future findings to be incorporated into guidelines and training for police, intermediaries, barristers and judges.

REFERENCES

Aging in the Americas into the 21st Century. www.census.gov/ipc/prod/ agegame.pdf. Retrieved 10 August 2010.

Allan, J. (2008). Older people and wellbeing. *Institute for Public Policy Research.*

Allen, D., Evans, C., Hider, A., Hawkins, S., Peckett, H., & Morgan, H. (2008). Offending behaviour in adults with Asperger syndrome. *Journal of Autism and Developmental Disorders, 38,* 748–758.

American Psychiatric Association (2000). *Diagnostic and Statistical Manual of Mental Disorders* (4th edn), *(DSM-IV).* Washington, DC: American Psychiatric Press.

Baird, G., Simonoff, E., Pickles, A., Chandler, S., Loucas, T., Meldrum, D., & Charman, T. (2006). Prevalence of disorders of the autism spectrum in a population cohort of children in South Thames: The Special Needs and Autism Project (SNAP). *Lancet, 368,* 210–215.

Baron-Cohen, S. (2001). Theory of mind and autism: A review. *International Review of Research in Mental Retardation: Autism, 23,* 169–184.

Bartlett, J.C., & Memon, A. (2007). Eyewitness memory in younger and older adults. In R.C.L. Lindsay, D.F. Ross, J.D. Read, & M.P. Toglia (Eds), *The Handbook of Eyewitness Psychology: Memory for People* (Vol. II, pp. 309–338), Hillsdale, NJ: Lawrence Erlbaum.

Beail, N. (2002). Interrogative suggestibility, memory and intellectual disability. *Journal of Applied Research in Intellectual Disabilities, 15,* 129–137.

Bennetto, L., Pennington, B.F., & Rogers, S.J. (1996). Intact and impaired memory functions in autism. *Child Development, 67,* 1816–1835.

Blair, R.J.R., Frith, U., Smith, N., Abell, F., & Cipolotti, L. (2002). Fractionation of visual memory: Agency detection and its impairment in autism. *Neuropsychologia, 40,* 108–118.

Bornstein, B.H., Witt, C.J., Cherry, K.E., & Greene, E. (2000). The suggestibility of older witnesses. In M.B. Rothman, B.D. Dunlop, & P. Entzel (Eds), *Elders, Crime, and the Criminal Justice System. Myth, Perceptions, and Reality in the 21st Century* (pp. 149–162). Series on Life Styles and Issues in Aging. New York: Springer.

Boucher, J., & Bowler, D. (2008). *Memory in Autism: Theory and Evidence.* New York, NY: Cambridge University Press.

Boucher, J., Mayes, A., & Bigham (2008). Memory, language and intellectual ability in low-functioning autism. In J. Boucher, & D.M. Bowler (Eds), *Memory in Autism* (pp. 330–349). Cambridge: Cambridge University Press.

Bowler, D.M., Gaigg, S.B., & Gardiner, J.M. (2008). Subjective organization in the free recall learning of adults with Asperger's syndrome. *Journal of Autism and Developmental Disorders, 38,* 104–113.

Bowler, D.M., Gardiner, J.M., & Berthollier, N. (2004). Source memory in adolescents and adults with Asperger's syndrome. *Journal of Autism and Developmental Disorders, 34,* 533–542.

Bowler, D.M., Gardiner, J.M., & Grice, S.J. (2000). Episodic memory and remembering in adults with Asperger's syndrome. *Journal of Autism and Developmental Disorders, 30,* 295–304.

Burack, J.A. (1994). Selective attention deficits in persons with autism: Preliminary evidence of an inefficient attentional lens. *Journal of Abnormal Psychology, 103*(3), 535–543.

Cardone, D., & Dent, H. (1996). Memory and interrogative suggestibility: The effects of modality of information presentation and retrieval conditions upon the suggestibility scores of people with learning disabilities. *Legal and Criminological Psychology, 1,* 165–177.

Cath, D.C., Ran, N., Smit, J.H., van Balkom, A.J.L.M., & Comijs, H.C. (2008). Symptom overlap between autism spectrum disorder, generalized social anxiety disorder and obsessive-compulsive disorder in adults: A preliminary case-controlled study. *Psychopathology, 41,* 101–110.

Cederborg, A.-C., Danielsson, H., La Rooy, D., & Lamb, M. (2009). Repetition of contaminating question types when children and youths with intellectual disabilities are interviewed. *Journal of Intellectual Disability Research, 53,* 440–449.

Cederborg, A.-C., Hultman, E., & La Rooy, D. (2012). The quality of details when children and youths with intellectual disabilities are interviewed about their abuse experiences. *Scandinavian Journal of Disability Research, 14,* 113–125.

Cederborg, A.-C., & Lamb, M. (2008). Interviewing alleged victims with intellectual disabilities. *Journal of Intellectual Disability Research, 52,* 49–58.

Ciesielski, K.T., Courchesne, E., & Elmasian, R. (1990). Effects of focused selective attention tasks on event-related potentials in autistic and normal individuals. *Electroencephalography & Clinical Neurophysiology, 75*(3), 207–220.

Clare, I.C., & Gudjonsson, G.H. (1993). Interrogative suggestibility, confabulation, and acquiescence in people with mild learning disabilities (mental handicap): Implications for reliability during police interrogations. *British Journal of Clinical Psychology, 32,* 295–301.

Clements, J. (1998). Development, cognition and performance. *Clinical Psychology and People with Intellectual Disabilities* (pp. 39–53). New York: John Wiley & Sons, Ltd.

Cohen, G., & Faulkner, D. (1989). Age differences in source forgetting: Effects on reality monitoring and on eyewitness testimony. *Psychology and Aging, 4,* 10–17.

Coxon, P., & Valentine, T. (1997). The effects of the age of eyewitnesses on the accuracy and suggestibility of their testimony. *Applied Cognitive Psychology, 11,* 415–430.

Crane, L., & Goddard, L. (2008). Episodic and semantic autobiographical memory in adults with autism spectrum disorders. *Journal of Autism and Developmental Disorders, 38,* 498–506.

Crane, L., Goddard, L., & Pring, L. (2009). Specific and general autobiographical knowledge in adults with autism spectrum disorders: The role of personal goals. *Memory, 17,* 557–576.

Cronbach, L.J. (1946). Response sets and test validity. *Educational and Psychological Measurement, 6,* 475–494.

Cutler, B.L., Penrod, S.D., & Stuve, T.E. (1988). Juror decision making in eyewitness identification cases. *Law and Human Behavior, 12,* 41–55.

Dawson, G., & Watling, R. (2000). Interventions to facilitate auditory, visual, and motor integration in autism: A review of the evidence. *Journal of Autism and Developmental Disorders, 30*(5), 415–421.

Dodson, C.S., & Krueger, L.E. (2006). I misremember it well: Why older adults are unreliable eyewitnesses. *Psychonomic Bulletin & Review, 15,* 770–775.

Ericson, K., Perlman, N., & Isaacs, B. (1994). Witness competency, communication issues and people with developmental disabilities. *Developmental Disabilities Bulletin, 22,* 101–109.

Eurostat (2010). http://epp.eurostat.ec.europa.eu/statistics_explained/index.php/Population_projections

Gabbert, F., Memon, A., & Allan, K. (2003). Memory conformity: Can eyewitnesses influence each other's memories for an event? *Applied Cognitive Psychology, 17,* 533–543.

Gabbert, F., Memon, A., Allan, K., & Wright, D.B. (2004). Say it to my face: Examining the effects of socially encountered misinformation. *Legal and Criminological Psychology, 9,* 215–227.

Gorgen, T. (2006). 'As if I didn't exist' – elder abuse and neglect in nursing homes. In A. Wahidn, & M. Cain (Eds), *Aging, Crime and Society* (pp. 71–89) Devon: Willan Publishing.

Gudjonsson, G.H. (1988). Interrogative suggestibility: Its relationship with assertiveness, social-evaluative anxiety, state anxiety and method of coping. *British Journal of Clinical Psychology, 27,* 159–166.

Gudjonsson G.H. (1992). *The Psychology of Interrogations, Confessions and Testimony*. Chichester: John Wiley & Sons, Ltd.

Gudjonsson, G.H. (2003). *The Psychology of Interrogations and Confessions: A Handbook*. New York: John Wiley & Sons, Ltd.

Gudjonsson, G.H., & Clare, I.C.H. (1995). The relationship between confabulation and intellectual ability, memory, interrogative suggestibility and acquiescence. *Personality and Individual Differences, 19,* 333–338.

Gudjonsson, G.H., Murphy, G.H., & Clare, I.C.H. (2000). Assessing the capacity of people with intellectual disabilities to be witnesses in court. *Psychological Medicine: A Journal of Research in Psychiatry and the Allied Sciences, 30,* 307–314.

Hare, D.J., Gould, J., Mills, R., & Wing, L. (1999). *A Preliminary Study of Individuals with Autistic Spectrum Disorders in Three Special Hospitals in England*. London: National Autistic Society.

Hashtroudi, S., Johnson, M.K., & Chrosniak, L.D. (1989). Aging and source monitoring. *Psychology and Aging, 4,* 106–112.

Hatton, C., Emerson, E., Bromley, J., & Caine, A. (1998). Intellectual disabilities and epidemiology and causes. In *Clinical Psychology and People with Intellectual Disabilities* (pp. 20–38). New York: John Wiley & Sons, Ltd.

Heal, L.W., & Sigelman, C.K. (1995). Response biases in interviews of individuals with limited mental ability. *Journal of Intellectual Disability Research, 39,* 331–340.

Henry, L., Cornoldi, C., & Mahler, C. (2010). Special issues on working memory and executive functioning in individuals with intellectual disabilities. *Journal of Intellectual Disability Research, 54,* 293–294.

Howlin, P. (1997). *Autism: Preparing for Adulthood*. London: Routledge.

Kanner, L. (1943). Autistic disturbances of affective contact. *Nervous Child, 2*, 217–250.

Karpel, M.E., Hoyer, W.J., & Toglia, M.P. (2001). Accuracy and qualities of real and suggested memories: Nonspecific age differences. *Journal of Gerontology, 56B*(2), 103–110.

Kebbell, M.R., & Hatton, C. (1999). People with mental retardation as witnesses in court: A review. *Mental Retardation, 37*, 179–187.

Kebbell, M.R., Hatton, C., & Johnson, S.D. (2004). Witnesses with intellectual disabilities in court: What questions are asked and what influence do they have? *Legal and Criminological Psychology, 9*, 23–35.

Kebbell, M.R., Milne, R., & Wagstaff, G.F. (1999). The cognitive interview: A survey of its forensic effectiveness. *Psychology Crime & Law, 5*, 101–115.

Klein, S. B., Chan, R. L., & Loftus, J. (1999). Independence of episodic and semantic self-knowledge: The case from autism. *Social Cognition, 17*, 413–436.

Lifshitz, H., Shtein, S., Weiss, I., & Vakil, E. (2011). Meta-analysis of explicit memory studies in populations with intellectual disability. *European Journal of Special Needs Education, 26*(1), 93–111.

Loftus, E.F., Levidow, B., & Duensing, S. (1992). Who remembers best? Individual differences in memory for events that occurred in a science museum. *Applied Cognitive Psychology, 6*, 93–107.

Luckasson, R., Borthwick-Duffy, S., Buntinx, W.H.E., Coulter, D.L., Craig, E.M., Reeve, A., Schalock, R. L., Snell, M.E., Spitalnik, D.M., Spreat, S., & Tassa, M.J. (2002). *Mental Retardation: Definition, Classification, and Systems of Supports* (10th edn). Washington, DC: American Association on Mental Retardation.

Maras, K.L., & Bowler, D.M. (in press). Eyewitness testimony in autism spectrum disorder: A review. *Journal of Autism and Developmental Disorders*.

Maras, K.L., & Bowler, D.M. (2011). Brief report: Schema consistent misinformation effects in eyewitnesses with autism spectrum disorder. *Journal of Autism and Developmental Disorders, 41*, 815–820.

McDowd, J.M., & Shaw, R.J. (2000). Attention and aging: A functional perspective. In F.I.M. Craik, & T.A. Salthouse (Eds), *The Handbook of Aging and Cognition* (2nd edn, pp. 221–292). Mahwah, NJ: Lawrence Erlbaum Associates Publishers.

Millward, C., Powell, S., Messer, D., & Jordan, R. (2000). Recall for self and other in autism: Children's memory for events experienced by themselves and their peers. *Journal of Autism and Developmental Disorders, 30*, 15–28.

Milne, R., Clare, I.C.H., & Bull, R. (2002). Interrogative suggestibility among witnesses with mild intellectual disabilities: The use of an adaptation of the GSS. *Journal of Applied Research in Intellectual Disabilities, 15*, 8–17.

Ministry of Justice (2011). *Achieving Best Evidence in Criminal Proceedings: Guidance on Interviewing Victims and Witnesses, and Guidance on using Special Measures* (3rd ed). London: Ministry of Justice.

Minshew, N.J., & Goldstein, G. (1993). Is autism an amnesic disorder? Evidence from the California Verbal Learning Test. *Neuropsychology, 7*, 209–216.

Mitchell, K.J., Johnson, M.K., & Mather, M. (2003). Source monitoring and suggestibility to misinformation: Adult age-related differences. *Applied Cognitive Psychology, 17*, 107–119.

Mueller-Johnson, K., & Ceci, S.J. (2004). Memory and suggestibility in older adults: Live event participation and repeated interview. *Applied Cognitive Psychology, 18*, 1109–1127.

Navah-Benjamin, M. (2000). Adult age differences in memory performance: Tests of an associative deficit hypothesis. *Journal of Experimental Psychology: Learning Memory and Cognition, 26*, 1170–1187.

Nerenberg, L. (2000). Forgotten victims of financial crime and abuse: Facing the challenge. *Journal of Elder Abuse & Neglect, 12,* 49–73.

Nettelbeck, T., & Wilson, C. (2002). Personal vulnerability to victimization of people with mental retardation. *Trauma, Violence, & Abuse, 3,* 289–306.

North, A.S., Russell, A.J., & Gudjonsson, G.H. (2008). High functioning autism spectrum disorders: An investigation of psychological vulnerabilities during interrogative interview. *Journal of Forensic Psychiatry & Psychology, 19,* 323–334.

Perlman, N.B., Ericson, K.I., Esses, V.M., & Isaacs, B.J. (1994). The developmentally handicapped witness: Competency as a function of question format. *Law and Human Behavior, 18,* 171–187.

Perske, R. (2004). Misunderstood responses in police interrogation rooms. *Intellectual and Developmental Disabilities, 48*(1), 75–77.

Petersilia, J.R. (2001). Crime victims with developmental disabilities: A review essay. *Criminal Justice and Behavior, 28,* 655–694.

Polczyk, R., Wesolowska, B., Gabarczyk, A., Minakowska, I., Supska, M., & Bomba, E. (2004). Age differences in interrogative suggestibility: A comparison between young and older adults. *Applied Cognitive Psychology, 18,* 1097–1107.

Prosser, H., & Bromley, J. (1998). Interviewing people with intellectual disabilities. In E. Emerson, C. Hatton, J. Bromley, & A. Caine (Eds), *Clinical Psychology and People with Intellectual Disabilities.* (pp. 99–113). New York: John Wiley & Sons, Ltd.

Rabinowitz, J.C., Craik, F.I., & Ackerman, B.P. (1982). A processing resource account of age differences in recall. *Canadian Journal of Psychology/Revue canadienne de psychologie, 36*(2), 325–344.

Reid, K.A., Smiley, E., & Cooper, S.-A. (2011). Prevalence and associations of anxiety disorders in adults with intellectual disabilities. *Journal of Intellectual Disability Research, 55*(2), 172–81.

Remington, A., Swettenham, J., Campbell, R., & Coleman, M. (2009). Selective attention and perceptual load in autism spectrum disorder. *Psychological Science, 20*(11), 1388–1393.

Schneider, B.A., & Pichora-Fuller, M.K. (2000). Implications of perceptual deterioration for cognitive aging research. In F.I.M. Craik, & T.A. Salthouse (Eds), *The Handbook of Aging and Cognition* (2nd edn, pp. 155–219). Mahwah, NJ: Lawrence Erlbaum Associates.

Sharrock, R., & Gudjonsson, G.H. (1993). Intelligence, previous convictions and interrogative suggestibility: A path analysis of alleged false-confession cases. *British Journal of Clinical Psychology, 32,* 169–175.

Shaw, J.A., & Budd, E.C. (1982). Determinants of acquiescence and naysaying of mentally retarded persons. *American Journal of Mental Deficiency, 87,* 108–110.

Sigelman, C.K., Budd, E.C., Spanhel, C.L., & Schoenrock, C.J. (1981). When in doubt, say yes: Acquiescence in interviews with mentally retarded persons. *Mental Retardation, 19,* 53–58.

Tager-Flusberg, H. (1991). Semantic processing in the free-recall of autistic children: further evidence for a cognitive deficit. *British Journal of Developmental Psychology, 9,* 417–430.

Ternes, M., & Yuille, J.C. (2008). Eyewitness memory and eyewitness identification performance in adults with intellectual disabilities. *Journal of Applied Research in Intellectual Disabilities, 21,* 519–531.

Tharinger, D., Horton, C.B., & Millea, S. (1990). Sexual abuse and exploitation of children and adults with mental retardation and other handicaps. *Child Abuse & Neglect, 14,* 301–312.

Thornton, A., Hatton, C., Malone, C., Fryer, T., Walker, D., Cunningham, J., & Durrani, N. (2003). *Distraction Burglary Amongst Older Adults and Ethnic*

Minority Communities. Home Office Research Study 269. Development and Statistics Directorate. London: Home Office.

White, R., & Willner, P. (2005). Suggestibility and salience in people with intellectual disabilities: An experimental critique of the Gudjonsson Suggestibility Scale. *Journal of Forensic Psychiatry & Psychology, 16,* 638–650.

Wilcock, R., Bull, R., & Milne, R. (2008). *Witness Identification in Criminal Cases: Psychology and Practice*. Oxford: Oxford University Press.

Willner, P. (2008). Clarification of the memory artefact in the assessment of suggestibility. *Journal of Intellectual Disability Research, 52,* 318–326.

Willner, P. (2011). Assessment of capacity to participate in court proceedings: a selective critique and some recommendations. *Psychology, Crime & Law, 17*(2), 117–131.

9

Acute Suggestibility in Police Interrogation: Self-regulation Failure as a Primary Mechanism of Vulnerability

DEBORAH DAVIS AND RICHARD A. LEO

KEY POINTS

This chapter aims to:

- Balance coverage of chronic personal characteristics impacting suggestibility by addressing the importance of acute situational sources of vulnerability to suggestion/influence.
- Provide evidence that depletion and impairment of the self-regulatory resources necessary for impulse control, regulation of emotions, and control of cognition constitute a primary mechanism of both chronic and acute vulnerability to suggestion/influence.
- Review the nature of forces of influence brought to bear on suspects in American police interrogation and the mechanisms of resistance necessary to counter them.

Suggestibility in Legal Contexts: Psychological Research and Forensic Implications,
First Edition. Edited by Anne M. Ridley, Fiona Gabbert and David J. La Rooy.
© 2013 John Wiley & Sons, Ltd. Published 2013 by John Wiley & Sons, Ltd.

- Review in detail the impact of three mechanisms of self-regulation failure common to many suspects in police interrogation:
  ○ Emotional distress
  ○ Glucose availability and regulation
  ○ Fatigue/sleep deprivation.

Shortly before 2 a.m. on the morning of 19 September 2004, police were called to a New York City apartment shared by lesbian couple Zahira Matos and Carmen Molina, and Matos's three children. When they arrived, officers found Matos kneeling over her naked, unconscious, bleeding and severely bruised 2-year-old son with a broken foot, trying to make him breathe. The boy was taken to the hospital, where he was later pronounced dead. The mother, Matos, told police that she herself had given the boy a bath earlier, and that he had fallen and hit his head in the empty bathtub. Though he cried sporadically throughout the evening, Matos reported that he seemed okay until he developed bloody diarrhoea around 11 pm. Matos was taken to the police station for questioning at around 3:00 a.m., and Molina was taken in around 3:50 a.m.

At this point, both women were read their rights under *Miranda* v. *Arizona* (1966) to refuse questioning, to have an attorney during questioning, and/or to have an attorney provided for them, and both women waived their rights and agreed to continue answering questions. Indeed, most suspects waive their *Miranda* rights, allowing police to subject them to interrogations that, for most, result in confessions: 42–76% according to English and American field studies of the confession rate (Gudjonsson, 2003; Thomas, 1996).

If suspects agree to be questioned, the interrogator is allowed to deploy powerful and sophisticated weapons of influence to manipulate their perceptions and emotions and convince them that a confession is in their best long-term legal interests. And, interrogators are largely free to interrogate severely compromised suspects, to use a variety of aversive and exhausting verbal interrogation tactics, and to continue the interrogation until the suspect exerts his *Miranda* rights and demands that it stop (see Davis, 2008; Davis & O'Donohue, 2004 for detailed explication of these tactics; Kassin *et al.*, 2010; Leo, 2008). In the case of Matos and Molina, neither woman understood what was to come: neither how long the interrogation might continue, nor how their own progressively deteriorating physical and emotional conditions might interact with interrogation tactics to lead them to act so dramatically against their own self-interests.

At the apartment and at the station, both women initially told officers that the boy had been injured during a bath with his mother, Matos, while Molina was out. But, this account was to be insistently and repeatedly challenged throughout the more than 24 hours of interrogation. As the two women were interrogated by multiple officers throughout the night and into the next day, Matos began to change her story, and eventually admitted to hitting the boy and causing him to fall and hit his head. But, this initial confession was not enough for the detectives. Even though Matos had a documented history of abusing her children, they seemed to suspect the rather 'butch' stepmother Molina instead, and challenged Matos's initial confession – asking why she wanted to stand up for Molina and protect her when Molina had killed her son. Well into the afternoon, Matos began to change her story again and accuse Molina, saying it was actually she (Matos) who was gone when Molina hurt her son. Matos completed a written statement and later a video statement with the now revised story between 5 and 6 p.m. (15–16 hours after police went to her residence and began the questioning). After another 6 hours of questioning and further shaping of the story by the interrogators, Matos completed a video-taped statement with the District Attorney at about 11.52 p.m. Matos had eaten once during the 22 hours she was questioned.

As Matos began to change her story to implicate Molina, police turned to Molina in earnest to challenge the story she had maintained throughout the afternoon. She continued to maintain her innocence until well after midnight. But the questioning continued until shortly after 3 a.m. on 20 September, 25 hours after questioning had begun at the apartment. At that time, Molina confessed on video to having hit the boy in the shower, thus causing his injuries – re-enacting the incident visually as she told the story. During these 25 hours, Molina had eaten only a bowl of soup at about 7 p.m. It was 7 hours later when she taped her confession.

Both Matos and Molina succumbed to a very lengthy and powerful set of interrogations and offered full video-taped and detailed confessions, complete with physical re-enactments of their final stories – confessions virtually guaranteed to secure their convictions. Yet, confessions against one's self-interest are not unusual. Of particular concern, while most confessions are presumably true, interrogation tactics are sufficiently powerful to elicit false confessions as well. Indeed, over the past few decades, several hundred confessions proven to be false to near or absolute certainty have been documented by scholars, independent researchers and journalists (Drizin & Leo, 2004; Garrett, 2010, 2011; Gudjonsson, 2003; Leo, 2008; Leo & Ofshe, 1998). Such false confessions have played a prominent role in documented wrongful convictions, as illustrated, for example, by close to 300 exonerations achieved by the Innocence Project (http://www.innocenceproject. org). In 20–25% of these cases, police-induced false confessions were implicated as a cause of wrongful conviction or false guilty pleas.

Though many suspects who offer confessions never contest them and may enter into plea agreements, others – such as Matos and Molina – later retract their confession or contest its admissibility into trial evidence, arguing that it was coerced, involuntary and or false. Once the confession is contested, the circumstances in which it was elicited must be judged for their potential to elicit an involuntary confession and/or to produce a false confession. Two general factors are relevant to such judgments: the nature of the interrogation; and the suspect's chronic and/or acute characteristics that may increase vulnerability to suggestion, or undermine rational decision-making and ability to resist.

Evidence suggests, however, that unless the defendant can be shown to suffer mental defects such as retardation or mental illness (and sometimes even then), the prejudicial impact of a confession is sufficient to assure that it will be judged as voluntary and admitted into trial evidence, judged as valid and provoke a conviction, and judged as sufficiently voluntary and credible to support appellate decisions to uphold these admissibility decisions and trial outcomes (Davis & Leo, 2010, 2011; Kassin *et al.*, 2010; Leo, 2008). In part, this overwhelming prejudicial impact is the result of failure at all levels to recognize the magnitude of the influences facing a criminal suspect in interrogation, including both the direct power of the persuasion brought to bear, and the indirect power of interrogative pressure to increase suggestibility and render the suspect more susceptible to the interrogator's attempts to influence.

Matos and Molina were the victims of such failures. Unlike many defendants, the women had no obvious vulnerabilities to coercion, such as youth, clear incapacitation through drugs or alcohol, or mental defect. Instead, they had to base their arguments for suppression of confession on the nature of the interrogation and circumstances surrounding it. Notwithstanding the stresses of the illness and the death of the child, the sleep deprivation leading up to and throughout the interrogation, and the excessive length of the interrogation, Judge Maxwell Wiley denied the motion to suppress.

It is exceedingly rare for judges to suppress a confession if *Miranda* warnings are administered and a valid waiver is obtained (Leo, 2008). Indeed, Judge Wiley pointed to the fact that both women had been read their *Miranda* rights a number of times and had agreed to continue to speak with police. Judges are likewise unlikely to suppress a confession obtained from a 'normal' suspect lacking obvious vulnerabilities such as youth or mental illness or defect. They tend to overestimate the capacity of normal adults to withstand excessively long or aversive interrogations and to resist the impulse to confess simply to escape (Davis & Leo, 2010; Wrightsman, 2010).

Accordingly, Judge Wiley seemed to give little weight to the severe emotional distress engendered by the death of the child, or to the excessive length of the interrogation or progressively increasing fatigue and sleep deprivation of the women. Instead, he noted:

> ... although defendants were at the precinct for much of the day, the interrogation was not continuous, they were offered food, drink and cigarettes, they were not deprived of the opportunity to rest and even nap.

In support of the latter, Judge Wiley noted that detectives had seen Molina sleeping in the interview room with her head on the table on two occasions during the first day of interrogation (Order November 2006; *New York* v. *Matos and Molina*).

The defendants then moved to offer expert testimony before the jury to explain the existence and causes of false confession. But, the interrogations were not video-taped, leaving only the sparsely documented accounts of the officers and those of the defendants as evidence of how the women were interrogated. Judge Wiley also denied the expert testimony (Order, April, 2007), in part on the basis that testimony on the impact of interrogation techniques on false confession was deemed speculative and not tied to the facts of the case since no objective record of the interrogations was available. He made no mention of the relevance of testimony regarding the impact of the length of the interrogations and the physical and emotional condition of the defendants.

Judge Wiley's rulings reflected an all-too-common problem of failure among police, attorneys, judges and juries to appreciate the magnitude of acute impairments of will and cognition in interrogation, and the degree to which they can render the suspect acutely suggestible and vulnerable to influence. The remainder of this chapter considers sources of enhanced susceptibility to interrogative influence triggered by the nature of the immediate circumstances of the suspect, rather than by his chronic personal characteristics, which we call '*acute interrogative suggestibility*'. Moreover, we consider in detail the role of '*interrogation-related regulatory decline*' or IRRD (Davis & Leo, in press) in producing acute interrogative suggestibility: that is, the decline in self-regulation resources necessary to control thinking and behaviour in service of resisting interrogative influence. In this context, we focus on three common but underappreciated sources of IRRD in police interrogation: acute emotional distress; fatigue and sleep deprivation; and glucose depletion.

UNDERPINNINGS OF RESISTANCE TO INTERROGATIVE INFLUENCE: INCREASING SUSCEPTIBILITY THROUGH EROSION OF RESISTANCE

Theories of social influence suggest that to successfully influence a person, one is best served by first establishing what it is that might provide resistance to the effort and then incorporating strategies to overcome the specific source of resistance. This proposition is perhaps most thoroughly and explicitly addressed by Eric Knowles and his colleagues (Knowles & Linn, 2004; Knowles & Riner, 2007), who outlined a theory of persuasion distinguishing between strategies of influence that attempt to increase the attractiveness of what is being advocated ('Alpha' strategies) versus those intended to reduce, deactivate or divert resistance toward what is being advocated ('Omega' strategies). The theory further suggests that resistance is the true target of persuasion:

> ... resistance is the key element in the persuasion process ... Persuasion is required only when people feel 'I don't like it!', 'I don't believe it!', or 'I won't do it!' Without this resistance, a goal would be selected and movement toward that goal would begin. It is the restraint, the resistance, the avoidance forces in the motivational system that inhibit change and make persuasion necessary. All persuasion, therefore, is implicitly aimed at resistance. Because of this, persuasion should rest on an understanding of the different forms of resistance operating to inhibit change. (Knowles & Riner, 2007, p. 84)

Such a view clearly implies the corollary that understanding susceptibility to influence likewise requires understanding of sources of resistance, and of how they can be undermined or impaired. Moreover, one must consider the specific forces of influence to be resisted to understand what resources of resistance are needed. Accordingly, we have previously offered theoretical analyses of the forces of influence in police interrogation, the resources necessary to resist them, and the personal characteristics and interrogation-related factors likely to undermine them (Davis & O'Donohue, 2004; Davis & Leo, in press; Follette, Davis, & Leo, 2007). We briefly review these theoretical propositions before turning to in-depth consideration of specific interrogation-related forces and their impact on vulnerability to interrogative influence.

WHAT ARE THE FORCES OF INFLUENCE IN INTERROGATION, AND HOW CAN THEY BE RESISTED?

Interrogation scholars have identified two general causes of confession: distress intolerance and confession to escape further interrogation, notwithstanding the consequences; and/or the mistaken conviction that confession is without consequences, or in one's best legal or other interests (Gudjonsson, 2003; Kassin *et al.*, 2010; Leo, 2008). Accordingly, understanding sources of acute interrogative suggestibility rests upon identification of the bases of resistance to these specific mechanisms promoting confession, as well as how interrogation tactics target them. Two major sources of resistance to influence – motivation and ability – have been identified by theories of persuasion (Knowles & Riner, 2007; Petty, Cacioppo, Strathman, & Priester, 2005), each applicable to causes of false confession identified by interrogation scholars.

Motivation to Resist

Susceptibility to stress-induced confession is most directly related to motivational impairments. The tendency to confess to escape an aversive situation will be a function of the strength of the more immediate need to escape the situation versus that of the motives or beliefs inhibiting confession – such as the expected social, personal or legal costs of confession. The likelihood of stress-induced confession should therefore be increased by chronic personal characteristics or acute situational influences that either increase distress (e.g. high dispositional anxiety, lengthy and aversive interrogation), reduce the suspect's ability to tolerate distress (e.g. chronic distress intolerance, acute fatigue and discomfort), or reduce the ability to control acute, potentially dysfunctional, impulses in favour of optimal long-term outcomes (e.g. youth, mental illness, fatigue).

Against these factors that undermine motivation to resist are others that fuel it. Knowles and Riner (2007) suggested that motivated resistance to influence, or psychological 'reactance', arises from the actual or threatened loss of personal freedom of belief, choice and/or behaviour and the desire to protect or restore such freedoms (Brehm, 1966). 'Reactance' is presumed to be greater as a function of the number and importance of the threatened freedoms, and of the coerciveness and obviousness of the influence attempt. It may also be motivated by a dislike of the source of influence.

Attempts to persuade are generally at risk of engendering reactance, as they are likely to be experienced as challenging one's preferred beliefs or behaviours, are often framed in a way easily identified as an influence attempt, and are often conducted in a manner experienced as coercive. Such is the case for police interrogation, where the importance of the freedom in question is very high (the freedom to avoid self-incrimination and potential incarceration), and the influence attempt is both obvious and coercive. The suspect is clearly aware of the attempt to induce a confession. The interrogator may be viewed as an enemy, and many behaviours of the interrogator – such as excessive length of interrogation, repetition, accusations of guilt and deception, invasion of personal space – are experienced as coercive (Davis, Leo, & Follette, 2010; Inbau, Reid, Buckley, & Jayne, 2001, 2011; Leo, 2008).

Interrogation tactics directly target the roots of reactance in several ways. Most directly, this occurs through efforts to undermine the perceived feasibility (therefore, eventually, the importance) of maintaining and defending one's innocence. Indeed, the first goal of interrogation is to take the suspect's goal of establishing innocence off the table and replace it with a sense of the futility of resistance. This is done by confronting the suspect with an absolutely confident accusation and various forms of real and/or fabricated damning evidence – and by failure to acknowledge claims of innocence by counter-arguing against or other-wise overwhelming them. Aronson (1999) dubbed reactions to a sense of futility the 'psychology of inevitability', and provided evidence that once an outcome is perceived as certain, cognitive/motivational forces are engaged to promote acceptance, compliance and approval of the situa-tion. Similar reactions are predicted by theories of learned helplessness (Seligman, 1975), self-efficacy (Bandura, 1997) and reasoned action (Fishbein & Ajzen, 2009) – all suggesting that behavioural motivation and attempts are jointly governed by the desirability and feasibility of an outcome. Thus, the motivation to defend innocence is undermined by reducing the perceived feasibility of success.

The interrogator next endeavours to reframe the purpose of the inter-action and redirect the suspect's motivation to the goal of minimizing consequences rather than exoneration. He tells the suspect that while guilt is firmly established, he still wants to talk to the suspect to estab-lish why the crime was committed, and 'what kind of person' the suspect is – with the implication that this information may affect what happens to the suspect. Simultaneously, the interrogator attempts to undermine reactance to himself as a potentially malevolent enemy working against the suspect's legal interests. He does this by casting himself as a benev-olent ally instead. In part, this is accomplished through a tactic dubbed the 'sympathetic detective with a time-limited offer' in which the detec-tive flatters the suspect, suggests that the suspect is not a bad person (but rather one who got caught up in a bad situation), states his desire to help, but notes that he can only help if the suspect 'tells the truth' during the interrogation, before the case is sent up the line to others who will be less sympathetic (Davis *et al.*, 2010).

If the suspect is still resistant to confession, the detective may threaten to withdraw his help. This has the effect of taking attention from the more complicated – and in some ways more remote – goals of defending innocence and avoiding legal consequences and redirecting it to the immediate goal of keeping the beneficent help of the interroga-tor. The only way to defend one's access to the detective's help is to comply with his demands to 'tell the suspect's side of the story'. Thus, reactance created by threats to the availability of the detective's help directly promotes confession. Such threats, and the other messages of the futility of resistance, combined with the sympathetic detective tac-tic are repeated throughout the interrogation as long as the suspect is resistant to admitting guilt – sometimes for many hours or even days.

These and other strategies have the cumulative effect of instilling a sense of hopelessness in the suspect that he might successfully defend his innocence and of turning his attention to how to minimize the consequences of being implicated in the crime. Moreover, they recast the interrogation as a negotiation in which the interrogator has the *authority* to affect what, if any, charges are filed against the suspect, and the *beneficent motivation* to help the suspect achieve the best legal outcomes (see Davis *et al*., 2010, for demonstrations of the effects of these tactics on the perceptions of authority and beneficence). In these ways, the primary source of reactance – the expectation of avoiding incrimination – is undermined and replaced by the goals of achieving the detective's help and minimizing the consequences of unavoidable incrimination.

Because interrogation entails multiple and sustained attempts to instil a strong sense of futility in the suspect and to redirect attention toward other goals of escape, minimizing the consequences of guilt and pleasing the interrogator and others, we have suggested that the motivation to resist interrogative influence is heavily dependent upon the abilities we turn to next (Davis & Leo, in press). To maintain this motivation, the suspect must focus on long-term goals serving his legal interests and resist diverting attention to goals promoted by the interrogator or the acute goal of escape prompted by distress intolerance. He must see through the deceptions of the interrogation, including the interrogator's misrepresentation of his own motives and his misleading suggestions that confession is wiser than resistance. Further, the suspect must possess the strength of will to persist in resisting despite growing discomfort, distress and fatigue.

Ability to Resist

Susceptibility to the second mechanism of confession – mistaken understanding of the consequences – essentially entails suscepti- bility to persuasion. Interrogation training manuals acknowledge their goal to convince suspects that confession is in their best inter- ests. A number of strategies are used to convey this message without explicitly threatening the suspect or promising leniency in exchange for confession. Some strategies endeavour to 'minimize' the apparent seriousness and consequences of the crime (thus lowering perceived costs of confession), and others attempt to 'maximize' the apparent negative consequences of denial (raising the costs of refusal to con- fess) (Kassin, 1997).

Vulnerability to such tactics will be a function of the suspects' ability to see through misrepresentations suggesting that confession is with- out consequences or that it is in the suspects' self-interest and to recog- nize that confession will, in fact, be harmful. In addition to vulnerability to confession (true or false), a suspect may be suggestible with regard to the details of the confession. Interrogations entail significant sug- gestion concerning such details as what happened (e.g. he fondled the outside of the girl's genitals versus penetrated with his fingers), how the crime was committed, how often, who was involved and which roles they each played (e.g. shooter versus get-away driver), why it occurred (e.g. revenge versus self-defence) and many others.

As theories of persuasion have suggested, the ability to resist persuasion depends upon knowledge that would contradict the persuasive message (in this case, knowledge relevant to the crime, the evidence and arguments of the interrogators and one's options other than confession), as well as the ability to process incoming information, to integrate it with existing knowledge, to hold all the relevant information in one's mind (i.e. in working memory) and to evaluate it rationally and effectively. Chronic (e.g. knowledge, intelligence) and acute (e.g. distraction, cognitive load, ego-depletion) impairments of these abilities render the suspect more susceptible to persuasion and more inclined to use heuristic rather than analytical modes of evaluation and decision-making (see Kahneman, 2011; Petty *et al.*, 2005, for reviews).

SELF-REGULATION AS A PRIMARY MECHANISM OF RESISTANCE TO INFLUENCE

The mechanisms of vulnerability identified in the preceding sections entail both chronic and acute failures of self-control and cognition. However, we suggest that *acute* interrogative suggestibility essentially entails acute failures of 'self-regulation': that is, the ability to control emotions, cognition and behaviour in service the of one or more specific goals (Baumeister, Schmeichel, & Vohs, 2007; MacDonald, 2008). One may have sufficient chronic assets of knowledge, intelligence, personal will, or self-regulatory control to resist interrogative influences under ideal circumstances, yet possess insufficient acute self-regulatory capacity to marshal or use them effectively under the circumstances at hand.

Baumeister and colleagues (Baumeister, Bratslavsky, Muraven, & Tice, 1998) suggested that self-regulatory capacity is limited, that it will be depleted through use (termed 'ego-depletion'), and that such 'ego-depletion' results in greater likelihood of failure on subsequent tasks also requiring self-regulatory resources. Substantial research supports these propositions, showing that prior use of self-regulatory resources does indeed impair performance on subsequent tasks, particularly those placing significant demands upon self-regulatory resources (see Hagger, Wood, Stiff, & Chatzisarantis, 2010; Vohs & Baumeister, 2011, for reviews). But how, exactly, does the specific task of resistance to interrogative influence demand and depend upon self-regulation?

We suggest that self-regulation is a primary mechanism of resistance: both chronic self-regulatory resources and acute ability to marshal them when needed. One must have the abilities to effectively assess relevant information to determine the best course of action, and to override acute impulses to exert one's will and act on that decision. These abilities depend, in turn, upon a number of specific functions. We suggest that the specific ability to resist interrogative influence requires intact functioning of at least: (1) the ability to maintain focus on the long-term goals of exoneration and avoidance of self-incrimination; avoiding diversion toward short-term goals such as pleasing the interrogator, conflict avoidance, immediate escape through confession and others; (2) the ability to control attention to focus on relevant and to ignore irrelevant information; (3) the ability to access information from long-term memory to provide a context for the evaluation of incoming information and suggestions; (4) the working memory capacity to hold all the relevant information in mind and use it to evaluate and decide how to respond to the interrogator's demands; (5) the willpower to resist and to act on what one considers best, rather than on what the interrogator demands, and to persist in such resistance for as long as required; and (6) the ability to control the emotions triggered by the context and the content of the interrogation to maintain the preceding functions (Davis & Leo, in press). These abilities depend upon chronic resources such as knowledge, intelligence and others, as well as upon the ability to marshal chronic abilities when acutely needed. All have been shown to depend upon intact self-regulatory resources.

Investigating Self-Regulation: The Dual Task Paradigm

Tests of the importance of self-regulatory resources for the above functions have largely been conducted using a dual-task depletion paradigm in which participants are first subjected to an 'ego-depleting' task presumed to consume self-regulatory resources, and subsequently to perform a second unrelated task that is also presumed to demand such resources. The general finding of such studies is that prior use of self-regulatory resources impairs performance on subsequent resource-demanding tasks, but does so less or not at all for less demanding tasks. Other studies have shown that poor physical or emotional condition promotes self-regulation failures. Generally, these studies have indicated that all self-regulation functions are interdependent, such that the depletion of resources through deployment of self-regulatory control in any domain affects the performance in any other domain that also requires self-regulatory control.

Accordingly, demanding cognitive tasks, emotion regulation and impulse control become more difficult through prior or contemporaneous depletion, regardless of the mechanism of depletion. Of particular relevance to interrogative suggestibility, ego-depletion promotes greater susceptibility to immediate impulses, to persuasion/suggestibility and to failures of rational decision making (see Davis & Leo, in press; Hagger et al., 2010; Hofmann, Friese, Schmeichel, & Baddeley, 2011; Kahneman, 2011; Otgaar, Alberts, & Cuppens, 2012; Vohs & Baumeister, 2011, for reviews). But, how exactly does interrogation impair self-regulation?

INTERROGATION-RELATED REGULATORY DECLINE AND THE ACUTE IMPAIRMENT OF RESISTANCE: THE BIG THREE

Many forces operate within a police interrogation and the circumstances surrounding it, to impair resistance to interrogative influence. Some are subtle and unlikely to be considered by those judging the voluntariness or validity of a confession: such as the depleting effects of threats to social identity or self-esteem, the operation of stereotype threat (the risk of conforming to the stereotype of one's own group), the effort required for resistance, aversive verbal interactions, and many others. Yet these are documented sources of self-regulation failures with effects including failures of impulse control, emotion regulation and rational thinking (see Davis & Leo, in press; Davis & O'Donohue, 2004; Follette *et al.*, 2007). Here, we focus on three significant causes of IRRD (interrogation-related regulatory decline) and acute suggestibility, one or more of which are present in most cases involving claims of involuntary or false confession: emotional distress, fatigue/sleep deprivation and glucose depletion. Effects of each tend to be under-appreciated by those judging the confession.

1. Emotional Distress

I found my daughter. She didn't even have eyes in her head. I was already broken. They didn't have to break me.
(False confessor Jerry Hobbs, quoted in Martin,
New York Times Magazine, 25 November 2011)

Stress during police interrogation may come from within and outside the interrogation itself. As was the case for Jerry Hobbs, and for Matos and Molina, many suspects are interrogated in the aftermath of emotionally devastating events involving the death of close friends or family, exposure to horrific violence and mayhem and other significant personal or financial losses. Indeed, many proven false confessions have been elicited under just such circumstances. These pre-existing stresses are supplemented by stressors inherent to the interrogation, such as: the fear and shame associated with being suspected and interrogated; confinement; social isolation; physical discomfort; the sense of powerlessness, helplessness and lack of control; the aversive nature of interrogation tactics; self-esteem and identity threat; and others (Davis & Leo, in press; Davis & O'Donohue, 2004; Najdowski, 2011).

At sufficiently high levels of emotion, arousal and stress there will be a catastrophic failure of self-regulation and cognition, as described in several prominent theories of stress and performance (e.g. the Yerkes–Dodson law, 1908), the catastrophe model of anxiety and performance (Fazey & Hardy, 1988), or the asymmetric neural control systems model

(Tucker & Williamson, 1984). The combination of pre-existing and interrogation-related stressors can and does reach this level for some suspects in interrogation. Some suspects have reached levels of stress sufficient to produce failures of reality monitoring severe enough to cause them not only to falsely confess but also to falsely remember having committed the crime (see Kassin, 2007, for examples and review).

Even short of such extremes, interrogation-related stressors can cause self-regulation failures sufficient to severely compromise cognition and impulse control. Adding to the direct effects of emotion, emotional distress will also operate in a vicious feedback loop with failures of self-regulation, such that emotional distress impairs self-regulation, which compromises emotion regulation and intensifies emotion, which further impairs self-regulation, and so on. Thus, strong negative emotions are likely to progressively impair cognition and impulse control as the interrogation proceeds (see Davis & Leo, in press for review). Such effects have been documented by decades of research in several traditions. A prolific line of research, for example, has investigated effects of strong negative emotions and stress in various domains (Driskell, Salas, & Johnston, 2006; Hammond, 2000; McNeil & Morgan, 2010; Phelps & Delgado, 2009; Thompson, 2010). Of particular relevance to interrogation, such studies have shown the negative effects of high stress on cognitive performance, decision-making, emotion regulation and impulse control. Research on stress and performance has further shown that high motivation and greater energy investment are necessary to compensate for the negative effects of stress. In their absence, stress will lead to greater declines in thinking and impulse control, which in turn further reduces the willingness to invest additional energy (Kruglanski & Webster, 1996; Roets & Van Hiel, 2011).

This is particularly problematic during interrogation because interrogation tactics specifically attempt to instill hopelessness in the suspect and because motivation is directly impacted by self-regulation failures, glucose depletion, sleep deprivation and fatigue (see following sections in this chapter). Moreover, energy itself is also compromised by these factors. Studies of self-regulation have also shown that stress leads to regulatory decline, and consequently to failures of impulse control and of inhibition of dysfunctional behaviours such as overeating, drinking or smoking; as well as failures to persist in desired behaviours such as exercise (see Vohs & Baumeister, 2011, for reviews).

Such failures are exacerbated by attempts to regulate negative emotions. Many studies in the dual-task depletion paradigm have used procedures in which the first task either requires the participant to suppress emotional reactions (such as emotional experience, overt expression of emotion or behavioural reactions to emotion) or to give them free rein. Emotional suppression – as is similarly true with efforts to cope with stress – leads to failures of self-regulation such as dysfunctional health behaviours; aggression; impairments in social functioning and communication; decrements in cognitive performance and decision-making; reduced persistence in the face of frustration; as well as paradoxical magnification of arousal and negative emotions and suppression of positive emotions. Conversely, initially depleting tasks of various sorts impair subsequent attempts to regulate emotions (see Davis & Leo, in press for review).

To summarize, the many emotionally distressing features of the personal context of the suspect and the nature of interrogation – and the attempts to regulate the resulting emotions – are likely to impair the additional self-regulatory resources needed to control immediate impulses to escape through compliance and to rationally evaluate the wisdom of confession versus other alternatives. Further, they are likely to impair the functions of memory and render the person more suscep- tible to suggestion regarding the details of the events in question. Finally, they are likely to do so at lower levels of distress than commonly recognized. Although the emotional distress of a suspect may be suffi- cient to create these effects alone, impairment can become much more profound when added to other common forces during interrogation.

2. Discomfort, Fatigue and Sleep Deprivation

Often, suspects face the combined effects of distress, fatigue and sleep deprivation – as was the case for Matos, Molina and Jerry Hobbs, all of whom lost children when already fatigued and sleep-deprived, before being interrogated for 24 hours or more. Sleep deprivation impairs all aspects of self-regulation. This includes a variety of cognitive functions necessary for information processing, memory, planning, prioritizing and decision-making; as well as emotion regulation and impulse con- trol (Barnes & Hollenbeck, 2009; Harrison & Horne, 2000; Walker & van der Helm, 2009; Wesensten & Balkin, 2010). Sleep deprivation ren- ders the original perception and encoding of information less accurate, even to the extent that at extreme levels the real can be confused with the unreal (Larsen, 2001). It also impairs the consolidation of new memories, and renders memories more vulnerable to distortion through suggestive influences over time (Blagrove, 1996; Blagrove, Alexander, & Horne, 1995; Blagrove, Cole-Morgan, & Lambe, 1994; Walker & van der Helm, 2009). It also compromises the many cognitive functions underlying rational analysis and evaluation of incoming information and decision making – such as attention, working memory, verbal flu- ency, logical reasoning, creative thinking, flexible updating of plans and priorities and others (Harrison & Horne, 2000; Wesensten & Balkin, 2010) – and thereby renders a person less able to resist persua- sion. Finally, in part due to its effects on underlying cognitive resources necessary for emotion-regulation and impulse control, sleep deprivation results in the disinhibition of a variety of dysfunctional behaviours ranging from over-indulgence to risk-taking, aggression and others (Walker & van der Helm, 2009; Wesensten & Balkin, 2010). In other words, the person becomes more responsive to immediate impulses than to long-term optimization of outcomes, the very process rendering the person more vulnerable to stress-induced confession. Despite such effects, however, as with emotional distress, the impact of sleep deprivation and fatigue tends to be underestimated and a host of confessions taken from severely compromised suspects have been admitted into evidence as voluntary and viewed as valid by juries.

3. Glucose Depletion

Whereas the Courts frown upon police who deny suspects nourishment and consider that it contributes to involuntary confession, if suspects decline offers of nourishment the Courts tend to weight the refusals on the side of voluntariness. Seemingly, the refusal to provide food and drink tends to be regarded as an improper form of inducement, rather than as a source of impairment and vulnerability in the suspect. Our analysis of IRRD and its effects on acute suggestibility suggests a different view of the role of nourishment in interrogation; that is, glucose depletion can lead directly to self-regulation failures rendering the suspect more vulnerable to influence and to failures of impulse control.

Judge Wiley clearly had the first view regarding the role of food and drink in Matos and Molina's interrogation. In his order denying the women's suppression motion, he repeatedly referred to the offers of food, drink and cigarettes as evidence that police did not deprive them of basic needs. Though the evidence suggested that the women ate only once between dinner the evening before Matos' son's death and more than 30 hours later, Judge Wiley viewed this as adequate to maintain the women's will and rational decision-making for up to 8 hours between dinner and the boy's death and through the following interrogation that lasted more than 24 hours. Moreover, such reasoning fails to take account of a significant implication of their refusals. That is, whereas under normal circumstances most individuals will eat three times or more during a typical day of roughly 16 hours, the suspects declined to eat even one-third of what would be expected during more than 24 hours without sleep. Refusals of normal food intake reflect, among other things, stress-related impairment of appetite – and as such, provided an important clue to the emotional state of the two women.

Between police failures to provide food and nourishing drinks and tendencies for suspects to refuse them when distressed, many suspects suffer progressive glucose depletion during interrogation. But, how easily is glucose depleted? How much glucose depletion is necessary to matter? And, *how* does it matter? These questions were addressed in a detailed review by Galliot and Baumeister (2007).

The authors noted that all brain processes – and therefore all cognition and control of behaviour – depend upon the consumption of energy from blood glucose. This would suggest that the availability, uptake and use of glucose by the brain will strongly affect these functions. The authors further suggested that self-control functions exert relatively high demands for energy and deplete glucose more rapidly than less demanding mental activities. These assumptions led to the prediction that chronic or acutely low glucose levels or poor glucose metabolism would be associated with impaired self-regulation.

Galliot and Baumeister (2007) reported a number of tests of the importance of glucose for self-regulation using the dual-task ego-depletion paradigm described earlier. Participants who engaged in various initial tasks involving self-control showed greater depletion of glucose than those who engaged in less demanding control tasks. Further, providing participants with replenishment of glucose between tasks mitigates the effects of the initial depletion task on subsequent performance. The authors reviewed substantial evidence that a number of the self-control functions central to performance in police interrogation fit this pattern: including executive functions such as control of cognition, regulation of emotion (including coping with stress) and impulse control.

Research has shown that glucose depletion is associated with poorer analytical reasoning and decision-making and greater reliance on automatic, heuristic-based processes (Masicampo & Baumeister, 2008). Police interrogation imposes very strong and sometimes overwhelming demands for cognitive, emotional and behavioural self-regulation activities that result in heavy glucose depletion, and that exacerbate the depletion occurring due to failure to replace glucose through eating and drinking.

These findings clearly suggest that glucose depletion can powerfully affect a suspect's thinking and impulse control during interrogation. However, regular ingestion of glucose can mitigate such effects. In much of the research using the dual-task depletion paradigm, the ingestion of a sugary drink between tasks reduced or eliminated impairments of performance on the second task. Other research has also shown that ingestion of glucose before demanding or distressing tasks can facilitate executive control, including various cognitive tasks involving control of attention, learning, working memory capacity, and episodic memory; and those involving emotion-regulation and behavioural self-control (Gagnon, Greenwood, & Bherer, 2010; Gailliot & Baumeister, 2007; McMahon & Scheel, 2010; Serra-Grabulosa, Adan, Falcon, & Bargall, 2010).

Such research suggests that the effects of glucose depletion can be largely mitigated through regular glucose replacement during lengthy interrogations – though this is not reliably the case. However, it is also important to note that the type of nourishment impacts glucose regulation, such that foods with low glycaemic indices (GI) provide more sustained release of glucose (Radulian, Rusu, Dragomir, & Posea, 2009), and therefore better minimize central fatigue and maintain self-control resources. Some additional direct evidence suggests that low-GI foods can more effectively maintain cognitive performance (e.g. Gilsenan, de Bruin, & Dye, 2009; Lamport, Hoyle, Lawton, Mansfield, & Dye, 2011). Such findings are important because suspects often drink sugary drinks during interrogation but fail to eat low-GI foods. This can produce an immediate improvement in cognitive performance, while impairing the longer-term maintenance of cognitive functions necessary for lengthy interrogations.

Finally, in assessing the potential role of glucose in interrogation it is important to consider when, during the course of the day, the interrogation is conducted. Glucose availability and functioning tend to be best after sleep and, more generally, in the morning and tend to be lower and used less effectively during the later hours of the day and evening (Gailliot & Baumeister, 2007), so much so that the term 'afternoon diabetes' was coined to describe the effect (Jarrett, Viberti, & Sayegh, 1978). This implies that the timing of interrogation, for this and other reasons, may have a significant impact on the suspect's self-regulatory resources and acute suggestibility in interrogation.

Although our primary concern here is the acute depletion of glucose in healthy suspects, it is important to note that chronic impairments in glucose tolerance and regulation can impair cognitive function and impulse control as well, posing a little-considered personal vulnerability to interrogative influence (Dahle, Jacobs, & Raz, 2009; Gailliot & Baumeister, 2007; Lamport, Lawton, Mansfield, & Dye, 2009; Messier, Awad-Shimoon, Gagnon, Desrochers, & Tsiakas, 2011). Such individual differences, even within normal glucose regulation, can affect self-regulation of cognition and behaviour (Dahle et al., 2009; Lamport et al., 2009). Those persons with diabetes are less able to use glucose effectively and, therefore, can be more strongly impaired. Hypoglycaemia can also be a source of individual vulnerability. Severely low glucose levels can result in relatively profound impairments in cognition and behaviour (see Galliot & Baumeister, 2007). Since hypoglycaemic individuals may begin an interrogation with lower glucose levels, they are likely to become more profoundly impaired during a long and depleting interrogation.

Some evidence indicates that impairments in the ability to *use* glucose – as opposed to simple fasting, blood glucose levels or glucose intolerance – better predict cognitive performance in both normal and diabetic adults Research participants who show greater glucose depletion after task performance produce better performance than those showing less depletion (Galanina, Surampudi, Ciltea, Singh, & Perlmuter, 2008). Thus, both the availability and the ability to use glucose seem crucial to self-regulation.

To summarize, the physical condition of the suspect matters during interrogation. Glucose depletion is an important but almost completely hidden and ignored aspect of physical condition. It is likely to be strongly affected by the nature and length of the interrogation itself, by the physiological disorders of the suspect related to glucose metabolism and by the circumstances preceding the interrogation. Experts called to testify regarding the suspect's vulnerability to interrogative influence should routinely investigate information relevant to this issue and testify concerning its effect. Judges and juries should also seriously consider this information in arriving at their findings.

THE BIG THREE IN CAHOOTS: SEVERE INTERROGATION-RELATED REGULATORY DECLINE

Research reviewed in the preceding sections has examined each of our 'big three' sources of regulatory failure separately. However, suspects in police interrogation are likely to experience multiple sources of distress, glucose depletion, fatigue and, often, sleep deprivation as well. Such circumstances cannot be studied easily in the laboratory, particularly using manipulations comparable in intensity to the experiences of suspects. The best information regarding such combined effects comes from military studies documenting what they refer to as the 'fog of war' or 'Operational Demand-Related Cognitive Decline' (Lieberman et al., 2005; McNeil & Morgan, 2010) – or decrements in cognitive performance and decision-making under extreme or dangerous environments (see also Gonzales, 2003 on cognition in other extreme circumstances). Of relevance to interrogation specifically, indices of physiological stress responses under extreme stress and sleep deprivation have been related to poorer performance in military interrogation training exercises (McNeil & Morgan, 2010).

McNeil and Morgan noted that the cognitive effects of the extreme stressors of SERE (Survive, Evade, Resist, Escape) training, for example, are sufficiently severe as to induce dissociative symptoms in more than 90% of cadets. Such extreme effects may also afflict some suspects in interrogation, particularly those subject to the full cocktail of the big three sources of regulatory decline reviewed here.

CONCLUSIONS

We have argued that self-regulation is a primary mechanism underlying resistance to influence and that impairment of self-regulation is a primary mechanism of suggestibility and failures of impulse control. These assertions suggest a largely overlooked, but important set of considerations for those evaluating the vulnerability of specific suspects to influence in interrogation. These include chronic individual differences related to self-regulatory capacity (e.g. glucose metabolism and other physiological and psychological underpinnings of self-control), as well as acute situational influences with the potential to impair self-regulation (glucose depletion, emotional stressors, etc.). Some such factors are subtle (identity threat and regulation of self-esteem) or hidden (glucose depletion, individual differences in chronic self-regulatory control) and have remained largely underestimated or unaddressed by interrogation scholars and by experts who evaluate individual suspects and testify in their hearings and trials. We encourage all who must evaluate the voluntariness or validity of a contested confession to recognize and to consider more fully the importance of self-regulation failures in undermining the will and rational decision-making of criminal suspects.

OVERALL SUMMARY AND CONCLUSIONS

- Both acute and chronic sources of vulnerability contribute to a given individual's susceptibility to suggestion and influence. Suspects of normal mental health and intelligence, and even of superior intelligence, may suffer acute impairment of personal resources sufficient to undermine resistance to influence.
- Intact self-regulatory resources provide a primary mechanism of resistance to influence, and in particular to interrogation-induced confession against one's self-interest.
  - Depletion of self-regulatory resources can impair impulse control and render the person vulnerable to confession as a means to escape the immediate distress of the interrogation.
  - Depletion of self-regulatory resources can also impair the cognitive functions underlying effective resistance to persuasion and decision-making, thereby rendering suspects more susceptible to the belief promoted by interrogators that confession will be in their best legal interests.
  - Finally, depletion of self-regulatory resources can impair emotion regulation, thereby impairing both impulse control and rational analysis and decision-making.
- A number of forces face police suspects in interrogation that can impair self-regulatory resources, including (but not limited to):
  - Pre-interrogation distress, fatigue, sleep deprivation, drug use
  - Stresses and fears caused by being accused of the crime and the anticipated social and legal consequences
  - The length and environmental stressors of the interrogation

○ Aversive interrogation tactics
○ Social isolation, lack of control.

- Three mechanisms of self-regulation failure are common to many suspects in police interrogation. Substantial empirical research links each of these mechanisms to failures of impulse control, emotion regulation and cognition, which has important implications for the resistance to influence during interrogation. These include:
  ○ Emotional distress
  ○ Glucose availability and regulation
  ○ Fatigue/sleep deprivation
- The American courts have established that confessions elicited under conditions rendering the confession 'involuntary' may not be admitted as evidence against the defendant in trial. In practice, most judges do not suppress interrogation-induced confessions unless the suspect possesses notable defects of mental health or cognition – and may often not suppress confession even then. The research reviewed herein suggests that much more weight should be given to issues of acute sources of vulnerability to influence and suggestion than is presently the case.

FORENSIC IMPLICATIONS

- Experts called to evaluate the voluntariness of a police-induced confession for a suppression hearing, or to testify before the jury to elucidate the causes of false confession and sources of individual vulnerability, should take care to evaluate the sources of acute vulnerability in addition to chronic vulnerabilities.
- Some experts stop their analysis with issues of chronic vulnerability, leaving 'normal' suspects with no basis for a motion to suppress a claim of false confession.
- Specific potential sources of acute impairment to be investigated include:
  ○ Emotional stressors due to the nature of the crime and its non-legal impact on the suspect
  ○ Other emotional stressors unrelated to the crime
  ○ The physical condition of the suspect going into the interrogation, including:
    ▪ Fatigue/sleep deprivation
    ▪ Drug (prescription or recreational) or alcohol use
    ▪ Glucose regulatory functions, and acute glucose depletion
    ▪ Illness or injury.
  ○ Interrogation-related stressors:
    ▪ The nature and severity of the accusations
    ▪ Emotions provoked by the interrogation and its circumstances

- Confinement, social isolation, physical discomfort, powerlessness and lack of control
- Threats to identity and self-esteem and their effortful management:
  - Caused by the nature of the accusations
  - Caused by stereotype threat and the expectation that others will view the suspect as guilty because of his or her category membership (e.g. blacks accused of crimes of violence or step-fathers accused of molesting their step-children)
- Aversive interrogation tactics:
  - Accusations
  - Interruptions, refusals to listen to or respect claims of innocence, repetition of demands, argumentative behaviour.
  - Excessive length
  - Failures to provide toilet facilities or refreshments
  - Multiple interrogators
  - Hostility and/or threats
- Progressive deterioration of physical and mental condition.

REFERENCES

Bandura, A. (1997). *Self-efficacy: The Exercise of Control*. New York: WH Freeman/Times Books/ Henry Holt & Co.

Barnes, C.M., & Hollenbeck, J.R. (2009). Sleep deprivation and decision-making teams: Burning the midnight oil or playing with fire? *Academy of Management Review, 34*(1), 56–66.

Baumeister, R.F., Bratslavsky, E., Muraven, M., & Tice, D.M. (1998). Ego depletion: Is the active self a limited resource? *Journal of Personality and Social Psychology, 74*(5), 1252–1265. doi: 10.1037/0022-3514.74.5.1252

Baumeister, R.F., Schmeichel, B.J., & Vohs, K.D. (2007). Self-regulation and the executive function: The self as controlling agent. In A.W. Kruglanski, & E.T. Higgins (Eds), *Social Psychology: Handbook of Basic Principles* (2nd edn, pp. 516–539). New York: Guilford Press.

Blagrove, M. (1996). Effects of length of sleep deprivation on interrogative suggestibility. *Journal of Experimental Psychology: Applied, 2*(1), 48–59.

Blagrove, M., Alexander, C.A., & Horne, J.A. (1995). The effects of chronic sleep reduction on the performance of cognitive tasks sensitive to sleep deprivation. *Applied Cognitive Psychology, 9*, 21–40.

Blagrove, M., Cole-Morgan, D., & Lambe, H. (1994). Interrogative suggestibility: The effects of sleep deprivation and relationship with field-dependence. *Applied Cognitive Psychology, 8*, 169–179.

Brehm, J.W. (1966). *A Theory of Psychological Reactance*. New York: Academic Press.

Dahle, C.L., Jacobs, B.S., & Raz, N. (2009). Aging, vascular risk, and cognition: Blood glucose, pulse pressure, and cognitive performance in healthy adults. *Psychology and Aging, 24*(1), 154–162. doi: 10.1037/a0014283

Davis, D. (2008). Selling confession: The interrogator, the con man, and their weapons of influence. *Wisconsin Defender, 16*(1), 1–16.

Davis, D., & Leo, R.A. (2010). Commentary: Overcoming judicial preferences for person-versus situation-based analyses of interrogation-induced confessions [Opinion]. *Journal of the American Academy of Psychiatry & the Law, 38*(2), 187–194.

Davis, D., & Leo, R.A. (2011). Three prongs of the confession problem: Issues and proposed solutions. In J. Epstein (Ed.), *The Future of Evidence* (pp. 233–264): Westlaw.

Davis, D., & Leo, R.A. (in press). 'Interrogation-related regulatory decline': Ego-depletion, self-regulation failure and the decision to confess. *Psychology, Public Policy & Law.*

Davis, D., Leo, R.A., & Follette, W.C. (2010). Selling confession: setting the stage with the 'sympathetic detective with a time-limited offer'. *Journal of Contemporary Criminal Justice, 26*(4), 441–457. doi: 10.1177/10439862103772

Davis, D., & O'Donohue, W. T. (2004). The road to perdition: Extreme influence tactics in the interrogation room. In W.T. O'Donohue, & E. R. Levensky (Eds.), *Handbook of Forensic Psychology: Resource for Mental Health and Legal Professionals* (pp. 897–996). New York: Elsevier Science.

Driskell, J.E., Salas, E., & Johnston, J.H. (2006). Decision making and performance under stress. In T.W. Britt, C.A. Castro, & A.B. Adler (Eds), *Military Life: The Psychology of Serving in Peace and Combat (Vol. 1): Military Performance*. (pp. 128–154). Westport, CT: Praeger Security International.

Drizin, S., & Leo, R.A. (2004). The problem of false confessions in the post-DNA world. *North Carolina Law Review, 82,* 891–1007.

Fazey, J.A., & Hardy, L. (1988). *The Inverted-U Hypothesis: A Catastrophe for Sport Psychology*. British Association of Sport Sciences Monograph 1. Leeds, UK: National Coaching Foundation.

Fishbein, M., & Ajzen, I. (2009). *Predicting and Changing Behavior: The Reasoned Action Approach*. New York: Psychology Press.

Follette, W.C., Davis, D., & Leo, R.A. (2007). Mental health status and vulnerability to interrogative influence. *Criminal Justice, 22*(3), 42–49.

Gagnon, C., Greenwood, C.E., & Bherer, L. (2010). The acute effects of glucose ingestion on attentional control in fasting healthy older adults. *Psychopharmacology, 211*(3), 337–346. doi: 10.1007/s00213-010-1905-9

Gailliot, M.T., & Baumeister, R.F. (2007). The physiology of willpower: Linking blood glucose to self-control. *Personality and Social Psychology Review, 11*(4), 303–327. doi: 10.1177/1088868307303030

Galanina, N., Surampudi, V., Ciltea, D., Singh, S.P., & Perlmuter, L.C. (2008). Blood glucose levels before and after cognitive testing in diabetes mellitus. *Experimental Aging Research, 34*(2), 152–161. doi: 10.1080/03610730701876979

Garrett, B. (2010). The substance of false confessions. *Stanford Law Review, 62,* 1051–1118.

Garrett, B.L. (2011). *Convicting the Innocent: Where Criminal Prosecutions Go Wrong*. Cambridge, MA: Harvard University Press.

Gilsenan, M., de Bruin, E.A. & Dye, L. (2009). The influence of carbohydrate on cognitive performance: A critical evaluation from the perspective of glycaemic load. *British Journal of Nutrition,101,* 941–949.

Gonzales, L. (2003). *Deep Survival: Who lives, Who Dies, and Why*. New York: W.W. Norton & Company.

Gudjonsson, G.H. (2003). *The Psychology of Interrogations and Confessions: A Handbook*. New York: John Wiley & Sons, Ltd.

Hagger, M.S., Wood, C., Stiff, C., & Chatzisarantis, N.L.D. (2010). Ego depletion and the strength model of self-control: A meta-analysis. *Psychological Bulletin, 136*(4), 495–525. doi: 10.1037/a0019486; 10.1037/a0019486.supp (Supplemental).

Hammond, K. R. (2000). *Judgments Under Stress*. New York: Oxford University Press.

Harrison, Y., & Horne, J.A. (2000). The impact of sleep deprivation on decision making: A review. *Journal of Experimental Psychology: Applied, 6*(3), 236–249. doi: 10.1037/1076-898x.6.3.236

Hofmann, W., Friese, M., Schmeichel, B.J., & Baddeley, A.D. (2011). Working memory and self-regulation. In K.D. Vohs, & R.F. Baumeister (Eds), *Handbook of Self-regulation: Research, Theory, and Applications* (2nd edn, pp. 204–225). New York: Guilford Press.

Inbau, F.E., Reid, J.E., Buckley, J.P., & Jayne, B.C. (2011). *Criminal Interrogation and Confessions* (5th edn). Gaithersburg, MD: Aspen Publishers.

Jarrett, R.J., Viberti, G.C., & Sayegh, H.A. (1978). Does "afernoon diabetes" predict diabetes? *British Medical Journal, 1,* 199–201.

Kahneman, D. (2011). *Thinking, Fast and Slow*. New York: Farrar, Straus and Giroux.

Kassin, S.M. (1997). The psychology of confession evidence. *American Psychologist, 52*(3), 221–233. doi: 10.1037/0003-066x.52.3.221

Kassin, S.M. (2007). Internalized false confessions. In M.P. Toglia, J.D. Read, D.F. Ross, & R.C.L. Lindsay (Eds), *The Handbook of Eyewitness Psychology, Vol I: Memory for Events* (pp. 175–192). Mahwah, NJ: Lawrence Erlbaum Associates.

Kassin, S.M., Drizin, S.A., Grisso, T., Gudjonsson, G.H., Leo, R.A., & Redlich, A.D. (2010). Police-induced confessions, risk factors, and recommendations: Looking ahead. *Law and Human Behavior, 34*(1), 49–52. doi: 10.1007/s 10979-010-9217-5

Knowles, E.S., & Linn, J.A. (2004). Approach-avoidance model of persuasion: Alpha and omega strategies for change. In E.S. Knowles, & J.A. Linn (Eds), *Resistance and Persuasion* (pp. 117–148). Mahwah, NJ: Lawrence Erlbaum Associates.

Knowles, E.S., & Riner, D.D. (2007). Omega approaches to persuasion: Overcoming resistance. In A.R. Pratkanis (Ed.), *The Science of Social Influence: Advances and Future Progress* (pp. 83–114). New York: Psychology Press.

Kruglanski, A.W., & Webster, D.M. (1996). Motivated closing of the mind: 'Seizing' and 'freezing'. *Psychological Review, 103*(2), 263–283. doi: 10.1037/0033-295x.103.2.263

Lamport, D.J., Hoyle, E., Lawton, C.L., Mansfield, M.W., & Dye, L. (2011). Evidence for a second meal cognitive effect: Glycaemic responses to high and low glycaemic index evening meals are associated with cognition the following morning. *Nutritional Neuroscience, 14*(2), 66–71. doi: 10.1179/1476830511y.0000000002

Lamport, D.J., Lawton, C.L., Mansfield, M.W., & Dye, L. (2009). Impairments in glucose tolerance can have a negative impact on cognitive function: A systematic research review. *Neuroscience and Biobehavioral Reviews, 33*(3), 394–413. doi: 10.1016/j.neubiorev.2008.10.008

Larsen, R.P. (2001). Decision making by military students under severe stress. *Military Psychology, 13*(2), 89–98. doi: 10.1207/s15327876mp1302_02

Leo, R.A. (2008). *Police Interrogation and American Justice*. Cambridge, MA: Harvard University Press.

Leo, R.A., & Ofshe, R.J. (1998). The consequences of false confessions: Deprivations of liberty and miscarriages of justice in the age of psychological interrogation. *Journal of Criminal Law & Criminology, 88*(2), 429–496.

Lieberman, H.R., Bathalon, G.P., Falco, C.M., Morgan, C.A., III, Niro, P.J., & Tharion, W.J. (2005). The fog of war: Decrements in cognitive performance and mood associated with combat-like stress. *Aviation, Space, and Environmental Medicine, 76*(7, Sect 2, Suppl), C7–C14.

MacDonald, K.B. (2008). Effortful control, explicit processing, and the regulation of human evolved predispositions. *Psychological Review, 115*(4), 1012–1031. doi: 10.1037/a0013327

Martin, A. (2011) The prosecution's case against DNA. *New York Times Magazine*, 25 November 2011. www.nytimes.com/2011/11/27/magazine/dna-evidence-lake-county.html

Masicampo, E.J., & Baumeister, R.F. (2008). Toward a physiology of dual-process reasoning and judgment: Lemonade, willpower, and expensive rule-based analysis. *Psychological Science, 19*(3), 255–260. doi: 10.1111/j.1467-9280.2008.02077.x

McMahon, A.J., & Scheel, M.H. (2010). Glucose promotes controlled processing: Matching, maximizing, and root beer. *Judgment and Decision Making, 5*(6), 450–457.

McNeil, J.A., & Morgan, C.A., III. (2010). Cognition and decision making in extreme environments. In C.H. Kennedy, & J.L. Moore (Eds), *Military Neuropsychology* (pp. 361–382). New York: Springer.

Messier, C., Awad-Shimoon, N., Gagnon, M.L., Desrochers, A., & Tsiakas, M. (2011). Glucose regulation is associated with cognitive performance in young nondiabetic adults. *Behavioural Brain Research, 222*(1), 81–88. doi: 10.1016/j.bbr.2011.03.023

Miranda v. *Arizona*, 384 US 436 (1966).

Najdowski, C.J. (2011). Stereotype threat in criminal interrogations: Why innocent black suspects are at risk for confessing falsely. *Psychology, Public Policy, and Law, 17*(4), 562–591. doi: 10.1037/a0023741

New York v. *Zahira Matos and Carmen Molina*: Ind. No. 5162 2004.

Otgaar, H., Alberts, H., & Cuppens, L. (2012). How cognitive resources alter our perception of the past: Ego depletion enhances the susceptibility to suggestion. *Applied Cognitive Psychology, 26*, 159–163. doi: 10.1002/acp.1810

Petty, R.E., Cacioppo, J.T., Strathman, A.J., & Priester, J.R. (2005). To think or not to think: Exploring two routes to persuasion. In T.C. Brock, & M.C. Green (Eds), *Persuasion: Psychological Insights and Perspectives* (2nd edn, pp. 81–116). Thousand Oaks, CA: Sage.

Phelps, E.A., & Delgado, M.R. (2009). Emotion and decision making. In M.S. Gazzaniga, E. Bizzi, L.M. Chalupa, S.T. Grafton, T.F. Heatherton, C. Koch, J.E. LeDoux, S.J. Luck, G.R. Mangan, J.A. Movshon, H. Neville, E.A. Phelps, P. Rakic, D.L. Schacter, M. Sur, & B.A. Wandell (Eds), *The Cognitive Neurosciences* (4th edn, pp. 1093–1103). Cambridge, MA: Massachusetts Institute of Technology.

Radulian, G., Rusu, E., Dragomir, A., & Posea, M. (2009). Metabolic effects of low glycaemic index diets. *Nutrition Journal, 8*(5). doi: 10.1186/1475-2891-8-5

Roets, A., & Van Hiel, A. (2011). Impaired performance as a source of reduced energy investment in judgement under stressors. *Journal of Cognitive Psychology, 23*(5), 625–632. doi: 10.1080/20445911.2011.550569

Seligman, M.E.P. (1975). *Helplessness: On Depression, Development, and Death.* New York: W.H. Freeman/Times Books/Henry Holt & Co.

Serra-Grabulosa, J.M., Adan, A., Falcon, C., & Bargallo, N.R. (2010). Glucose and caffeine effects on sustained attention: An exploratory fMRI study. *Human Psychopharmacology: Clinical and Experimental, 25*(7–8), 543–552.

Thomas, G.C.I. (1996). Plain talk about the Miranda empirical debate: A "steady-state" theory of confessions. *UCLA Law Review, 43*, 933–959.

Thompson, H.L. (2010). *The Stress Effect: Why Smart Leaders Make Dumb Decisions, and What To Do About It.* San Francisco, CA: Jossey-Bass.

Tucker, D.M., & Williamson, P.A. (1984). Asymmetric neural control systems in human self-regulation. *Psychological Review, 91*(2), 185–215. doi: 10.1037/0033-295x.91.2.185

Vohs, K.D., & Baumeister, R.F. (2011). *Handbook of Self-regulation: Research, Theory, and Applications* (2nd edn). New York: Guilford Press.

Walker, M.P., & van der Helm, E. (2009). Overnight therapy? The role of sleep in emotional brain processing. *Psychological Bulletin, 135*(5), 731–748. doi: 10.1037/a0016570

Wesensten, N.J., & Balkin, T.J. (2010). Cognitive sequelae of sustained operations. In C.H. Kennedy, & J.L. Moore (Eds), *Military Neuropsychology* (pp. 297–320). New York: Springer.

Wrightsman, L.S. (2010). The Supreme Court on Miranda rights and interrogations: The past, the present, and the future. In G.D. Lassiter, & C.A. Meissner (Eds), *Police Interrogations and False Confessions: Current Research, Practice, and Policy Recommendations* (pp. 161–177). Washington, DC: American Psychological Association.

Yerkes, R.M., & Dodson, J.D. (1908). The relation of strength of stimulus to rapidity of habit-formation. *Journal of Comparative Neurology and Psychology, 18*, 459–482.

10

Suggestibility and Witness Interviewing using the Cognitive Interview and NICHD Protocol

DAVID J. LA ROOY, DEIRDRE BROWN AND MICHAEL E. LAMB

KEY POINTS

- This chapter reviews two interview approaches developed (in part) to minimize suggestive influences within an interview situation.
- First, we review research evaluating the efficacy of the Cognitive Interview (CI), which was developed for police officers to use when interviewing cooperative adult witnesses, and has since been applied to a variety of witness groups.
- Next, we describe the NICHD Investigative Interviewing Protocol, which was developed to assist forensic interviewers adhere to best practice guidelines in the conduct of interviews with children.
- The CI and NICHD Protocol are supported by large established literatures and their core recommendations are the result of significant consensus among researchers regarding effective interviewing.
- The two approaches share many features, although the NICHD Protocol focuses on interviews with children and is much more thoroughly structured than the CI.

Suggestibility in Legal Contexts: Psychological Research and Forensic Implications,
First Edition. Edited by Anne M. Ridley, Fiona Gabbert and David J. La Rooy.
© 2013 John Wiley & Sons, Ltd. Published 2013 by John Wiley & Sons, Ltd.

- While the CI has largely been examined in laboratory-based studies, the NICHD Protocol has been the focus of extensive field research.

As shown throughout this volume, there are many varieties of suggestibility and the effects of suggestive influence should be taken very seriously during investigations. Our memories can be influenced and distorted in many ways because they are vulnerable to decay, inner biases, social demands and expectations, confusion between similar (yet different) experiences, leading questions, misleading information, conversations with other witnesses, conformity and mental disability. To make matters even more complex, there are also individual differences in the susceptibility to suggestibility (Bruck & Melnyk, 2004) making it more difficult to pinpoint exactly where and when the effects of suggestibility are likely to manifest themselves (see Chapters 5, 7 and 8). Because suggestibility can have Kafkaesque and tragic consequences within the legal system – for example, false confessions, identification and conviction – considerable efforts have been made to develop practical means of minimizing the possible effects. It is important for investigators to understand the processes involved and the ways in which they can avoid suggestion and its effects.

In this chapter we review two research-based approaches to investigative interviewing – the Cognitive Interview (CI) and the National Institute of Child Health and Human Development (NICHD) Investigative Interview Protocol. As we make clear herein, these two approaches use many of the same key concepts derived from a wealth of experimental and applied research on memory. However, there are also important differences that have affected the development of these two approaches. In particular, the CI was developed largely to *enhance* the memory of adults who are *willing witnesses*; they may be witnesses who have either knowingly or unknowingly witnessed a crime, and therefore be asked about events of which they may have little or no recollection as well as those they actually remember very well. One important function of the CI is to advance the investigation by providing investigators with many accurate leads to follow up.

By contrast, the NICHD Protocol was developed primarily for use with children who are alleged victims of sexual and/or physical abuse and who are often unwilling to talk because they are scared, frightened or ashamed. There are often very long delays before interviews are conducted as a result of delayed disclosure and children are often presumed to be less credible and more suggestible. Importantly, children's developing cognitive abilities must be considered so that we have realistic expectations of what we can expect from them in interviews. In many jurisdictions, interviews with children are electronically recorded and serve a dual purpose within the legal system: they both advance investigations by providing leads and also are often used in court, sometimes replacing live testimony. The CI and Protocol approaches to interviewing are discussed herein with emphasis on the minimization of suggestibility.

ENHANCING ADULT EYEWITNESS MEMORY: THE COGNITIVE INTERVIEW

The Cognitive Interview (CI) was designed to improve the way police officers interviewed cooperative adult witnesses (Fisher, Geiselman, Raymond, Jurkevich, & Warhaftig, 1987). Research in the late 1980s and early 1990s examining the content and style of police interviews identified such problems as: minimal development of rapport, premature use of focused questions (including leading and/or suggestive questions) to elicit details, and frequent interruption of witness narratives and recall (Fisher, Geiselman, & Raymond, 1987; George & Clifford, 1992). Moreover, some officers interviewed witnesses in the same suggestive ways that they interviewed suspects, invoking many preconceived presumptions about case characteristics. As a result, the original aim of the CI was to improve police interviewing practices and to help witnesses provide detailed reports by incorporating strategies derived from research regarding the principles of memory and cognition. Most prominent were those relating to: (1) encoding specificity (Tulving & Thomson, 1973) which holds that maximizing the similarity between the psychological contexts in which encoding and retrieval take place is likely to enhance memory; and (2) the multicomponent view of memory encoding (Bower, 1967; Wickens, 1970), suggesting that memory traces each comprise many features, not all of which are equally accessible at any one time. For this reason, multiple retrieval attempts may allow additional details to be accessed (but see Dando, Ormerod, Wilcock, & Milne, 2011).

The original CI involved four strategies: (1) instructions to report everything recalled (even partially) whether or not the witness believed that the information was relevant or important; (2) attempts to mentally reinstate the context (including both emotive and sensory aspects) of the event; (3) recalling events in different temporal sequences; and (4) recalling the event from multiple perspectives, including those of other people, and from different locations within the scene. Although initial research suggested that the CI did, indeed, enhance witness informativeness, many of the difficulties faced by police officers were not addressed (Köhnken, Milne, Memon, & Bull, 1999). These included a tendency to control the flow of information reporting via directive questioning to follow up potential leads, a limited range of prompts and retrieval strategies, the frequent interruption of witness narratives, and limited rapport building and emphasis on the importance of witness

---

Box 10.1 An Example of the Memory Enhancing CI Technique

Investigator: 'I need a high level of detail from you, so I want you to concentrate really hard. I wasn't there so I do not know what happened. You are the one with all the information, so I need you to tell me everything that you can remember. I want you to tell me everything you can about what happened last night, even the things you think are not important, and even if you cannot remember something completely or can only remember it partially. Everything which comes to mind I want you tell me in your own time and pace. I want you to think back to a point in time on that night. It is like when you have lost something and you try to picture in your mind where you last had it, it is like that. What I want you to do is build a picture in your mind. Think of where you were. How were you feeling? What could you hear? What could you smell? Think of all the people who were present. Think about all the objects there. Think of the layout of where you were. Get a really good picture in your mind. Tell me everything you can, even the little things you think are not important. Remember I was not there, so just tell me everything in your own time.' (Westera *et al.*, 2011)

---

contributions. The CI was thus further revised to address the social factors influencing interview dynamics and to encourage interviewers to seek witness-directed narratives (Fisher & Geiselman, 1992). Increased emphasis was placed on the development of rapport-building and witness preparation, the transfer of control over the interview to the witness, the use of pauses and non-verbal behaviour, the exploration of many types of prompts and retrieval cues (e.g. imagery) and the inclusion of witness-compatible questioning and responding (e.g. by using other forms of communication such as sketches to describe spatial layouts). Box 10.1 illustrates what an investigator might say in an effort to re-build memory context and enhance a witness's memory (Westera, Kebbell, & Milne, 2011). In this example, the investigator aims to enhance memory by having the witness build the best possible picture in his/her mind of the remembered event before telling investigators what happened.

Two meta-analyses have summarized the research on various forms of the CI. Köhnken *et al.* (1999) analysed the effects of the CI (original and revised) relative to control or standard interview procedures as reported in studies (published and unpublished) conducted between 1984 and 1999. A standard interview is one that simply uses verbal prompting (open and direct questioning) without any particular preparation of the witness or any directed use of retrieval strategies or mnemonics. Their analysis indicated that the CI indeed enhanced the amount of correct information reported by participants (children and adults), with no studies showing the CI to be less effective than the comparison condition. The size of the effect was influenced by factors known to affect recall (e.g. adults seemed to benefit more than children and effects were greater after shorter delays and when the witnesses were more actively involved in the target events). The CI also produced higher levels of incorrect recall, although the pattern was less consistent across studies (e.g. some showed the CI elicited fewer incorrect details) and the effect size was markedly smaller. When overall accuracy was considered (the amount of correct information relative to the total amount reported), there were no differences. Put another way, the CI improved the amount of recall without any detrimental effect on the quality or reliability of the information reported.

More recently, Memon, Meissner, and Fraser (2010a) conducted a meta-analysis including studies published since 1999. The earlier findings were replicated, even with the variability produced by the numerous variations of the CI used in recent research. That is, use of the CI had a substantial effect on the amount of correct information elicited. There was a small effect on the numbers of incorrect details reported, but overall accuracy rates were not affected. This is likely a result of the overall increase in information reported. That is, as witnesses report more information, the opportunity to include erroneous details increases. The increased reporting is probably a result of both the effectiveness of the cognitive retrieval strategies (e.g. context reinstatement) and the instructions to report all details (Memon, Wark, Bull, & Köhnken, 1997). The 'report everything' instruction aims to lower witness response thresholds and minimize the likelihood of respondents withholding information because they do not consider it to be important (Koriat & Goldsmith, 1996). Importantly, the accuracy rates (proportion of correct information) are the same as with any other interview the CI has been compared to. The effects of the CI were strongest for recall-based tasks, especially during the follow-up questioning phase (where the various mnemonic techniques were used). Thus there is substantial evidence, mostly from research in laboratory/analogue contexts, that the CI can help witnesses provide elaborative details about their experiences.

Although most studies examining the CI have involved adults (primarily university students), its effectiveness in supporting more vulnerable witnesses have also been examined with studies of children, older adults, adults with intellectual disabilities and children with intellectual or other developmental disabilities. The CI does not help child witnesses as consistently as it helps adults but improved recall has been demonstrated with children ranging in age from 4 years

(Holliday & Albon, 2004) to middle childhood (Akehurst, Milne, & Köhnken, 2003; Geiselman & Padilla, 1988; Holliday, 2003; Larsson, Granhag, & Spjut, 2003; Milne & Bull, 2003; Saywitz, Geiselman, & Bornstein, 1992). As with adults, some researchers have reported increases in the numbers of erroneous details reported (Memon et al., 1997), although the proportion of incorrect to correct information seems to remain constant (McCauley & Fisher, 1995). Other researchers have reported no improvements in recall when children were interviewed using the CI (Memon, Cronin, Eaves, & Bull, 1996). Studies of older adults also show benefits (e.g. Holliday et al., in press), even when significant cognitive deficits are present (Wright & Holliday, 2007), although at least one study failed to show any advantage when older adults were interviewed using the CI (McMahon, 2000).

Few researchers have studied adults and children with intellectual or other disabilities (e.g. Autistic Spectrum Disorders (ASD)). Children with mild intellectual disabilities provide more correct and incorrect details when interviewed using the CI, with no detrimental effect on overall accuracy (Milne & Bull, 1996; Robinson & McGuire, 2006). Adults with cognitive impairments that fell within the borderline/mild intellectual disability range recalled more information when interviewed using the CI although they also reported more inaccurate information (Brown & Geiselman, 1990) and similar results were obtained by Milne, Clare, and Bull (1999) in a study of adults who had mild intellectual disabilities.

There has only been one study to date looking at the effectiveness of the CI when the witnesses have specific developmental disabilities. Maras and Bowler (2010) compared how well adults with and without ASD recalled a short video clip when interviewed using either the CI or standard interview practices. Contrary to findings with other vulnerable groups, the CI not only failed to enhance correct recall but also affected accuracy adversely, leading the authors to caution that the particular cognitive and social challenges associated with ASD may make the CI particularly unsuitable for this group. Thus, with the possible exception of ASD, the CI seems to be effective when used to interview vulnerable witnesses.

But, what of suggestibility? Witnesses may encounter suggestion from a range of sources including inappropriate (leading or misleading) questioning during an interview, misinformation by co-witnesses or the media and/or explicit suggestions or coaching by interested parties (e.g. parents). These influences may be encountered before a witness is first interviewed, or in the interim between an interview and subsequent interviews and/or testifying in court. Several researchers have therefore examined the extent to which the CI may reduce the incorporation of misinformation into witness accounts, or assist witnesses in resisting suggestive questions. The findings regarding suggestibility are not as uniform as those relating to the recall of events. Some studies show that use of the CI helps children resist suggestive questioning at the conclusion of an interview (Memon, Holley, Wark, Bull, & Köhnken, 1996; Milne & Bull, 2003) and misinformation provided before the interview (Holliday, 2003, Experiment 2; Holliday & Albon, 2004), while others show that children are still vulnerable to post-event misinformation (Hayes & Delamothe, 1997; Holliday, 2003, Experiment 1; Milne, Bull, Köhnken, & Memon, 1995). Recently Holliday *et al.* (in press) demonstrated that older (but not younger) adults interviewed with the CI were less susceptible to the effects of misinformation encountered before interview. Other studies with younger adults, however, have shown protective effects against incorporation of suggested information into reports, particularly when the CI occurs *prior* to rather than *following* the misinformation. That is, an early interview conducted with the CI may protect against later suggestion but its use after contamination does not overcome or 'cure' the effects of misinformation (e.g. Centofanti & Reece, 2006; Geiselman, Fisher, Cohen, Holland, & Surtes, 1986; Memon, Zaragoza, Clifford, & Kidd, 2010b). It has been suggested that an early CI may exert a protective effect because it increases the amount of information retrieved, strengthens the memory for the original event details (through rehearsal) and allows rejection of suggestion through more accurate source monitoring (e.g. Geiselman *et al.*, 1986; Holliday *et al.*, in press). The instructions contained within it may also lead to witnesses interviewed with the CI feeling more confident about rejecting suggestive questions; that is, the social instructions emphasize the expert role of the witness (and conversely, the naivety of the interviewer). This may be particularly important for children given their vulnerability to agreeing with interviewers to create a positive impression and their assumptions that adults are knowledgeable about their experiences (Lamb & Brown, 2006).

To what extent do these studies tell us how well the CI works in the real world of police investigative interviewing? Studies of interviewing quality have consistently demonstrated that without regular supervision and ongoing training, interviewers have difficulty maintaining post-training standards of practice. Research indicates that police officers may not consistently use the CI in its entirety (e.g. Kebbell, Milne, & Wagstaff, 1999) and have expressed scepticism about the utility of some of the strategies contained within it. Furthermore, time constraints faced by officers often make the use of a full CI impracticable. In response to this concern, researchers have examined shortened versions of the CI (e.g. Davis, McMahon, & Greenwood, 2005; Dando, Wilcock, Milne, & Henry, 2009) as well as a self-administered interview protocol (SAI) that can be used to interview multiple witnesses as quickly as possible (Gabbert, Hope, & Fisher, 2009). Both sorts of modifications seem to be effective.

While the positive effects on witness recall and reporting have been demonstrated despite variations in the populations sampled and the specific CI components included, some important methodological limitations remain. Memon *et al.* (2010a) identified a range of factors that have received little attention and many of the same points were mentioned by Köhnken *et al.* (1999) a decade earlier. First, variability in the specific components of the CI studied makes it difficult to determine which components are especially important. Memon *et al.* (2010a) note that 44% of the studies that have been conducted used modified versions of the CI, with little consistency about which strategies were included. As a result, it is still unclear which components are effective – or indeed whether some components are more or less productive than others – for which witnesses and under which conditions (Fisher, 2010; Fisher & Schreiber, 2007). Second, few studies involve delays akin to those that witnesses (especially children) may encounter in the forensic system: most involve delays of a mere day or so, with few involving delays longer than 2 weeks. Third, most studies ask witnesses to recall short video clips, with few using personally experienced events and none using events that elicit high levels of emotional arousal or are traumatic. Fourth, surprisingly few studies involve transcripts of real-world investigative interviews. Finally, although witnesses are typically required to recount their experiences in the context of multiple interviews, whether formal or informal (e.g. with family and friends), researchers have seldom studied the effect of more than one CI interview. Thus, there remain many opportunities for researchers eager to expand our understanding of the CI and its effects.

In summary, the CI is buttressed by a substantial and growing evidence base, although considerable scope remains for ecologically valid research to refine the content and broaden the application of the CI. It has support from researchers and practitioners alike and is included in many police training programmes around the world (Fisher, 2010; Fisher, Milne, & Bull, 2011; Fisher & Schreiber, 2007). As with other interview protocols, however, the CI cannot 'cure' the effects (i.e. suggestion) of inappropriate prior interviewing – although it may ameliorate some of these effects – and it does not uniformly offer protection with all groups of witnesses. Those at the forefront of research on the CI caution that, as with other protocols, the CI should be viewed as a toolbox of techniques to address issues that may arise in the course of an interview rather than as a rigid recipe for interviewing (Fisher, 2010; Fisher, Milne, & Bull, 2011; Fisher & Schreiber, 2007). Not all components of the CI are effective for all witnesses and for all witness tasks. Merely training in or using the CI does not replace the need for careful planning of an interview, taking into consideration witness characteristics and the nature of the target event. Interviewers must also flexibly adapt the interview to the needs of specific witnesses.

OBTAINING CHILDREN'S TESTIMONY:
THE NICHD PROTOCOL

The NICHD Protocol was developed in the mid-1990s with input from a wide range of professionals including lawyers, developmental, clinical and forensic psychologists, police officers; and social workers, and has been the focus of intensive forensic evaluation and research ever since (see Lamb, Hershkowitz, Orbach, & Esplin, 2008; Bull, 2010). Its development was prompted in part by various very high-profile child-abuse cases that sparked concerns throughout the psychological and legal worlds about the suggestive ways in which children were being interviewed. In a series of 'day care' child-abuse cases (including the oft-cited McMartin and Michaels cases described by Ceci & Bruck, 1993 and Bruck & Ceci, 1995), for example, suggestive interviews yielded allegations that children had been raped, genitally penetrated with knives, forced to consume faeces, buried alive, transported through underground tunnels, and witnessed murders, all during normal working hours when parents were free to come and go as they pleased from the day care centre. In these cases, and others like them, no corroborative evidence was ever found. Nowadays, it may seem obvious that the ways children are interviewed can foster false allegations but, in the past, widely held but erroneous beliefs about children's memories were fuelled by social hysteria and diagnostic therapies that seemed to 'prove' the 'widespread' nature of the problem (e.g. Bass & Davis, 1988). It was commonly assumed in the 1980s and 1990s that: 'all men are rapists'; 25% of females were severely abused; sex 'rings' and satanic ritual abuse were commonplace; most people were in denial about their abuse history; it was possible to recover previously repressed memories; and that behavioural indicators could reveal that abuse had taken place, even when the supposed victims could remember nothing about it. Ultimately, many courts failed to convict because so much evidence was obtained using suggestive interview and therapy techniques but, nonetheless, the everyday lives of many of those involved were ruined by the accusations.

What followed came to be known as the 'memory wars' during which our understanding of children's suggestibility (and the danger of therapist 'interventions') was greatly advanced. We now know from experimental research that misleading questions (Baker-Ward, Gordon, Ornstein, Larus, & Clubb 1993; Pipe, Sutherland, Webster, Jones, & La Rooy, 2004), misleading information (Bruck, Ceci, Francoeur, & Barr, 1995), misleading props (Leichtman & Ceci, 1995), repeated questions (Krähenbühl & Blades, 2006; Poole & White, 1991, 1993), social pressure (Melnyk & Bruck, 2004), peer pressure (Bruck, Ceci, & Hembrooke, 2002; Principe & Ceci, 2002), imagination and fantasy (Ceci, Huffman,

Smith, & Loftus, 1994), inappropriate encouragement and praise (Bruck *et al.*, 2002), asking about things we know didn't happen (Ceci *et al.*, 1994; Erdmann, Volbert, & Bohm, 2004), negative reinforcement (Powell, Jones, & Campbell, 2003) and encouraging guessing and speculation (Erdmann *et al.*, 2004) can all lead children to report inaccurately. In many of these studies, various combinations of suggestive techniques were used to produce large effects; in one study, for example, as many as 73% of the children falsely agreed that fictitious events had taken place (Erdmann *et al.*, 2004).

In addition to explaining when children are likely to provide unreliable information during investigations, researchers have also allowed us to define developmentally appropriate expectations about children's capabilities and to identify the conditions in which children are most likely to describe their experiences of abuse accurately. The universal emphasis on the superior value of narrative responses elicited using open-ended prompts is rooted in the oft-replicated results of laboratory analogue studies demonstrating that information elicited using such prompts is much more likely to be accurate than information elicited using more focused recognition prompts (Dale, Loftus, & Rathbun, 1978; Dent, 1982, 1986; Dent & Stephenson, 1979; Goodman & Aman, 1990; Goodman, Bottoms, Schwartz-Kenney, & Rudy, 1991; Hutcheson, Baxter, Telfer, & Warden, 1995; Oates & Shrimpton, 1991; Ornstein, Gordon, & Larus, 1992), probably because open-ended questions force the respondent to recall information from memory, whereas more focused prompts often require the respondent to recognize one or more options suggested by the interviewer.

Given the clarity of research on children's memory and suggestibility, the developers of the NICHD Protocol sought to create forensic interviewing guidelines that clearly specified the types of interviewer prompts that were appropriate to use in interviews with children, while at the same time restricting as much as possible opportunities for interviewers to fall into the suggestibility trap by asking focused questions based on their own assumptions about things that may not have happened. Developers of the Protocol thus sought to reduce reliance on focused prompting and encourage reliance on open-ended prompting to allow children to control the recall process and to increase the likelihood that the information recalled would be accurate. The goal was to create an interview Protocol that could be used by interviewers around the world with varying levels of experience and training and, importantly, that could be used by interviewers who didn't have a specialized knowledge of suggestibility research and memory development! Moreover, the Protocol also needed to be robust enough to withstand legal challenge. The solution lay in providing not only guidance regarding general concepts about memory and suggestibility but also specific and structured guidance about exactly the sorts of

Box 10.2 An Example of the Stages of the Structured NICHD Protocol

The NICHD Protocol is printed in full in Kuehnle and Connell (2009), Lamb *et al.* (2008) and Lamb, La Rooy, Malloy, and Katz (2011).

- Introduction
- Ground rules:
  - Truth and lies
  - Transfer of control (e.g. 'don't know,' 'don't guess,' 'correct me if I am wrong.')
- Rapport (e.g. 'What do you like to do? [wait for and answer] Tell me about that.')
- Practice interview (memory training/cognitive support)
- Transition to substantive phase
- Investigate incidents:
  - Open-ended prompts (e.g. 'Tell me what happened.')
  - Separation of incidents (e.g. 'Did this happen one time, or more than one time?)
- Focused questions about information not already mentioned
- Disclosure information (Who did the child initially tell? Who else knows what happened?)
- Closure (e.g. 'Anything else you want to tell?' 'Do you have any questions you want to ask?')
- Neutral topic (e.g. 'What are you going to do when you leave?')

things that should be said and in what order. The advantage of this structured approach was that it promised to level the playing field by providing all children with equal opportunities to recount their experiences regardless of individual interviewer biases and pre-existing beliefs about children's capabilities and case similarities (see Box 10.2).

The Protocol developed in the mid-1990s covers all stages of the investigative interview. The introductory phase was influenced by various law enforcement agencies in different jurisdictions who requested the inclusion of questions designed to establish that children understood the difference between true and false statements in anticipation of legal challenges to children's credibility. For example, interviewers tell children that they will be required to describe events in detail and that they should 'tell the truth', and say, 'I don't remember', 'I don't know', 'I don't understand', when they don't understand what the interviewer is saying. This initial phase, sometimes called 'ground rules', is designed to remove potential 'pressure' that could manifest itself as suggestive influence later in the interview should the children feel that they must acquiesce to leading questions or suggestive utterances. These ground rules can also serve as a form of protection for the interviewer when, as invariably happens, a suggestive or leading question is inadvertently asked – it is actually good to see children saying 'I don't know' in interviews.

Interviewers then create a relaxed, supportive environment while trying to gauge the children's social and emotional needs. Rapport building is further extended during what is known as the 'practice interview' (also described as 'memory training', 'narrative elaboration training' or 'episodic memory training'). In this phase, children are prompted to describe a real experience in detail in response to open-ended prompts. This allows interviewers to introduce the kinds of prompts that will be used when the events of interest are later discussed, thereby demonstrating to the children the level of detail required and that interviewers are naive or ignorant regarding the children's experiences. The significance of this phase is that it also focuses children on 'real' events because they are asked to provide specific details about things that really happened – not things that they, for example, have been told to say by others (interviewers can sometimes pre-plan suitable events to discuss by talking to parents and guardians; they thus already know a little about what happened before the interview begins). Importantly, the Protocol from the outset moves conversation away from topics and activities that could facilitate suggestibility and foster fantasy, such as including discussions of movies, stories, favourite games, imaginary friends, as well as drawings and opportunities to play with toys.

The transition between the introductory, rapport-building and practice narrative phases (collectively, the pre-substantive phase) and the substantive phase of the interview is particularly pertinent to concerns about suggestibility. In this phase, a series of prompts are used to identify the target event/s under investigation as non-suggestively as possible. Because suggestive questions are defined as any information introduced by the interviewer that has not already been mentioned by the child, the interviewer cannot be the first to raise the topic. Hence, in an effort to be non-suggestive, the interviewer should simply ask the child if they know why they are here and, if the child indicates that they do, the interviewer should try to obtain an account by using an open-ended prompt such as 'Tell me what happened', followed by further open-ended prompting.

Some commentators have suggested that open-ended prompts such as 'Tell me more about that' are actually suggestive because they could be seen to imply that something more *has* happened when the child has already exhausted his/her memory. This concern is obviously important because children can, and do, provide information about non-events when they are questioned about them (Bruck *et al.*, 2002;

Ceci *et al.*, 1994). However, it is important to consider the context for which the 'Tell me' prompt is recommended. In real child abuse investigations, unlike research studies, children are not intentionally interviewed about suggested events that investigators know didn't really happen. Rather, the trigger for many interviews is that children have made a prior disclosure that raises suspicion of abuse. In a forensic context, therefore, it is important to realize that children are often aware of the reason that the interview is taking place because they have made previous disclosures. Moreover, false allegations by children are very rare and there is no evidence that children make up information when asked to 'tell' what happened to them in an appropriate context. This differs, of course, from the highly suggestive interview context and false allegations in the McMartin case discussed earlier.

Sometimes, however, when children do not provide any information to the interviewer's initial prompt 'Tell me why you came to see me today', the interviewer needs to needs to ask another open question; according to Sternberg, Lamb, Davies, & Wescott *et al.* (2001) four-fifths of the children who make allegations do so in response to a completely open-ended prompt. For this reason, interviewers should *always* allow children to raise the topic themselves. If children do not make allegations and the investigators have good reason to suspect that they were indeed abused, however, the interviewer may need to move on to use a series of increasingly focused prompts, perhaps including a prompt like 'Your teacher told me that you said someone has touched your privates. Tell me about that.' This prompt is suggestive because it refers to information that the child has not told the investigator, so should be used only if necessary, and in such a way as to focus attention without identifying the alleged perpetrator, the location, or other details about the suspected incidents. If the child agrees with the investigator's assertion, it is crucial that the investigator resume using open-ended prompts, starting with: 'So someone touched your privates. Tell me everything about that.' Open-ended prompts like this allow the child to report details not suggested by the investigator and to regain control of the interview. As noted above, some children do not make allegations in response to such prompts when they are first given the opportunity to do so and investigators should always consider whether it would be best to abort the interview rather than ask contaminating suggestive questions. Of course, when there are child protection concerns, it is often necessary to proceed with caution, despite the attendant risks.

Whenever children make allegations, interviewers are encouraged to elicit further information using additional open-ended prompts such as 'Then what happened?', 'Tell me more about that', and 'You said X, tell me more about that', for example. Once the child has provided an initial account, it is sometimes necessary to prompt the child to indicate whether the abuse occurred 'one time or more than one time' to clarify the components of specific incidents. Research showing the difficulty children (and adults) have with source monitoring has influenced the expectations we should have about the number of separate incidents that interviewers can hope children will describe accurately (Brubacher, Glisic, Roberts, & Powell, 2011; Brubacher, Roberts, & Powell, 2011; Powell, Roberts, & Guadagno, 2007). Rather than asking the children to recall all the incidents in a specific order (as suggested in some variants of the CI), interviewers are encouraged to focus on the times that are likely to be the best remembered – the first time, the last time and another time.

After children have provided sufficiently detailed accounts, interviewers can use focused questions to explore important details that may have been left out. These may include focused questions of the who/how variety, which are preferable because they leave control with the children, or closed questions. The latter include questions that can be answered yes/no or ask children to choose between interviewer-provided options, for example, 'Was it A or B?' Research shows that questions like these may mislead children, causing them to acquiesce to non-experienced events and details suggested by the interviewer (Bruck, Ceci, Francouer, & Renick, 1995; Ceci & Huffman, 1997; Pipe *et al.*, 2004; Poole & Lindsay, 1998). Hence, it is particularly important that interviewers only ask these questions when absolutely necessary and that they follow up with open-ended questions that transfer control back to the child and minimize contamination (e.g. 'So it hurt. Tell me everything about that.').

All questions need to be constructed simply and carefully to avoid misunderstanding and investigators need to remain sensitive to cues that they have been misunderstood. For example, the question 'What colour was the car?' may seem fairly straightforward but the child may wonder whether the question pertains to the inside or outside of the car (e.g. Jones & Krugman, 1986). Moreover, the ease with which focused questions can be answered varies: a question such as 'What is your brother's name?' may be quite easy to answer because it refers to well-learned semantic information, whereas 'What finger did he touch you with?' may be difficult to remember and thus encourage a guess response.

Suggestive utterances, which strongly communicate desired responses, are discouraged by the NICHD Protocol. Research conducted in the early 2000s has shown clearly how dangerous such questions can be and most professionals agree that there has been a general decline in the frequency with which such questions are used. Several studies show that the number of suggestive questions asked in forensic interviews is actually quite low (e.g. < 10%; Cederborg, La Rooy, & Lamb, 2008; Orbach *et al.*, 2000; Sternberg *et al.*, 2001). The challenge for the future is to encourage the use of open-ended prompting to elicit the most accurate information in interviews.

In summary, our understanding of the issues surrounding investigative suggestibility has shaped many professional recommendations about interviewing children (e.g. American Professional Society on the Abuse of Children (APSAC), 1997; Achieving Best Evidence (ABE), Home Office, 2002, 2007; Ministry of Justice, 2011; Jones, 2003; Lamb *et al.*, 2008, 2011; Law Commission, 1997; Poole & Lamb, 1998; Sattler, 1998; Scottish Executive, 2003, 2011). Because our knowledge of memory and suggestibility is now so advanced, core recommendations made by professional bodies worldwide reveal remarkable consensus and are unlikely to change dramatically. Differences in recommended procedures used by professionals usually arise out of regional idiosyncratic legal constraints rather than disagreements about the true nature of memory, children's developing abilities, and the best ways of eliciting information from them.

CONCLUSIONS

- The Cognitive Interview (CI) and the National Institute of Child Health and Human Development (NICHD) Investigative Interview Protocol have both been developed by researchers as approaches to interviewing that minimize suggestive influence.
- The CI is incorporated into professional guidelines in England and Wales, Canada and New Zealand.
- The NICHD Protocol is mandated in parts of the USA, Canada and Israel, is taught, built into and/or underpins formal guidelines in Sweden, Norway, England, Wales, Scotland and Finland and is currently being implemented in Korea, Japan and Portugal.
- The CI and the Protocol can be readily incorporated into existing training programmes and are freely available.
- For reference, the NICHD Protocol is printed in full in Kuehnle & Connell, (2009), Lamb *et al.* (2008) and Lamb *et al.* (2011).

FORENSIC IMPLICATIONS

- Investigators must be aware of research-based guidelines for interviewing and strive to implement them in full.
- Being knowledgeable about research-based guidelines is important for defending practice when challenged. Interviewers need to be able to identify *when* and *why* departures from guidelines occur.

REFERENCES

Akehurst, L., Milne, R., & Köhnken, G. (2003). The effects of children's age and delay on recall in a cognitive or structured interview. *Psychology, Crime & Law, 9,* 97–107.

American Professional Society on the Abuse of Children (1997). *Guidelines for Psychosocial Evaluation of Suspected Sexual Abuse in Young Children* (Revised). Chicago, IL: APSAC.

Baker-Ward, L., Gordon, B.N., Ornstein, P.A., Larus, D., & Clubb, P. (1993). Young children's long-term retention of a pediatric examination. *Child Development, 56,* 1103–1119.

Bass, E., & Davis, L. (1988). *The Courage to Heal.* New York: Harper & Row.

Bower, G.H. (1967). A multicomponent view of a memory trace. In K.W. Spence, & J.T. Spence (Eds), *The Psychology of Learning and Motivation* (Vol 1. pp. 299–325). New York: Academic Press.

Brown, C.L., & Geiselman, R.E. (1990). Eyewitness testimony of the mentally retarded: Effect of the cognitive interview. *Journal of Police and Criminal Psychology, 6,* 14–22.

Brubacher, S.P., Glisic, U., Roberts, K.P., & Powell, M. (2011). Children's ability to recall unique aspects of one occurrence of a repeated event. *Applied Cognitive Psychology, 25,* 351–358.

Brubacher, S.P., Roberts, K.P., & Powell, M. (2011). Effects of practicing episodic versus scripted recall on children's subsequent narratives of a repeated event. *Psychology, Public Policy, and Law, 17,* 286–314.

Bruck, M., & Ceci, S.J. (1995). Amicus brief for the case of *State of New Jersey* v. *Michaels* presented by Committee of Concerned Social Scientists. *Psychology, Public Policy, and Law, 1,* 272–322.

Bruck, M., Ceci, S. J., Francoeur, E., & Barr, R. (1995). "I hardly cried when I got my shot!" Influencing children's reports about a visit to their pediatrician. *Child Development, 66,* 193–208.

Bruck, M., Ceci, S.J., Francoeur, E., & Renick, A. (1995). Anatomically detailed dolls do not facilitate pre-schoolers' reports of a paediatric examination involving genital touch. *Journal of Experimental Psychology: Applied, 1,* 95–109.

Bruck, M., Ceci, S.J., & Hembrooke, H. (2002). The nature of children's true and false narratives. *Developmental Review, 22,* 520–554.

Bruck, M., & Melnyk, L. (2004). Individual differences in children's suggestibility: A review and synthesis. *Applied Cognitive Psychology, 18*(8), 947–996.

Bull, R. (2010). The investigative interviewing of children and other vulnerable witnesses: Psychological research and working/professional practice. *Legal and Criminological Psychology, 15,* 5–23.

Ceci, S.J., & Bruck, M. (1993). Suggestibility of the child witness: A historical review and synthesis. *Psychological Bulletin, 113,* 403–439.

Ceci, S.J., & Huffman, M.L.C. (1997). How suggestive are preschool children? Cognitive and social factors. *Journal of the American Academy of Child and Adolescent Psychiatry, 36,* 948–958.

Ceci, S.J., Huffman, M.L.C., Smith, E., & Loftus, E.F. (1994). Repeatedly thinking about a non-event-source misattributions among preschoolers. *Consciousness and Cognition, 3,* 388–407.

Cederborg, A.-C., La Rooy, D., & Lamb, M. (2008). Repeated interviews with children who have intellectual disabilities. *Journal of Applied Research in Intellectual Disabilities, 21,* 103–113.

Centofanti, A.T., & Reece, J.E. (2006). The cognitive interview and its effect on misleading post-event information. *Psychology, Crime & Law, 12,* 669–683.

Dando, C.J., Ormerod, T.C. Wilcock, R., & Milne, R. (2011). When help becomes hindrance: Unexpected errors of omission and commission in eyewitness memory resulting from change temporal order at retrieval? *Cognition, 121,* 416–421.

Dando, C., Wilcock, R., Milne, R., & Henry, L. (2009). A modified cognitive interview procedure for frontline police investigators. *Applied Cognitive Psychology, 23,* 698–716.

Dale, P.S., Loftus, E.F., & Rathbun, L. (1978). The influence of the form of the question of the eyewitness testimony of preschool children. *Journal of Psycholinguistic Research, 74,* 269–277.

Davis, M.R., McMahon, M., & Greenwood, K.M. (2005). The efficacy of mnemonic components of the cognitive interview: Towards a shortened variant for time-critical investigations. *Applied Cognitive Psychology, 19,* 75–93.

Dent, H.R. (1982). The effects of interviewing strategies on the results of interviews with child witnesses. In A. Trankell (Ed.), *Reconstructing the Past: The Role of Psychologists in Criminal Trials* (pp. 279–297). Stockholm: Norstedt.

Dent, H.R. (1986). Experimental study of the effectiveness of different techniques of questioning child witnesses. *British Journal of Social and Clinical Psychology, 18,* 41–51.

Dent, H.R., & Stephenson, G.M. (1979). An experimental study of the effectiveness of different techniques of questioning child witnesses. *British Journal of Social and Clinical Psychology, 18,* 41–51.

Erdmann, K., Volbert, R., & Bohm, C. (2004). Children report suggested events even when interviewed in a non-suggestive manner: What are the implications for credibility assessment? *Applied Cognitive Psychology, 18,* 589–611.

Fisher, R.P. (2010). Interviewing cooperative witnesses. *Legal and Criminological Psychology, 15,* 25–38.

Fisher, R.P., & Geiselman, R.E. (1992). *Memory-enhancing Techniques for Investigating Interviewing: The Cognitive Interview.* Springfield, IL: Charles C. Thomas.

Fisher, R.P., Geiselman, R.E., & Raymond, D.S. (1987). Critical analysis of police interviewing techniques. *Journal of Police Science & Administration, 15,* 177–185.

Fisher, R.P., Geiselman, R.E., Raymond, D.S., Jurkevich, L.M., & Warhaftig, M.L. (1987). Enhancing enhanced eyewitness memory: Refining the cognitive interview. *Journal of Police Science and Administration, 15,* 291–297.

Fisher, R.P., Milne, R., & Bull, R. (2011). Interviewing cooperative witnesses. *Current Directions in Psychological Science, 20,* 16–19.

Fisher, R.P., & Schreiber, N. (2007). Interviewing protocols to improve eyewitness memory. In M. Toglia, J. Reed, D. Ross, & R. Lindsay (Eds), *The Handbook of Eyewitness Psychology: Volume 1. Memory for Events* (pp. 53–80). Mahwah, NJ: Erlbaum Associates.

Gabbert, F., Hope, L., & Fisher, R.P. (2009). Protecting eyewitness evidence: Examining the efficacy of a self-administered interview tool. *Law and Human Behavior, 33,* 298–307.

Geiselman, R.E., Fisher, R.P., Cohen, G., Holland, H., & Surtes, L. (1986). Eyewitness responses to leading and misleading questions under the cognitive interview. *Journal of Police Science and Administration, 14,* 31–39.

Geiselman, R.E., & Padilla, J. (1988). Cognitive interviewing with child witnesses. *Journal of Police Science and Administration, 16,* 236–242.

George, R.C., & Clifford, B. (1992). Making the most of witnesses. *Policing*, *8*, 185–198.

Goodman, G.S., & Aman, C. (1990). Children's use of anatomically detailed dolls to recount an event. *Child Development, 61*, 1859–1871.

Goodman, G.S., Bottoms, B.L., Schwartz-Kenney, B.M., & Rudy, L. (1991). Children's testimony about a stressful event: Improving children's reports. *Journal of Narrative and Life History, 1*, 69–99.

Hayes, B.K., & Delamothe, K. (1997). Cognitive interviewing procedures and suggestibility in children's recall. *Journal of Applied Psychology, 82*, 562–577.

Holliday, R. (2003). Reducing misinformation effects in children with cognitive interviews: Dissociating recollection and familiarity. *Child Development, 74*, 728–751.

Holliday, R.E., & Albon, A. (2004). Minimising misinformation effects in young children with cognitive interview mnemonics. *Applied Cognitive Psychology, 18*, 263–281.

Holliday, R.E., Humphries, J.E., Milne, R., Memon, A., Houlder, L., Lyons, A., & Bull, R. (in press). Reducing misinformation effects in older adults with Cognitive Interview mnemonics. *Psychology and Aging*.

Home Office (2002). *Achieving Best Evidence in Criminal Proceedings: Guidance for Vulnerable or Intimidated Witnesses, Including Children*. London: Home Office.

Home Office (2007). *Achieving Best Evidence in Criminal Proceedings: Guidance on Interviewing Victims and Witnesses, and Using Special Measures*. London: Home Office.

Hutcheson, G.D., Baxter, J.S., Telfer, K., & Warden, D. (1995). Child witness statement quality: Question type and errors of omission. *Law and Human Behavior, 19*, 631–648.

Jones, D.P.H. (2003). *Communicating with Vulnerable Children*. London: Gaskell and Royal College of Psychiatrists.

Jones, D.P.H., & Krugman, R.D. (1986). Can a three-year-old child bear witness to her sexual assault and attempted murder? *Child Abuse & Neglect, 10*, 253–258.

Kebbell, M., Milne, R., & Wagstaff, G. (1999). The cognitive interview: A survey of its forensic effectiveness. *Psychology, Crime and Law, 5*, 101–116.

Köhnken, G., Milne, R., Memon, A., & Bull, R. (1999). The cognitive interview: A meta-analysis. *Psychology, Crime & Law, 5*, 3–27.

Koriat, A., & Goldsmith, M. (1996). Monitoring and control processes in the strategic regulation of memory accuracy. *Psychological Review, 103*, 490–517.

Krähenbühl, S., & Blades, M. (2006). The effect of question repetition within interviews on young children's eyewitness recall. *Journal of Experimental Child Psychology, 94*, 57–67.

Kuehnle, K., & Connell, M. (2009). *The Evaluation of Child Sexual Abuse Allegations: A Comprehensive Guide to Assessment and Testimony*. Chichester: John Wiley & Sons, Ltd.

Lamb, M.E., & Brown, D.A. (2006). Conversational apprentices: Helping children become competent informants about their own experiences. *British Journal of Developmental Psychology, 24*, 215–234.

Lamb, M.E., Hershkowitz, I., Orbach, Y., & Esplin, P.W. (2008). *Tell Me What Happened*. Chichester,: John Wiley & Sons, Ltd.

Lamb, M.E., La Rooy, D.J., Malloy, L. C., & Katz, C. (2011). *Children's Testimony: A Handbook of Psychological Research and Forensic Practice* (2nd edn). Oxford: Wiley-Blackwell.

Larsson, A., Granhag, P.A., & Spjut, E. (2003). Children's recall and the Cognitive Interview: Do the positive effects hold over time? *Applied Cognitive Psychology, 17,* 203–214.

Law Commission (1997). *The Evidence of Children and Other Vulnerable Witnesses.* Wellington, NZ: Law Commission.

Leichtman, M.D., & Ceci, S.J. (1995). The effects of stereotypes and suggestions on preschoolers' reports. *Developmental Psychology, 31,* 568–578.

Maras, K.L., & Bowler, D.M. (2010). The Cognitive Interview for eyewitnesses with autism spectrum disorder. *Journal of Autism and Developmental Disorders, 40,* 1350–1360.

McCauley, M.R., & Fisher, R.P. (1995). Facilitating children's eyewitness recall with the revised cognitive interview. *Journal of Applied Psychology, 80,* 510–516.

McMahon, M. (2000). The effect of the Enhanced Cognitive Interview on recall and confidence in elderly adults. *Psychiatry, Psychology and Law, 7,* 9–32.

Melnyk, L., & Bruck, M. (2004). Timing moderates the effects of repeated suggestive interviewing on children's eyewitness memory. *Applied Cognitive Psychology, 18,* 613–631.

Memon, A., Cronin, O., Eaves, R., & Bull, R. (1996). An empirical test of the mnemonic components of the cognitive interview. In G.M. Davies, S. Lloyd-Bostock, M. McMurran, & J.C. Wilson (Eds), *Psychology and Law: Advances in Research* (pp. 135–145). Berlin: De Gruyter.

Memon, A., Holley, A., Wark, L., Bull, R., & Köhnken, G. (1996). Reducing suggestibility in child witness interviews. *Applied Cognitive Psychology, 10,* 503–518.

Memon, A., Meissner, C.A., & Fraser, J. (2010). The Cognitive Interview: A meta-analytic analysis and study space analysis of the past 25 years. *Psychology, Public Policy & Law, 16,* 340–372.

Memon, A., Wark, L., Bull, R., & Köhnken, G. (1997). Isolating the effects of the cognitive interview techniques. *British Journal of Psychology, 88,* 179–197.

Memon, A., Zaragoza, M., Clifford, B.R., & Kidd, L. (2010b). Inoculation or antidote? The effects of cognitive interview timing on false memory for forcibly fabricated events. *Law and Human Behavior, 34,* 105–117.

Milne, R., & Bull, R. (1996). Interviewing children with mild learning disability with the cognitive interview. *Issues in Criminological and Legal Psychology, 26,* 44–51.

Milne, R., & Bull, R. (2003). Does the cognitive interview help children to resist the effects of suggestive questioning? *Legal and Criminological Psychology, 8,* 21–38.

Milne, R., Bull, R., Köhnken, G., & Memon, A. (1995). The cognitive interview and suggestibility. In N.K. Clark, & G.M. Stephenson (Eds), *Criminal Behaviour: Perceptions, Attributions and Rationality.* Leicester: British Psychological Society.

Milne, R., Clare, I.C.H., & Bull, R. (1999). Using the cognitive interview with adults with mild learning disabilities. *Psychology, Crime and Law, 5,* 81–99.

Ministry of Justice (2011). *Achieving Best Evidence in Criminal Proceedings: Guidance on Interviewing Victims and Witnesses, and using Special Measures.* London: Ministry of Justice.

Oates, K., & Shrimpton, S. (1991). Children's memories for stressful and non-stressful events. *Medical Science and Law, 31,* 4–10.

Orbach, Y., Hershkowitz, I., Lamb, M.E., Sternberg, K.J., Esplin, P.W., & Horowitz, D. (2000). Assessing the value of structured protocols for forensic interviews of alleged child abuse victims. *Child Abuse and Neglect, 24,* 733–752.

Ornstein, P.A., Gordon, B.N., & Larus, D.M. (1992). Children's memory for a personally experienced event, Implications for testimony. *Applied Cognitive Psychology, 6,* 49–60.

Pipe, M.-E., Sutherland, R., Webster, N., Jones, C.H., & La Rooy, D. (2004). Do early interviews affect children's long-term recall? *Applied Cognitive Psychology, 18,* 1–17.

Poole, D.A., & Lamb, M.E. (1998). *Investigative Interviews of Children: A Guide for Helping Professionals.* Washington, DC: American Psychological Association.

Poole, D.A., & Lindsay, D.S. (1998). Assessing the accuracy of young children's reports: Lessons from the investigation of child sexual abuse. *Applied and Preventive Psychology, 7,* 1–26.

Poole, D.A., & White, L.T. (1991). Effects of question repetition on the eyewitness testimony of children and adults. *Developmental Psychology, 27,* 975–986.

Poole, D.A., & White, L.T. (1993). Two years later: Effects of question repetition and retention interval on the eyewitness testimony of children and adults. *Developmental Psychology, 29,* 844–853.

Powell, M.B., Jones, C.H., & Campbell, C. (2003). A comparison of preschoolers' recall of experienced versus non-experienced events across multiple interviews. *Applied Cognitive Psychology, 17,* 935–952.

Powell, M., Roberts, K., & Guadagno, B. (2007). Particularisation of child abuse offences: Common problems when questioning child witnesses. *Current Issues in Criminal Justice, 19,* 64–74.

Principe, G.F., & Ceci, S.J. (2002). 'I saw it with my own ears': The effects of peer conversations on preschoolers' reports of nonexperienced events. *Journal of Experimental Child Psychology, 83,* 1–25.

Robinson, J., & McGuire, J. (2006). Suggestibility and children with mild learning disabilities: The use of the cognitive interview. *Psychology, Crime & Law, 12,* 537–556.

Sattler, J. (1998). *Clinical and Forensic Interviewing of Children and Families.* San Diego, CA: Jerome M. Sattler Publishing.

Saywitz, K.J., Geiselman, R.E., & Bornstein, G.K. (1992). Effects of cognitive interviewing and practice on children's recall performance. *Journal of Applied Psychology, 77,* 744–756.

Scottish Executive (2003). *Guidance Interviewing Child Witnesses and Victims in Scotland.* Edinburgh: Scottish Executive.

Scottish Executive (2011). *Guidance on Joint Investigative Interviewing of Child Witnesses in Scotland.* Edinburgh: Scottish Executive.

Sternberg, K.J., Lamb, M.E., Davies, G.M., & Westcott, H.L. (2001). The Memorandum of good practice: Theory versus application. *Child Abuse and Neglect, 25,* 669–681.

Tulving, E., & Thomson, D.M. (1973). Encoding specificity and retrieval processes in episodic memory. *Psychological Review, 80,* 359–380.

Westera, N.J., Kebbell, M.R., & Milne, R. (2011). Interviewing rape complainants: Police officers' perceptions of interview format and quality of evidence. *Applied Cognitive Psychology, 25,* 917–926.

Wickens, D. (1970). Encoding categories of words: An empirical approach to meaning. *Psychological Review, 77,* 1–15.

Wright, A.M., & Holliday, R.E. (2007). Interviewing cognitively impaired older adults: How useful is a cognitive interview? *Memory, 15,* 17–33.

11

Suggestibility in Legal Contexts: What Do We Know?

ANNE M. RIDLEY, FIONA GABBERT AND DAVID J. LA ROOY

In this final chapter we summarize the key points about suggestibility reviewed in this book and consider the forensic implications of suggestibility for practitioners.

REVIEW OF KEY POINTS

In the first three chapters of this book the early history of suggestibility in legal contexts as well as the methods and theories from the resurgence of research in the area in the 1970s and 1980s are discussed in depth. The currency of the early work on suggestibility in children by Binet, Stern, and others in the early twentieth century (Chapter 1) is striking. This work was a clear forerunner of what was to come some 70 years later. During the intervening years, the focus of research turned to identifying whether suggestibility was one or more phenomena but without particular focus on, or relevance to, eyewitness testimony. Throughout this volume, the two conceptualizations of suggestibility in legal contexts have been defined in three different ways. These definitions are broadly, but not entirely, the same as each other.

Suggestibility in Legal Contexts: Psychological Research and Forensic Implications, First Edition. Edited by Anne M. Ridley, Fiona Gabbert and David J. La Rooy.

Table 11.1 Summary of different approaches to suggestibility and findings from individual differences research

Conceptualization	Characteristics	Evidence of association with:
Experimental Delayed Investigative	Experimentally induced using the misinformation paradigm: tests incorrect recall for previously encountered misleading information, including that suggested in leading questions.	Anxiety (negative relationship) Memory distrust Memory (variable findings)
Trait Immediate Interrogative	Measured by the GSS Linked to the social interaction and negative feedback/coercive interview techniques, (that may include leading questions)	Anxiety (positive relationship) Self-esteem Life adversity Memory (negative relationship, particularly for misleading questions)

To clarify, they are summarized in Table 11.1, along with 'individual differences' findings reviewed in Chapter 5. Ridley and Gudjonsson conclude that research into these different conceptualizations of suggestibility has frequently been conducted in parallel rather than in an integrated way. Studies using the new definitions of *interrogative* versus *investigative* suggestibility, proposed in Chapter 1, combined with individual difference factors might further clarify the extent to which they are distinct or overlapping constructs.

In Chapter 2, Chrobak and Zaragoza focus on the experimental misinformation paradigm introduced in the 1970s to induce *investigative* suggestibility. Their chapter provides a review and a critical evaluation of different theoretical explanations for this type of suggestibility. A recent programme of research by the authors is also outlined. This line of work has developed the misinformation paradigm to reflect more pressured or coercive interview techniques, thereby inducing *interrogative* suggestibility. Across a series of studies, the authors examine whether it is possible that witnesses can come to believe events that they themselves have fabricated under pressure from the interviewer. They point out that being urged to speculate in this way may well occur in police interviews and therefore potentially has serious forensic implications.

Moving away from the experimental work on suggestibility, Gudjonsson outlines the development of the Gudjonsson Suggestibility Scales (GSS) to measure the extent to which individuals are likely to cede to leading questions or change their responses after negative feedback. The proposed mechanisms behind this have been set out in a theory of interrogative suggestibility that encompasses the coping strategies and expectations of the witness or suspect and interpersonal trust with the interviewer. The author also explains the notion of compliance and its close relationship with suggestibility; the main difference is that, unlike suggestibility, compliant responses are not privately accepted to be true. Also, compliance is more difficult than suggestibility to measure accurately using standardized tests. The author points out that the GSS should be used as part of a battery of assessment tools when assessing witnesses and suspects in forensic contexts. Using the newly proposed *investigative* and *interrogative* distinctions, we would argue that while suggestibility resulting from negative feedback is definitely *interrogative* suggestibility, the Yield measure of the GSS (resulting from misleading questions) might be better conceptualized as *investigative* suggestibility. This is borne out by the differing patterns of findings noted in Chapter 5, with Yield being related to memory and Shift being more reliably associated with psychosocial factors.

Closely related to the misinformation paradigm is the effect of co-witness discussion on memory conformity, which is covered in Chapter 4 by Gabbert and Hope. As discussed in this chapter, memory conformity refers to people's memories for an event becoming similar following a discussion. The difference between 'memory conformity' studies and more general 'misinformation studies' is that participants are exposed to misleading post-event information in the social context of a discussion. As both social and cognitive factors can play a role in determining whether someone will become influenced, exposure to misleading post-event information during discussions with others results in a particularly powerful form of suggestion. The chapter considers both social and cognitive factors when presenting theoretical accounts of why memory conformity occurs. Investigative interviewers should be aware that witnesses who have discussed an incident together might have unintentionally influenced each other's memories. Future research should take into consideration the role a person plays in an event when assessing eyewitness evidence, as recent evidence from Carlucci, Kieckhaefer, Schwartz, Villalba, and Wright (2011) shows that bystanders are more susceptible to memory conformity than witnesses who have been actively involved in an incident.

What is clear is that suggestibility involves complex phenomena that can interact in complex ways; for example, suggestibility may be present in social interactions where a suggested message may, or may not, be privately believed to be true. Suggestibility is also, at least in part, the result of memory-related factors such as the inability to identify correctly the original source of misleading information, poor memory for correct details when confronted with misleading questions, or a combination of the two.

In the second part of the book, the issue of vulnerability to suggestive influence is explored in detail. Contributors focus on various populations including children, adults with intellectual disabilities, older witnesses, individuals with contentious recovered memories of childhood sexual abuse, and suspects in coercive interviews.

James Ost reviews the evidence for whether abuse in childhood can be 'forgotten' and later recovered in adulthood – sometimes during therapy. His chapter presents the various mechanisms whereby a victim might believe they have rediscovered a traumatic event from their childhood for the first time but argues that these can generally be explained by normal cognitive and metacognitive functions such as forgetting and individual beliefs. Of central relevance to this book is the question of whether recovered memories can be the result of suggestive therapy techniques. If so, this has important forensic implications. Ost reviews several experimental studies that show it is possible to induce recall for details of traumatic events that were never actually witnessed and even for entire suggested events from childhood. In the light of this, it is recommended that in legal contexts recovered memories of childhood trauma should be supported by corroborating evidence, but this remains a controversial issue.

Chapter 7 by London, Henry, Conradt and Corser provides an in-depth review of areas of recent research on individual differences in suggestibility in children. In the ongoing pursuit of improving interview techniques, there is promising research indicating that training in narrative skills may provide some protection against suggestibility. Nevertheless, children who possess advanced narrative skills may also understand social cues better. This, paradoxically, may render them more susceptible to accepting an interviewer's incorrect version of events. Another complex set of findings has emerged for the association between theory of mind and suggestibility. The balance of evidence indicates that the ability to infer the intentions of others is associated with reduced suggestibility; however, more research is needed. In the final section of this chapter, evidence suggests that children with intellectual disabilities tend to be more suggestible than children of the same chronological age but generally no more so than children of a similar mental age. When questioned appropriately, however, all children – including those with intellectual disabilities – can provide accurate testimony.

At the other end of the lifespan, Maras and Wilcock summarize the literature on older witnesses, concluding that older adults are somewhat more suggestible than young adults, although the extent of this may be masked by poorer memory generally. That said, suggestibility within this population is variable with many aging witnesses able to give very accurate evidence. A consistent finding that has emerged is that when older witnesses are suggestible, they tend to be more confident of their accuracy than younger witnesses. This is a concern because, in legal contexts, confidence is often assumed to mean accuracy. One weakness of research among the elderly is that the literature to date tends to focus on participants without serious cognitive impairments. However, there is a clear need for research among individuals who are less able – including those with dementia – as such groups are vulnerable to crime, even within the care system, as recent reports in the UK media suggest.

Maras and Wilcock review various studies indicating that individuals with intellectual disabilities are more suggestible to misleading questions than control groups but no more suggestible than comparison groups when given negative feedback. A special group with a particular pattern of cognitive and social impairments are individuals with autism spectrum disorder (ASD). A new area of research by Maras and her colleagues among high-achieving individuals with ASD indicates that they are no more suggestible than controls. This finding is not inconsistent with the lack of understanding of the intentions of others and the cognitive inflexibility that are typical in ASD. These impairments might reduce the tendency to, for example, change responses in the presence of negative feedback. More research is needed including studies using lower functioning ASD participants.

An interesting theoretical point is lurking in the research among children and those with ASD, and that is related to understanding the actual intentions of an interviewer. With children, it has been proposed that both good narrative ability and advanced theory of mind (ToM) may lead to greater understanding of the intentions of others. This can be at the same time both helpful and counterproductive for its impact on suggestibility: if a child understands the intentions of the experimenter and wants to please them, they may willingly and knowingly accept misleading information. However, it could equally be assumed that they understand that they are being 'tricked', in which case the opposite can occur and the misleading information will be rejected. By contrast, the pattern of cognitive and social impairments in adults with ASD renders them *less* likely than control groups to understand the intentions of an interviewer. The limited evidence so far available from this group is that it does *not* increase their suggestibility in either *investigative* or *interrogative* paradigms. Whether this is because the interpersonal aspects of the interview are less important or because participants with ASD do not have the cognitive flexibility to change their responses is not yet clear. Further research into the importance of understanding the intentions of the interviewer among child and adult populations with and without specific intellectual disabilities should help to deconstruct this important aspect of suggestibility.

Suggestibility in suspect interviews is discussed in depth by Davis and Leo in Chapter 9. A particular issue arises when the suspect is classed as vulnerable. True confessions are, understandably, a desirable outcome of police interviews. Nevertheless, they are not always in suspects' best interests, particularly if the extent of their involvement in the offences becomes exaggerated. Further, suggestibility is argued to be a factor in false confessions and the interrogation techniques advocated in countries such as the United States make this a particular concern. Davis and Leo argue that such interrogation techniques can lead to acute interrogative suggestibility. The authors outline a new theoretical account where by this occurs as a result of a combination of impaired self-regulation related to glucose depletion, emotional stress, sleep deprivation and subtle threats to self-esteem. It is important to mention that although there are several factors related to increased suggestibility, the opposite is also true: many people are highly resistant to suggestion. What leads to such resilience has been somewhat neglected in research to date.

In Chapter 10, La Rooy, Brown and Lamb describe research-based approaches to appropriate interviewing in legal contexts that reduce concerns about suggestibility. The approaches considered are the Cognitive Interview (CI), which has been incorporated into professional guidelines in England and Wales, Canada and New Zealand, and the NICHD Protocol, which is mandated in parts of the USA, Canada and Israel, and is taught, built into, and/or underpins formal guidelines in Sweden, Norway, England, Wales, Scotland and Finland, and is currently being implemented in Korea, Japan and Portugal. The two approaches share many features, although the NICHD Protocol focuses on interviews with children and is much more thoroughly structured than the CI. The advantage of these approaches are that they focus interviewers on recommended good practice in interviews and restrict behaviours that are likely to contaminate memory.

FORENSIC IMPLICATIONS

In each chapter, the forensic implications of the research reviewed are highlighted. In Table 11.2, we incorporate these findings in a timeline of suggestibility in legal contexts and summarize the overall forensic implications.

Table 11.2 Timeline of suggestibility

Stage of process	Risk	Witness, victim or Suspect	Action to minimize suggestibility	Chapter reference
The crime	Trauma, arousal, attention, viewing conditions	All	N/A	6, 7, 9
The aftermath	Co-witness discussion, exposure to incorrect information, e.g. inaccurate press coverage, non-disclosure, inappropriate initial questioning, forgetting, trauma, emotion	Victim Witness	Discourage witnesses from discussing event. Obtain witness statements as soon as possible.	2, 4, 6, 7, 8, 9
Police interview	Leading questions, interviewer demeanour, pressurized or coercive interview situation, witness vulnerability	All	Encourage free recall as far as possible. Avoid option posing and leading questions, explain why repeated questions are necessary.	2, 3, 5, 6, 7, 8, 9, 10
Court appearance	Leading, complex questions pressurized situation, arousal, emotion, witness vulnerability.	All	For vulnerable witnesses ensure phrasing of question does not imply the answer. Explain why repeated questions are necessary.	3, 5, 7, 8, 9, 10

Once a crime has taken place, there is an entirely understandable tendency for fellow victims and/or witnesses to want to discuss what happened while waiting for the police to arrive. Take, for example, an incident in which the first author of this chapter was herself recently a witness to an armed bank robbery.

Anne Ridley recalls:

The presence of the gun and the loud and threatening behaviour of the robber made this quite traumatic and a number of people in the bank were wailing. Once the perpetrator had fled the scene, the bank was closed down and those present started to discuss what had happened. Being a psychologist with expertise in memory and suggestibility, I was in the strange position of knowing that people shouldn't run the risk of contaminating each others' memories in this way, and decided to speak out. I convinced the bank staff to distribute paper and pens so people could write down what they remembered. Having the Self-Administered Interview (SAI; Gabbert, Fisher & Hope, 2009) to hand would have been very useful! Rapid response police who arrived at the scene immediately asked for the information they needed from witnesses in order to get the initial search underway (details of getaway motor cycle, race and number of perpetrators). Detectives from Scotland Yard arrived some 45 minutes later to take over the investigation and carry out the main evidence-gathering interview. This was conducted using the mental reinstatement of context element of the Cognitive Interview (Fisher, Geiselman, Raymond, Jurkevich & Warhaftig, 1987), followed by more specific questions about details such as race, dress and height of the perpetrator, and length of the incident. As far as I know, after nine months, no arrests have been made, so I have not been called to give evidence in court, but I am very aware that the passage of time and repetitions of the story may have altered somewhat from the original recollections. Certainly they have become more gist-like. One thing in particular strikes me in terms of suggestibility. Because I was focussing on the gun (I am now a firm believer in weapon-focus), I did not get a good look at the perpetrator's face as he came towards me. He was wearing a crash helmet, but the visor was up so I could have looked at his face. However, when asked about his race I said I was not sure, but based on his voice thought he was probably white. CCTV footage later showed that he was black. Now, when I create a mental image of the perpetrator, he always has a black face even though I know I did not see him as such at the time.

Despite the use of CI techniques in my interview, I would argue that the process of an initial interview in such circumstances is problematic. During the interview, the police officer wrote notes, he then transcribed his notes in handwriting onto an official statement form and I had to read and sign it. While I am not saying this happened in my case, this process makes it entirely possible that incorrect details could creep in based on misunderstanding or assumptions by the interviewing officer – effectively the officer himself being suggestible. These inaccuracies could subsequently become "facts" in the case either if the witness believes them to be true (and there is much evidence for such beliefs presented in this book) or if the witness does not carefully read the written statement. The self-administered interview has been developed to help police deal with multiple witnesses in such situations, and enables witnesses to give a statement in their own words, thus overcoming the problems associated with having an investigating officer write the statement. Furthermore, the SAI can help protect against the effects of subsequently encountered misinformation and leading questions (Gabbert, Hope, Fisher, & Jamieson, 2012). It is currently in regular use in some UK forces and is being trialled by other forces in the UK and abroad. However, it is not yet widely adopted despite its promise for reducing the impact of suggestibility.

Research throughout this book points clearly to a number of factors that should keep suggestibility to a minimum in police interviews:

- Awareness that memories, even for personally experienced events, will have gaps that are particularly vulnerable to being filled by incorrect information.
- Avoid telling witnesses information about the case that they may not already know.
- Awareness that if witnesses have discussed a case with each other, incorrect details may have been shared. Warnings of this possibility may help if the interview takes places fairly soon after the event.
- Consideration of the role and relationships of the interviewee(s) – witnesses are somewhat more likely than victims to believe information from other witnesses is true, and witnesses are more likely to accept another's account if they know them than if they are a stranger.
- Information from witnesses, victims and suspects should be elicited using free recall questions and open-ended prompts as far as possible.
- Leading and misleading questions should be avoided completely.
- Complex and option-posing (e.g. yes/no) questions or prompts should be used only after open-ended prompts have been exhausted.
- Explain to witnesses that the interviewer does not 'know' what actually happened.
- If it is necessary to repeat questions, explain why, so that the witness does not assume that their initial responses were wrong.
- Accept 'don't know' responses.
- Awareness that vulnerability, however caused, (e.g. age, trauma, intellectual disability, personality, stress) may increase suggestibility.
- Do not give witnesses negative feedback (either verbally or non-verbally).

These guidelines should also be followed as far as possible for suspect interviews, although it is accepted that suspects are not usually as willing as cooperative witnesses to provide a detailed account through free recall. Therefore, more specific questions may be necessary.

In addition, the following is recommended to minimize suggestible responding and, potentially, false confessions:

* avoid conducting very long interviews if possible.
* allow suspects adequate rest and meals/drinks, etc.
* awareness of the potential effects of the traumatic nature of many crimes on the suspect themselves.
* recognizing that vulnerable suspects may be particularly susceptible to falsely confessing to something they did not do.

The final stage of the timeline of a crime is the court appearance. After all the good work of a well-conducted evidence gathering interview by the police or other appropriate professionals, both witnesses and suspects encounter a very different kind of interview in court, particularly in countries with an adversarial legal system such as that in Great Britain and the United States. Here, free recall is not invited (and if a witness attempts to provide it, they are frequently interrupted by counsel). Instead, complex, option posing and suggestive questioning predominate. This is a challenging environment for anybody, but particularly for vulnerable witnesses and suspects. When cross-examining witnesses, the role of the defence barrister is to challenge their evidence, so questions are framed to make it as difficult as possible for the witness to disagree. When witnesses give in to such questions or even change their testimony in court, this can be likened to suggestibility and/or compliance.

Relatively little research about the extent to which witnesses change their responses in court has been conducted but experimental studies with children have shown that when questioning techniques similar to cross-examination are used, children are highly likely to alter their responses from those they gave during an initial 'evidence gathering' phase (e.g. Bettenay, 2010; Zajac & Hayne, 2003). Mark Kebbell and his colleagues conducted a series of studies using transcripts of real court cases comparing those for witnesses with intellectual disabilities with a sample of cases with witnesses from the general population. Findings indicated that there was no difference between the two groups in terms of the questioning techniques used. Furthermore, the group with intellectual disabilities were more likely to agree with leading questions (Kebbell, Hatton, & Johnson, 2004). It was also found that judges were no more likely to intervene to stop inappropriate questioning for the group with intellectual disabilities (O'Kelly, Kebbell, Hatton, and Johnson, 2003). Special measures introduced in many jurisdictions have addressed some of the more intimidating court practices for vulnerable witnesses, such as giving evidence via a live link (video from another room) and the introduction of intermediaries to both advise on appropriate questioning techniques for particular witnesses and to assist those witnesses in court if they do not understand the questions. Nevertheless, further training and advice for judges, lawyers, barristers and intermediaries about questioning in such as way as to test the evidence without simply forcing a suggestible or compliant response are highly desirable in the interests of fairness and justice (see also Kebbell, Hatton, Johnson, & O'Kelly, 2001; Pigot, 1989; Spencer, 2011).

Finally, we have presented a necessarily bleak picture of the effects that inappropriate questioning can have on the suggestibility of witnesses, particularly those with vulnerabilities. However, not all witnesses are suggestible or compliant in the face of cross-examination, as this example of a witness with an intellectual disability shows:

> LAWYER: Near the front door? Do you remember at your house there used to be meat hooks?
> WITNESS WITH LDS [LEARNING DISABILITIES]:   No.
> LAWYER: Metal meat hooks?
> WITNESS WITH LDS: Didn't have no meat hooks.
> LAYWER: No meat hooks at all?
> WITNESS WITH LDS: None at all.
> LAWYER: Big S-shape, like that?
> WITNESS WITH LDS: No
> LAWYER: Metal?
> WITNESS WITH LDS: We ain't got none of them.
> LAWYER: You do not remember three of them being in the hall?
> WITNESS WITH LDS: No, none.
> LAWYER: Do you not remember your little sister coming back one day holding the three meat hooks? Someone had given them to her?
> WITNESS WITH LDS: No.
>
> (Kebbell *et al.*, 2001, pp. 99–100)

FUTURE DIRECTIONS

Research to investigate suggestibility and mitigate its effects is still evolving even after many decades and many hundreds of studies having been conducted. Each chapter in this volume has been written by experts in the field of suggestibility research, outlining the current state of play regarding present knowledge and focus, as well as areas in need of research attention. Authors have also discussed new and emerging areas of research, sparking ideas for promising future developments.

As always, there is a need for both more ecologically valid methodologies in the study of suggestibility and the triangulation of findings with studies based on observation and transcripts of police interviews (both at the crime scene and later) and court proceedings so that both psychologists and legal professionals can better understand the extent to which experimental and real-world research into suggestibility map onto each other.

Suggestibility is a fascinating and important aspect of human behaviour. A full understanding of its causes and relationships with social, cognitive and individual difference variables is of considerable theoretical and applied interest. It is particularly important that practitioners in legal contexts are aware of its potentially insidious effects.

REFERENCES

Bettenay, C. (2010). Memory under cross-examination of children with and without intellectual disabilities. Unpublished doctoral dissertation, London South Bank University.

Carlucci, M.E., Kieckhaefer, J.M., Schwartz, S.L., Villalba, D.K., & Wright, D.B. (2011). The South Beach Study: Bystanders' memories are more malleable. *Applied Cognitive Psychology, 25,* 562–566.

Fisher, R.P., Geiselman, R.E., Raymond, D.S., Jurkevich, L.M., & Warhaftig, M.L. (1987). Enhancing enhanced eyewitness memory: Refining the cognitive interview. *Journal of Police Science and Administration, 15,* 291–297.

Gabbert, F., Hope, L., & Fisher, R. P. (2009). Protecting eyewitness evidence: Examining the efficacy of a Self-Administered Interview tool. *Law & Human Behavior, 33,* 298–307.

Gabbert, F., Hope, L., Fisher, R.P., & Jamieson, K. (2012). Protecting against susceptibility to misinformation with the use of a Self-Administered Interview. *Applied Cognitive Psychology,* doi: 10.1002/acp.2828.

Kebbell, M.R., Hatton, C., & Johnson, S.D. (2004). Witnesses with intellectual disabilities in court: What questions are asked and what influence do they have? *Legal and Criminological Psychology, 9,* 23–35.

Kebbell, M.R., Hatton, C., Johnson, S.D., & O'Kelly, C.M.E. (2001). People with learning disabilities as witnesses in court: What questions should lawyers ask? *British Journal of Learning Disabilities, 29*(3), 98–102.

O'Kelly, C.M.E., Kebbell, M.R., Hatton, C., & Johnson, S.D. (2003). Judicial intervention in court cases involving witnesses with and without learning disabilities. *Legal and Criminological Psychology, 8,* 229–240.

Pigot, T. (1989). *Report of the Advisory Group on Video-Recorded Evidence.* Chairman His Honour Judge Thomas Pigot, QC; London: Home Office, 1989.

Spencer, J.R. (2011). Evidence and cross-examination. In M.E. Lamb, D.J. La Rooy, L.C. Malloy, & C. Katz (Eds), *Children's Testimony: A Handbook of Psychological Research and Forensic Practice* (pp. 285–307). Oxford: Wiley-Blackwell.

Zajac, R., & Hayne, H. (2003). I don't think that's what really happened: The effect of cross-examination on the accuracy of children's reports. *Journal of Experimental Psychology: Applied, 9,* 187–195.

Index

accuracy-oriented research 12
accusations of guilt 177–8
Achieving Best Evidence (Ministry of Justice) 11
acquiescence 52, 87, 150–3
acute suggestibility 171–95, 222
  ability to resist 176, 179–80
  agreeableness 87
  discomfort, fatigue and sleep deprivation 172–4, 184–5, 190–1
  dual task paradigm 181, 183–4, 186
  emotional states 171–2, 174, 182–4, 190
  erosion of resistance to interrogation 175–6
  forces of influence 176–80
  forensic implications 190–1
  glucose depletion 172–4, 185–8, 190
  legal context in *New York v. Matos and Molina* 172–5, 185
  motivation to resist 176–9
  self-regulation as primary mechanism of resistance 180–1
  severe IRRD 188

ADHD *see* attention deficit hyperactive disorder
admissibility 174
adolescents 97–8
adverse life-events
  individual differences 85, 87, 93–4, 101, 130
  recovered memories 107–10, 121, 220
alien abduction 112–13
alpha strategies 176
altered states of consciousness 8
anxiety 87, 88–91, 98, 101, 218
arousal 130
ASD *see* Autism Spectrum Disorder
Asperger syndrome 155
Associative Deficit Hypothesis 158
attachment theory 94
attention 11–13
  interrogative suggestibility 55–6
  vulnerable witnesses 155, 158
attention deficit hyperactive disorder (ADHD) 55–6, 93, 100
attribution theory 30–1
authority
  acute suggestibility 178–9
  historical development 8
  social factors 14
  vulnerable witnesses 150

Suggestibility in Legal Contexts: Psychological Research and Forensic Implications, First Edition. Edited by Anne M. Ridley, Fiona Gabbert and David J. La Rooy.
© 2013 John Wiley & Sons, Ltd. Published 2013 by John Wiley & Sons, Ltd.